Performance-Based Assessment for Middle and High School Physical Education

Jacalyn Lea Lund, PhD
Ball State University

Mary Fortman Kirk, PhD
Northern Kentucky University

Human Kinetics

Library of Congress Cataloging-in-Publication Data

Lund, Jacalyn Lea, 1950-
    Performance-based assessment in midddle and high school physical education / Jacalyn
Lund, Mary Fortman Kirk.
        p.   cm.
    Includes bibliographical references and index.
    ISBN 0-7360-3270-3
    1. Physical education and training--Study and teaching (Secondary)--Examinations. 2.
Education tests and measurements. I. Kirk, Mary Fortman, 1946- II. Title.

GV362.5 .L86 2002

613.7'0712--dc

ISBN: 0-7360-3270-3   2002017211

Acquisitions Editor: Scott Wikgren
Developmental Editor: Judy Park
Assistant Editor: Lee Alexander
Copyeditor: Scott Weckerly
Proofreader: Erin Cler
Indexer: Bobbi Swanson
Permission Manager: Dalene Reeder
Graphic Designer: Stuart Cartwright
Graphic Artist: Angela K. Snyder
Photo Manager: Leslie A. Woodrum
Cover Designer: Jack W. Davis
Photographer (cover): Tom Roberts
Photographer (interior): Tom Roberts, except where otherwise noted. Photograph on page 119 provided by Jacalyn
Lea Lund.
Art Manager: Carl D. Johnson
Illustrators: Dick Flood (line art) and Tom Roberts (Mac art)
Printer: Versa Press

Printed in the United States of America

10   9   8   7   6   5   4   3   2   1

Human Kinetics
Web site: www.humankinetics.com

United States: Human Kinetics
P.O. Box 5076
Champaign, IL 61825-5076
800-747-4457

Canada: Human Kinetics
475 Devonshire Road Unit 100
Windsor, ON N8Y 2L5
800-465-7301 (in Canada only)
e-mail: orders@hkcanada.com

Europe: Human Kinetics
107 Bradford Road
Stanningley
Leeds LS28 6AT, United Kingdom
+44 (0) 113 255 5665

Australia: Human Kinetics
57A Price Avenue
Lower Mitcham, South Australia 5602
08 8277 1555
e-mail: liahka@senet.com.au

New Zealand: Human Kinetics
P.O. box 105-231, Auckland Central
09-523-3462
e-mail: hkp@ihug.co.nz

To Mom . . . Thanks for your support and everything you've done!

In memory of my Aunt Edna Epstein . . . For always making me feel so special!

In memory of my parents, Joseph and Lois Fortman . . .
who were always my greatest fans and supporters.

CONTENTS

Physical education teachers can do one of two things: resist educational reform and the new forms of assessment, or embrace them. We have chosen to embrace them. This book is the result of our work as teachers who have stumbled onto alternative ways of assessing students while in the gym and refined these ideas as teacher educators in a state immersed in education reform. Before writing this book, we spent many years in public schools (26 years, if you combine our experience), which helped us to learn the problems facing physical educators in the field. We have both been on state assessment task force writing teams and have learned the information we are about to present in a hands-on, discovery learning mode. Those experiences have convinced us of the value of assessment. Our years in the trenches have given us opportunities to see how assessment and instruction can work together to increase student learning.

In this book, we offer assessment how-to's as well as examples of what can be done. By explaining the process of developing performance-based assessments, we give you strategies for creating assessments for your own gymnasium settings. We recognize that every program is different and as such, our ideas will need modification and tailoring to fit your situation and needs. Our suggestions and ideas are designed to provide a springboard for your own imagination and creativity. We present our ideas as a starting point and challenge you to take the plunge with assessment-based teaching. To help get you started, actual models of continuous performance-based assessments are presented in chapters 7, 8, and 9.

Teachers offer a variety of reasons for not using assessment in physical education. Some teachers feel that assessment takes too much time away from instruction. Given the limited amount of time allocated to physical education, teachers are reluctant to devote those precious minutes to assessing students. Other teachers feel that large numbers of students in classes prevent them from doing assessments. We hope that part I helps change the minds of those who feel that assessments are impractical or unnecessary.

Most physical education teachers complete a test and measurement class as part of their instructional preparation. In that class, they learn about administering skill and fitness tests, along with other traditional testing formats. As teacher educators, we realize that assessment is underused in physical education, despite the training most teachers have in measurement and evaluation. The purpose of this book is to provide some new assessment ideas and inspire physical education teachers to use assessments more effectively and more often with their classes.

We have focused on performance-based assessments that, if used properly, can provide instructional feedback for both teachers and students. By providing many options and ideas for using performance-based assessment and guiding the reader through the process, this book can become a resource for making physical education instruction and assessment more efficient and effective.

In an article in JOPERD, Hensley et al. (1987) asked, "Is evaluation worth the effort?" The authors of the article reported that teachers were not using the evaluation techniques learned in test and measurement classes. The article cited Dunham, who a year earlier contended that "most teachers initially engage in formal evaluation, but quickly realize that the time expenditure required by the current procedures is not worth the value of the results attained" (59). Hensley and his coauthors called for fixing the "evaluation pothole" by doing the following:

▶ Adopting a criterion-reference approach to evaluation that is founded on the identification of important educational objectives and student behaviors that are inherent in a healthy and productive life

▶ Moving more toward a formative evaluation model that better facilitates the teaching-learning process

▶ Evaluating the process, not just the product

- Developing an evaluation model that makes more appropriate use of professional judgments; that is, subjective evaluation
- Adhering to a self-management approach that includes self-assessment of ability and behavior . . . which may eventually lead to long-term behavior change (61)

Assessment in this text is approached from a very different perspective than most assessment books and embraces the suggestions offered by Hensley and his associates. We believe that assessment should be continuous and done throughout a unit rather than tacked on after all instruction has finished. Using this approach, assessment can inform the instructional process, resulting in optimal learning situations. Goals are criterion-referenced and designed to make students competent in the activities and sports covered in physical education classes. By using continuous assessment, students have feedback about their progress on the quality of their skills. Teachers can take the assessment information to determine the next step in the teaching-learning process. Formative assessments allow students opportunities to self- and peer-assess, as well as provide students with many chances to demonstrate competence. They also provide teachers with many lenses from which to view student progress.

This book is designed to provide middle and secondary physical education teachers as well as undergraduate preservice teachers with a step-by-step method for assessing students. It bridges the theory-practice gap, putting assessment theory in understandable language that is easy to implement. A variety of performance-based assessments are given along with helpful hints should teachers decide to implement them into their curriculums.

When used to its maximum potential, assessment can do a variety of things. Our objective is to illustrate these unlimited possibilities to give physical education teachers the necessary skills and tools to incorporate assessment into their classroom, at whatever level they deem appropriate. This book explains and gives examples of how to:

- incorporate national, state, and local standards into assessments;
- use assessment to evaluate student progress toward goals;

- design appropriate assessments that include stated criteria;
- identify assessment tasks that are authentic and real-to-life to students;
- plan assessment throughout instruction units;
- use assessment to evaluate the effectiveness of instruction and curriculum;
- connect assessment with grades; and
- link assessment with instruction.

The many examples provided illustrate just exactly how to implement continuous assessment. You will be guided through the process of developing assessments for your own units of instruction.

Learning new skills in physical education is often a slow process. Students can become discouraged when they fail to see results. Assessments help measure progress, thus inspiring students to work harder. By giving goals for instruction, then measuring student progress toward achieving them, students can be challenged to work harder and produce even greater results. Assessment can thus be motivational for students. Instead of dreading assessments, students can look forward to using them as opportunities to measure progress toward stated goals. Assessments can also add accountability to help ensure student learning.

Our intention as authors is to provide impetus for changing both your approach to doing assessment as well as your attitudes concerning it. We have witnessed many positive changes using continuous performance assessment and wish to share these with you. By looking at learning from multiple perspectives you can demonstrate to others (i.e., parents, administrators, students), just how much students have actually achieved through instruction.

Grant Wiggins offers the following advice: "Nothing worth understanding is mastered the first time, the first year, or the first course of study." (Wiggins 1998a, 15) We encourage you to use that philosophy as you begin changing assessment practices. Change takes time, and good change takes even longer. You will no doubt experience frustration from things not working as they should. However, if you keep working at the process we have presented, you will begin to experience satisfaction in seeing how assessment can enhance instruction. We encourage you to begin your journey to change assessment practices with small steps. By thinking big, but starting small, the task seems less onerous.

We hope that you enjoy this book and that it encourages you to expand your assessment horizons by following our various suggestions and hints. The power of assessment came alive for one of us during a field experience involving a preservice elementary classroom teacher. After teaching a series of lessons, the perspective teacher arranged assessments to show students how much they had pro-gressed. At the end of the lesson, she told of her success and finished by stating, "I never realized how motivational assessment could be." Her high rate of time on task and the excitement generated when students could visually see their progress was a huge *a-ha!* moment for her. We encourage readers to make a similar discovery and become just as excited about the potential assessment holds. Remember that improvement implies that some type of change must occur. On behalf of both of us, we wish you good luck on your new assessment adventure!

ACKNOWLEDGMENTS

Many thanks to our friends, colleagues, and families who have supported us throughout this project. For Bill, Nicholas, and Jeff, your patience and understanding were much appreciated. For Jan Montague, for your encouragement, patience, understanding, and taking on my share of the "household chores."

Additionally, we'd like to recognize many individuals for the following contributions:

▶ Marilyn Buck and Margaret Pentecost for the chapters you read and the advice and suggestions you offered

▶ Margaret Pentecost for contributing an event task to chapter 2

▶ Tara Scanlan and her students, who created the brochure for chapter 2

▶ Our students and student teachers, who taught us many things about assessment and who continue to challenge and inspire us

▶ Our cooperating teachers, who have shared information about the assessment process

▶ Les Abramson, a mentor and friend, who helped me focus a research agenda

PART

I

Introduction to Performance-Based Assessment

This section is designed to give an overview of performance-based assessments and introduce you to some of the terminology we use throughout this book. The standards reform movement has been instrumental in calling for changes in how students are assessed. In the past, physical education teachers had limited ways to assess student performance. The intent of this part of our book is to present to you the many options that are now available and explain how they can be used to enhance student learning.

CHAPTER ONE

The Need for Change

It is not our classroom assessments that draw all of the news coverage and editorial comment. All the visibility and political power honors go to our large-scale standardized tests. Nevertheless, anyone who has taught knows that it is classroom assessments—not standardized tests—that provide the energy that fuels the teaching and learning engine. For this reason, our classroom assessments absolutely must be of high quality. (Stiggins 1997, p. vi)

A huge educational reform is currently under way, calling for teachers to revamp curriculums, teaching strategies, and assessment practices. This reform touches all curricular areas, including physical education. The sweeping changes are in part a reflection of the many changes that have occurred in today's society. For example, people are no longer satisfied with waiting three to five days for surface mail to arrive because correspondence is transmitted almost instantaneously via e-mail and fax machines. Letters and packages can be sent via overnight delivery and arrive around the world the following day. People hire personal trainers to become physically fit faster and

more efficiently. Cell phones connect people at all times, with international phone calls as clear as those coming from across the street. Changes in communication have led to a more global economy, making policy leaders concerned about how students compare to their international counterparts. Computer capabilities increase almost daily, and increases in information are nearly logarithmic. Since the demands on graduates have changed over the past 100 years, the demands on schools are changing as well. The knowledge explosion alone would have necessitated change, but other factors have also led to changes in the way schools do business.

The Call for Change in Physical Education

Although many factors contributed to the call for change in education, some seem more significant than others. At the end of the 19th century, the percentage of students graduating from high school was significantly lower than that of today. Some students left school out of a need to supplement family income. Others who didn't do well in school dropped out in favor of manual labor jobs and other well-paying positions that did not require a high school education. As the economy shifted to one using more technology, fewer jobs were available for dropouts and more students remained in school. Schools began dealing with greater numbers of students and in some instances with lower performing students. Although this statement is an oversimplification of the problem, the net result was a gradual erosion of standards and requirements for graduation.

In the early 1980s, a report titled *A Nation at Risk* was issued that stated that the educational system in the United States was in serious decline (National Commission on Excellence in Education 1983). Students were unable to perform the basic functions assumed of capable high school graduates—such as the ability to read, write, and solve mathematics problems. A diploma, in some cases, really represented "seat time." In other words, students had attended school enough days to satisfy attendance requirements while, in some instances, acquiring content that represented a rather minimal body of knowledge. Because students were awarded credit for having completed a certain number of classes, a diploma didn't represent a body of knowledge or competency; rather, it meant that the student had simply been present at school.

Additionally, jobs that 10 years ago only required basic skills today require technical expertise. Auto technicians are a prime example of drastic change in job requirements. The skills of today's technicians are a far cry from those required of stereotypical backyard mechanics whose basic knowledge of engines 30 years ago enabled them to fix almost any make or model of car. Today's technicians use very sophisticated equipment to diagnose automobile problems as many of today's autos have computers to increase efficiency. Auto technicians must understand these machines to diagnose very complex problems.

Those in power began calling for the establishment of standards in many subject areas after reports critical of education were issued. "The major reason that national and state leaders have coalesced around the need for defining content and student performance standards is that the quality of American education must be improved, and the current system of relying on local decision-making power over curriculum is failing to bring about that improvement" (Jennings 1995, 768). National content organizations put together teams to write standards in subject areas such as math, social studies, science, and language arts. In 1995, the standards for physical education were released in a National Association for Sport and Physical Education (NASPE) publication titled *Moving Into the Future—National Standards for Physical Education: A Guide to Content and Assessment* (NASPE 1995). The physical education standards have been widely distributed, adopted, or modified by many states for use as physical education standards (see figure 1.1).

So what are standards in relation to education? The term *standards* generally represents information that students should know and be able to do relative to a given subject. When people use the term *standards*, they typically

---

A physically educated person:

1. Demonstrates competency in many movement forms and proficiency in a few movement forms.

2. Applies movement concepts and principles to the learning and development of motor skills.

3. Exhibits a physically active lifestyle.

4. Achieves and maintains a health-enhancing level of physical fitness.

5. Demonstrates responsible personal and social behavior in physical activity settings.

6. Demonstrates understanding and respect for differences among people in physical activity settings.

7. Understands that physical activity provides opportunities for enjoyment, challenge, self-expression, and social interaction.

Figure 1.1   Content standards in physical education.

Reprinted from *Moving Into the Future: National Standards for Physical Education* (1995) with permission from the National Association for Sport and Physical Education (NASPE), 1900 Association Drive, Reston, VA 20191-1599.

are talking about either content standards or performance standards. **Content standards** specify what students should know and be able to do (NASPE 1995). "Content standards establish what should be learned in various subjects . . . [and] emphasis is apt to be on learning content more through critical thinking and problem solving strategies than through rote learning of discrete facts" (Lewis 1995, 746). They incorporate the most important and enduring ideas that represent the knowledge and skills necessary to the discipline. The NASPE physical education standards are content standards as are most state standards. **Performance standards**, on the other hand, seek to answer the question, "How good is good enough?" They define a satisfactory level of learning (Lewis 1995). A performance standard indicates both the nature of the evidence that is accepted as documentation of student achievement as well as the quality of student performance necessary to satisfy the performance standard. Grant Wiggins (1998a) uses the high jump as an analogy to illustrate the difference between content

and performance standards (see figure 1.2). If one thinks of the high jump as the content standard, then the performance standard is where the teacher places the bar. Jumping a bar placed at three feet is much less demanding than one placed at a six-foot height. Performance standards for physical education have not yet been written at the national level, leaving it up to teachers in the various states to decide figuratively where to "place the bar."

The establishment of standards gave schools a way of comparing students' performance with a standard of learning rather than the work of other students. Under **standards-based instructional formats**, students are required to demonstrate competence in a variety of subject areas. With standards-based education, it doesn't matter how well students perform in comparison with others, as standards are **criterion referenced** (based on a set standard) rather than **norm referenced** (compared to a population) (see figure 1.3). Many national achievement tests are norm referenced. They tell teachers and administrators how students in that school compare with others taking

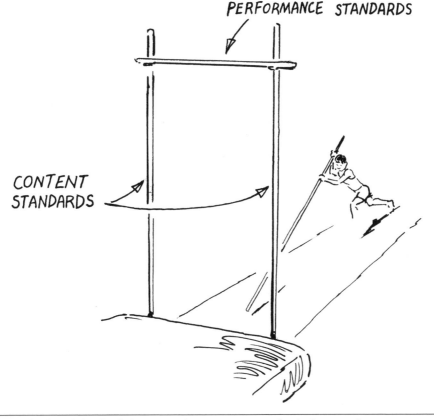

Figure 1.2   If one thinks of the high jump as the content standard, then performance standard is where the teacher places the bar.

the same test. When a teacher uses a curve to grade a class, a norm-referenced grading system is being used, as students are compared with one another. The curve depends on the performance of others and can change what the teacher expects students to know. The curve makes the goal for learning a moving target because the performance of other students determines the standard for learning. The best students get the best grades and the poorest students get the lowest grades, but no one is really sure how much they learn. Comparing students with one another isn't always negative, especially when top students are of high quality. However, when students are not of a high caliber, comparing mediocre students with one another doesn't give you much information on their level of achievement.

Standards were therefore developed to give teachers a measuring stick to assess student learning more accurately as well as to know the additional work students must do to reach this level of achievement. Learning expectations are clear to both students and teachers. When students are judged via a criterion score or standard, there is no limit to the number of students who can reach the goal. If the criterion score or standard for the 100-meter dash were set at 12 seconds, all students reaching that would have achieved the goal or competence (see figure 1.3). It doesn't matter how they place in the rank order of the class; they are competing to meet a criterion score rather than against one another. This paradigm represents a philosophical shift in the way many teachers plan and conduct classes.

Standards-Based Instruction

This textbook is about improving student learning and achievement in physical education by using **standards-based instruction** and performance-based assessments for students. In standards-based instruction, the teacher identifies a unit goal that is often based on state or national standards, then uses this goal to determine progress toward expectations for student learning. When educators use performance-based assessments with standards-based instruction, the assessments are determined before instruction begins. The students' performances either meet the standards or they don't. When assessment is not planned before the implementation of the unit, it often fails to occur or the attempt at assessment is

Figure 1.3 With standards-based education, it doesn't matter how well students perform in comparison with others because standards are criterion referenced (based on a set standard) rather than norm referenced (compared with a population).

piecemeal at best. Chapters 7, 8, and 9 of this book provide examples of developing these standards-based units of instruction.

Types of Assessment in Standards-Based Instruction

The standards movement has brought with it new ways to document student learning. Until recently, tests were created by psychometricians rather than teachers (Stiggins 1997). Tests from instructor guides typically used traditional testing formats (e.g., true-false, matching, multiple choice) and were written by outside people who used only the text as a source for testing information. The instructional process, or what the teacher did to present knowledge, was not included in writing the tests. The tests had to be generic because the test authors had no idea how teachers would present information or what points would be emphasized. These questions were typically designed to measure student recall of information rather than require them to think critically.

Members of the educational reform movement began calling for changes in assessment practices because too often students were graduating with a wealth of information but were incapable of applying it in the workplace or world of business. Because standards-based instruction is an attempt to improve current education practices, it makes sense that different ways to measure achievement should accompany it. The need to document a different type of learning (application versus recall of information) led to the development of new, alternative forms of assessment. Grant Wiggins (1989b) called for the use of authentic tests that would approximate tasks done by people in the real world. Performance-based testing is closely associated with both the standards movement and the need for students to apply knowledge while demonstrating mastery of content material. Because much of physical education is based on performance or behavior that is observable, physical educators have been very comfortable with using these new assessment forms.

We like Lambert's (1999) definition of **standards-based assessment**:

> *Standards-based assessment is the process of determining if and to what degree a student can demonstrate in context, his/her understanding and ability relative to identified standards of learning. (p. 6)*

Since students are to demonstrate their understanding and knowledge, some type of observable action or tangible product is required of the student. Although traditional forms of assessment could be used, standards-based assessments are more likely to be the new, alternative forms of assessment that involve students doing something and being assessed using predetermined criteria, rather than just selecting a correct answer.

The alternative assessments referred to in this book are called *performance-based assessments*. Authors often use the terms *performance-based assessment,* **alternative assessment,** and **authentic assessment** synonymously (Herman, Aschbacher, and Winters 1992), while others (Marzano, Pickering, and McTighe 1993) use them to define different types of assessment. In this book, the terms

will be used synonymously. Performance-based assessments require students to *generate* rather than *select* a response (Herman, Aschbacher, and Winters 1992). They have two essential parts—the performance tasks or exercises that students are to do and the criteria by which to judge the product or performance. Although some authors have made a rather liberal interpretation of the term *performance-based assessments*, we are using a more conservative definition that requires the assessment to be complex, involving integrative tasks to determine whether students have reached desired outcomes or standards. The key elements or dimensions of performance are called *performance criteria*. Clear criteria are essential to the assessment process.

Effect on Teaching When Standards Are Used

Before using standards as a basis for instruction, some teachers were only concerned with educating upper-level and more capable students or athletes. Those of lesser ability were encouraged to learn whatever they could; if they did not reach a certain level of achievement or competence, teachers accepted it and moved on to new lessons. Implementing standards-based learning brings with it changes in instructional methods and practices. These include the following:

- ▶ Beginning the planning process by identifying what students should know and be able to do
- ▶ Having students work to meet clearly defined and acknowledged standards or goals
- ▶ Informing students about the criteria of evaluation
- ▶ Letting assessment and instruction work together
- ▶ Connecting assessment with real-world tasks
- ▶ Attempting to identify an audience outside the realm of the school
- ▶ Using evaluation to assess student ability in areas of application and higher-level thinking skills

Using these outlined points, the following sections compare the differences between standards-based instructional practices with those used in traditional teaching formats. Many beginning teachers plan lessons on a day-by-day basis. The results are lessons that may keep students engaged but lack a sense of purpose or learning. These lessons are similar to children's exploring the interesting sights and sounds of the neighborhood as they make their way home. In contrast, adults often walk the distance in a direct path. Both arrive at the same destination; however, the adult gets there in far less time. The adult path described here is analogous to the teaching strategies used in standards-based instruction. It follows a direct path to desired student learning without extraneous activity that is irrelevant to final goals (see figure 1.4).

Planning Process

With traditional teaching, physical educators first select activities and drills using fun, engaging activities that practice the skills. Physical educators then build a unit around these skills and determine assessments after instruction has taken place. Many educators

Figure 1.4 When teachers know where they are headed, the path to student learning is much more direct.

choose activities because students simply enjoy doing them, not for their contribution to developing competent performers. Although teachers intend for students to become competent movers or to be able to play a given sport, criteria for achieving success are often not explicitly defined. As such, teaching is not done with a final concrete goal in mind.

Lesson planning with standards-based instruction begins with determining solid educational goals. Because assessments designed to measure these final goals are chosen before the unit begins, criteria necessary to meet the goals are defined before actual instruction starts. Teachers inform students of the final objectives and activities, which provide an opportunity for students to reach these goals, and are chosen using a technique referred to as **backward mapping**. By considering the impact that an activity has on reaching the goal, teachers avoid frivolous lessons that do not contribute to student learning.

An example of choosing activities before identifying goals for students occurred for one of us when a group of preservice teachers were planning a badminton unit. One young man, a baseball coach, had access to a radar gun. His lesson revolved around using the radar gun to time the speed of badminton strokes for beginning students. Although this might be a novel way to motivate advanced players, using a radar gun for students just learning how to perform an overhead clear in badminton were inappropriate. After considering his goals for the unit, the coach changed the lesson to one that emphasized critical elements of the stroke rather than racket speed. With standards-based assessment, the goal is selected first, then the unit activity that allows one to reach that goal is selected second. Although it may seem obvious, it is important to mention that activities that do not contribute to student learning are not included in the unit. All instruction is built around getting students to reach criteria set by the teacher for student learning. Learning becomes more focused with the use of standards-based assessment.

Defining Standards and Goals

The standards-based instructional planning process begins by identifying what students should ultimately know and be able to do. When a teacher fails to specify this final outcome, goals may change as the instruction evolves. When the teacher clearly defines what the final outcome or product should look like and all instruction is built around getting students to reach this goal, the instructional focus is maintained.

In secondary schools, many teachers want students to be competent in game play, dance, or some other movement form. With standards-based teaching, the assessments are determined before instruction begins. By determining the final assessments and sharing these with students, teachers define what competence means relative to student performance. Because teachers identify what students must know and be able to do to demonstrate competence before beginning a unit, a clear picture of the final outcome or product is created. With traditional instruction teachers may sometimes have a general idea about what they would like student performance on an assessment to look like, but they have not defined specific criteria. By clearly identifying the assessments and criteria, teachers are forced to think through the teaching and learning process, making lessons purposeful and meaningful for students.

Students Know Criteria

Students know the criteria of evaluation with standards-based instruction. When teachers clarify what they want students to know and be able to do as the result of instruction (e.g., the assessment), the guessing games are over and students have a clearly defined target to aim at (see table 1.1). With traditional instruction, teachers don't always communicate their expectations to students, so students try to clarify the assessment by asking questions. With performance-based assessments, students are given the criteria necessary for success along with the assessment. Assessment is no longer a guessing game because students no longer need to solve the mystery of trying to figure out what is important. When we give students criteria for scoring the assessment as instruction begins, they can work toward reaching and attaining these without false starts or wasted efforts created by pursuing the wrong path. Students can use peer evaluation or self-evaluation techniques to compare themselves or others with the stated goals, then work toward achieving them. Thus, students have multiple teachers from which to receive feedback; they do not rely solely on evaluation or information from the physical educator.

Assessment Linked to Instruction

With performance-based assessment, teaching and assessment are intertwined, sometimes becoming impossible to distinguish between the two. Students have the opportunity to work on meaningful projects and tasks that are later assessed. For example, choreographing a dance allows students to apply knowledge of the elements of dance design as they create different levels, shapes and patterns of movement, while combining various dance steps and locomotor movements to music. When the dance is completed, the teacher evaluates this dance to determine whether students understand the principles of choreography while at the same time assessing dance ability. Thus, the task is both a learning experience and a way to assess students.

Many physical education teachers complain that assessment requires too much time

Table 1.1 Differences in Planning Between Traditional and Standards-Based Assessment

Typical assessment	Standards-based assessment
Select the activity or unit (e.g., dance, badminton)	Select a goal or target (may already be selected for you)
Determine goals	Precisely define the standard and the indicators
Decide what will be taught	Choose appropriate course of study
Assess	Determine how you will know if the standard has been met (assessment)
Move to the next unit	Write the rubric
	Choose activity
	Practice continuous assessment and instruction to reach the goal or target

to complete. Assessment is especially seen as a burden in situations where class size is large. With performance-based assessment, instruction and assessment are linked. Game play allows students to apply the information and skills learned during a unit and increase their levels of competence. Student knowledge of the rules, use of strategy, selection of the correct psychomotor skill, execution of psychomotor skills, and teamwork are just some of the components that can be assessed during game play. By creating criteria for assessing various aspects of student performance, teachers can assess game play skills while students are continuing to learn.

Real-World Connections

Standards-based assessments attempt to connect assessment with real-world tasks and identify an audience outside the realm of the school. With traditional assessments, teachers sometimes have students complete assessments that are perceived as superficial and do little to pique student interest. Those assessments have little meaning and students complete them only to receive points toward their grade. Students do what is expected and little more, often making student performance minimal. With standards-based assessments, teachers create tasks that approximate something that people would do in a real-world setting. Instead of only using skill tests for evaluation of psychomotor skill, students play games in a tournament. In lieu of taking a written test that covers rules, students have the opportunity to demonstrate their knowledge while creating a brochure or pamphlet, officiating, keeping statistics, or reporting on games. Students are asked to do real-world tasks. Since these assessments are perceived as meaningful, students are willing to devote more time to them.

Recently while teaching a badminton unit, I used skill tests to indicate performance on some of the skills taught as well as performance-based tests to assess playing ability, content knowledge, and affective domain dispositions. At the end of the unit, I asked students which type of test best measured their abilities. The overwhelming response was that the performance-based assessments were better indicators of their ability to play the game than were the more traditional ones. They enjoyed being evaluated with multiple lenses that gave them many opportunities to demonstrate skill and learning.

In an attempt to make the assessment more "real world," it is important to identify, when possible, an audience outside the realm of the school, rather than using assessments that have only the teacher as the audience. **Traditional assessments** typically assess the knowledge and skills presented in class with no thought or consideration as to how these apply to the real world. With performance-based assessments, students are given an opportunity to expand their horizons by performing tasks and solving problems for others. The brochure mentioned in the previous example could capitalize on this concept by identifying potential clientele for a summer sport camp as a target audience. Thus, students would not just be writing a brochure for a primary audience of one (the teacher); they would also be writing it for the secondary audience of many (the parents and students they are trying to interest in attending their camp).

Identifying an audience is important because different audiences require different types of performance. The skill needs of a soccer player in elementary school are not the same as the skill needs of a soccer player in high school. An aerobic dance routine choreographed for high school freshmen would be quite different from one done for people in their fifties. A tennis clinic might be organized for a group of immigrant students who had never played before, or a play-by-play broadcast of an in-class game might be done for an audition with a large radio station in the Midwest. By creating an outside audience for the assessments, teachers broaden the scope and increase the importance of the assessment. Of course, a real audience is always preferred, but a contrived audience can also help focus the intent of the product, gearing it to a more specific knowledge base. The audience can then contribute to the meaningfulness of the assessment, extending knowledge beyond the walls of the gymnasium, something very different from what traditional assessments do.

Higher-Level Thinking Skills

Bloom's Taxonomy (figure 1.5) calls for students to use higher-order thinking skills. Although tests can be written that require students to use analysis, synthesis, and evaluation, many written tests for physical education merely measure knowledge and comprehension. Standards-based instruction calls for the use of higher-order thinking skills. Performance-based assessments give students an opportunity to develop these skills. For example, game play can develop student ability to analyze opponent's strengths and weaknesses and synthesize or create plays to give his or her team a playing advantage. An analysis of a dance performance requires students to evaluate what is observed with pre-established criteria and evaluate whether characteristics were present or omitted.

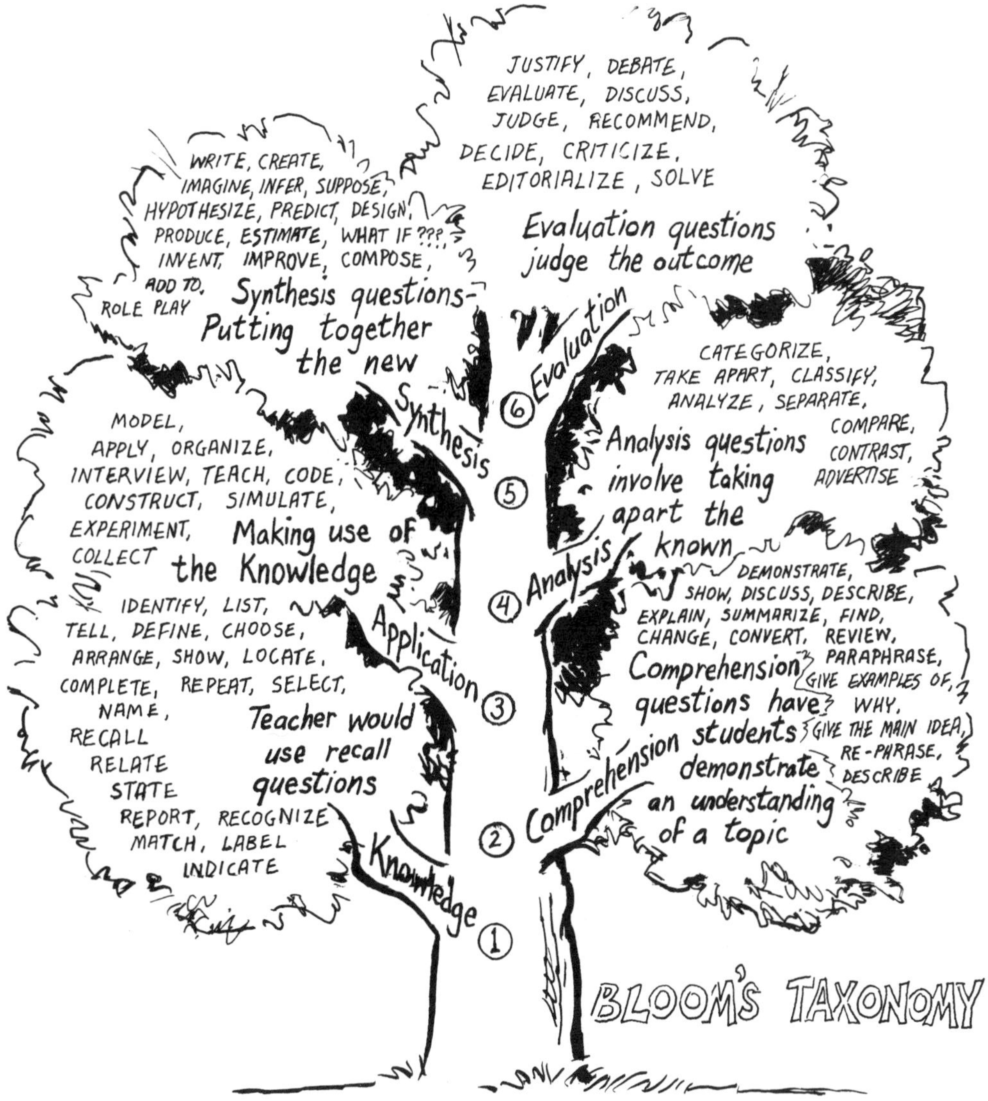

Figure 1.5 Bloom's Taxonomy. The type of questions asked, and the verbs used when asking them, affects the level of student learning.

You are a talent scout looking for new pieces for an upcoming 10-city modern dance tour. Today several dancers will be auditioning in hopes that you will select the dance they choreographed for your tour. You are to watch the dancers perform and use the following criteria to evaluate the performance:

- Dance uses both locomotor and nonlocomotor movements.
- Elements of good dance performance are present (e.g., force, time, space).
- Dance was well-rehearsed and performed smoothly.
- Members of the group worked together.
- Dancers moved in time to the rhythm or musical accompaniment.
- Dancers demonstrated creativity with movement combinations.

A quantitative **analytic rubric** uses the following descriptors for rating each of the above elements:

   0—No dance was performed.
   1—The dance did not demonstrate this element.
   2—The dance element was present some of the time.
   3—The dance element was clearly present.
   4—Outstanding use of the dance element; it took your breath away.

The Need to Increase the Use of Assessment in Physical Education

The American Federation of Teachers, the National Council on Measurement in Education, and the National Education Association published a set of standards for evaluating teacher competence in student assessment in 1987 (Cunningham 1998). The standards were based on two fundamental assumptions. The first of these assumptions is that student assessment is a key part of a teacher's role. Teachers must determine, through evaluation, whether students have met the goals set for them. The second assumption is that effective teaching and effective evaluation go together. Evaluation should inform instruction and determine what pathways teachers should follow to make learning most effective. In other words, effective teachers use assessments to increase the quality of instruction.

Assessment is a key component of standards-based learning. Educators cannot merely say that a student had learned something or met a standard; district and state officials want proof. This proof implies some type of measurement. Increased testing of students to obtain this proof was inevitable in

the standards movement because assessments were seen as keys to promoting change and educational reform. Administrators and those encouraging change wanted to document the improvement in concrete ways rather than relying on subjective information. "Standards-based assessment is the process of determining if and to what degree a student can demonstrate, in context, his/her understanding and ability relative to identified standards of learning" (Lambert 1999, 6).

Physical educators have not always done a good job using assessments with their programs. Some physical education teachers equate assessment with determining student grades and use assessments only for grading purposes. This usage was exemplified when one of us asked a student teacher to administer skill tests during a field experience. The student teacher replied that she was unable to give skill tests because the district in which she was teaching only allowed physical education teachers to grade students on attendance and written tests. When assessments are viewed from this narrow standpoint, they lose their potential to become powerful instructional tools.

In 1987, approximately 1,400 physical educators (98% of the respondents) reported that participation was the most frequently used factor in determining student grades (Hensley et al. 1987). Despite the fact that most physical education teacher preparation programs include a course on measurement and evaluation, slightly less than one-half of those surveyed reported using written tests with their classes. Other subjective factors used to determine grades included attitude, effort, improvement, and potential. The article noted the heightened demand for accountability and the need to develop and use better evaluation techniques. The authors said, "It is likely that the survival of our profession may, to some extent, depend upon the efficacy of our measurement and evaluation efforts" (Hensley et al. 1987, 61). The call for reform in assessment practices was clearly stated in this article.

Assessments have many purposes in education and in physical education programs. In physical education, assessments can effectively do the following:

► Measure student learning to show progress and motivate students

► Measure student progress to plan future instruction

► Provide feedback to students

► Document program effectiveness

► Formalize the observation process

► Inform and document student learning for parents and administrators

Too many times teachers only assess students when they calculate grades. Assessment can enhance instruction because it increases teacher effectiveness. The benefits of assessment to your physical education program clearly call for their use beyond calculation of grades.

Measure Student Learning

For students, assessment provides a means of measuring progress. In the acquisition of motor skills or sports, learning happens in minute steps. Progress can be slow and students can become discouraged. This frustration is especially true for lower-skilled students who may have difficulty learning motor activities, and a lack of previous success can lead directly to lack of motivation. Measuring progress along the way motivates students because they can see concrete evidence of their improvement. Through assessments, students can track improvement and see gains. Measurement becomes a powerful means for improving student learning.

Plan Future Instruction

Student progress should be measured to plan future instruction. Much of instruction tends to be progressive as one lesson builds on the next, moving students toward a teacher's final goal. Teachers build tomorrow's lessons based on what students learned today. For teachers, planning for the next lesson without measuring student progress is like trying to hit a target without knowing where to aim. Sometimes lessons are taught, but students fail to learn the desired material. Assessments let teachers know which concepts students grasped and what needs to be presented again. Student needs should determine lesson content and how it is taught. Without some type of systematic measurement or assessment, determining the content for the next lesson is merely a guessing game.

Provide Feedback

The primary reason to assess should be to give feedback to students about progress toward meeting learning goals of the teacher and program. Because of the overt nature of physical activity, teachers frequently give feedback to students to improve their performance. Feedback is inadequate when teachers fail to inform students of their expectations. When teachers explain their assessment strategies and procedures as they give learning objectives, students have a clearer picture of what teachers ultimately expect them to learn. Using assessments to measure student learning provides concrete feedback to students; it informs them of what they must do to achieve mastery and competence.

Document Program Effectiveness

It no longer is sufficient to say that students learn because they attended a given class (i.e., seat time). Learning must be documented. Accountability is currently a concern in education. People in charge (e.g., state officials, school boards, district superintendents, district curriculum specialists, principals) are held accountable by states for documenting student learning. Therefore, assessment is no longer an option; it is a necessity.

As academic requirements increase, physical educators must be prepared to justify the time spent learning physical activity in a school curriculum. Classes must be educative rather than recreational, and learning must be documented. Teachers can no longer say, "I taught today; therefore, my students must have learned." Success must be documented in education as it is in other sectors. Salespeople know they're successful when customers buy the product. Figuratively speaking, assessment tells us whether students browsed or if they bought.

Although physical education has not been held accountable with a rigorous testing format like that found in math, reading, or science, it has faced accountability in terms of decreasing requirements for secondary students. Many states have decreased the high school graduation requirement for physical education. According to the 1996 Surgeon General's Report, currently only 25% of all high school students are enrolled in physical education classes (U.S. Department of Health and Human Services 1996). Illinois is the only state with a K-12 daily physical education requirement, and even there exemptions are allowed (NASPE 2001). These requirement changes are the result in some instances of a perceived need by educators to spend more time on the basics (math, science, social studies, and language arts). However, some of the changes are a reaction to poor physical education programs. Some teachers don't really teach; they simply organize games and activities for students or provide a recreational setting and allow students to play (i.e., they throw out the ball and watch them play). Other teachers organize classes into activity units lasting one to two weeks with some instructional days, but the majority of the class time is spent playing games. Thinking that students can learn complex motor skills in one day is ludicrous; nonetheless, some teachers expect students to do so. Their intent is to cover activities rather than expect students to become competent performers and achieve levels of excellence. In these situations, little learning occurs. These teachers say that they don't have time to assess student learning. Given the relatively short period used to cover information concerning the activity, little if any learning occurs anyway.

Formalize the Observation Process

Physical education teachers have used observation for years to provide feedback to students. Through assessments, teachers record this feedback and document student performance to help both teacher and student in future lessons. Teachers have records or proof with which to document student improvement and achievement to parents and administrators. Informal (unwritten) feedback can be fleeting and is not always accurate; sometimes teachers are surprised by their observations. When a teacher watches a class systematically during an assessment, it may become evident that not all students are participating equally. Some aggressive students may have more opportunities than passive students to respond. Students who play certain positions may have more opportunities than others to respond. Sometimes competent bystanders appear to be engaged and on task, but when viewed through an assessment lens, they rarely have opportunities to respond (Tousignant 1981). By formalizing the observation, teachers can concretely identify student behaviors that they sensed were occurring but could not necessarily prove—as well as noting other things that were less apparent. This information can provide proof of what is occurring in class.

Informing Others

Assessments inform and document student learning for parents and administrators. Grades are probably the most common use of assessment. At the secondary level, physical education teachers are usually required to give students a grade, which symbolizes the degree to which students met either teacher or program learning objectives. Grading is an important function of assessment, and teachers must use methods to ensure that it is done validly and reliably. Chapter 10 of this book discusses grading in depth.

The Need to Change the Type of Assessments Used

Although some physical education teachers do a good job of using assessment to augment learning in their classes, it has been our observation that a majority of teachers could improve their current practices. These problems range from not using any assessments to using assessments ineffectively. For physical educators who do assessment, the three most common test formats used before the inception of performance-based assessments included written tests, fitness tests, and skill tests. These tests were often flawed, leaving much room for improvement in assessment practices. The following section discusses some of the problems that we have observed with assessment. These problems lead us to conclude that other assessment formats, such as performance-based assessments, are needed.

No Assessments Given

Some physical education teachers do not do assessments. They determine grades through attendance, dressing for class, and a difficult-to-define category called effort. With this method, physical educators have failed to document student achievement, making themselves vulnerable to budget and time cuts. Effort is difficult to assess with low-fit students without some way to monitor heart rate. Low-fit students perceive that they are working hard and giving 100% effort, but in comparison with other more fit students, their output is much lower. Documenting student achievement with performance-based assessments can produce tangible, observable results; thus, it is an excellent way to measure achievement for all students.

Written Tests

Many of the written tests used in physical education measure basic knowledge of rules and definitions. Questions evaluate student recall of knowledge and sometimes understanding (levels one and two of Bloom's Taxonomy, respectively). They rarely address a student's ability to think critically about various aspects of a sport or activity, nor do they address complex scenarios that can create problems and disagreements during game play when students are unsure about how to proceed or make a call. Questions on written tests that assess the upper levels of Bloom's Taxonomy are difficult to write, which is probably why most teachers don't include them on

written tests. Although it is important for students to know basic facts, it is also important for them to know other things relative to skill performance. Performance-based assessments can be used to determine a student's ability to use the knowledge presented in class in an applied setting.

Fitness Tests

Many physical education teachers administer fitness tests every fall and spring, only to let results sit on the shelf for the remainder of the year. Fitness test results can tell teachers whether students are unfit and can be used in planning future lessons. If a teacher's goal is to have students reach a criterion set by a standardized fitness test, then fitness testing should be done and future lessons geared toward helping students achieve this goal. Unless results of fitness testing are used to improve student learning, testing should not be done. Additionally, the Physical Education Content Standards call for students to use this information to develop personal fitness improvement programs (NASPE 1995). Performance-based assessments might call for students to create such a plan based on the analysis of personal fitness test results and knowledge of what optimal levels of fitness should be causing students to use fitness results in a manner that would be helpful to them as adults.

Skill Tests

Standardized skill tests present several problems. First, they are time consuming to set up and administer when test protocol is followed. When, for instance, a volleyball serving test is to be valid, the net must be set to an exact height, which presents problems in schools with unofficial equipment: The server has to stand a given distance from the net; the ball must fall within certain zones on the opposite court; and so on. The second problem is that many skill tests are actually not developmentally appropriate for children. If we consider the volleyball serving test, weaker students have difficulty getting the ball over the net from the specified distance (French et al. 1991).

A third problem is that skill tests are representations of a student's ability to play a game. At the secondary level, a teacher's goal is usually to teach a student how to play a game or do an activity. Skill tests may evaluate discrete skills in a fairly closed (unchanging) environment, but they do not evaluate a student's ability to use these skills during game play. Game play involves decisions about which skill to use, requiring students to make choices dependant on evaluation of a complex environment. Skill tests do not measure these decisions. Performance-based assessments designed to assess student ability during game play evaluate this ability more directly than do conventional skill tests.

Although skill tests have their place in the instructional process by measuring student performance of skills necessary for game play, some teachers do not utilize them effectively in the instructional process. Figure 1.6 illustrates examples of how skill tests can be used ineffectively.

Because one of the essential components of performance-based assessments is the inclusion of criteria by which to judge performance, some of the problems alluded to in this section are eliminated. Also, because performance-based assessments can be administered multiple times, assessments can provide feedback and encourage students to improve skills.

Ineffective Uses of Skill Tests

- Teachers typically administer skill and written tests at the completion of the unit, making the tests summative. Since instruction is completed, any feedback gleaned from the test about deficiencies in student learning or performance is not used in the instructional process.

- If teachers show students the tests on the testing day for the first time, then students have little chance to practice and improve skills. Students frequently learn test protocols and complete the test on the same day.

- If a teacher used skill tests as part of a student's grade and the student had a "bad day" on the skill tests, then the grade for the unit suffers. Despite stellar performances on other parts of the unit, poor test scores adversely affect the student's grade.

- Teachers don't always explain what they are looking for on the skill tests. For instance, a teacher was observed skill testing the volleyball set and forearm pass, giving students 10 chances to return a tossed ball to him. Students assumed that the number of balls returned to the teacher determined their score. When interviewed after the testing, the teacher revealed that he was evaluating process, or correct form, and 10 opportunities gave him ample chance to determine student ability, but it had nothing to do with the final grade.

Figure 1.6   Unless properly administered, skill tests don't assess student learning or achievement.

We do not claim that performance-based assessments cure all the assessment problems associated with physical education. However, we *are* saying that when used appropriately, performance-based assessments can address some of the concerns detailed here. When assessment is incorporated into the learning process, student achievement improves.

Conclusion

Education is usually a reflection of society. Just as society is experiencing much change today, reformers are calling for change in the educational system as well. New criteria are being written to specify what students should know and be able to do. Reformers also state that we must find better methods for teaching and assessment. Accountability is being mandated for both teachers and students; much of this pressure comes from groups outside the field of education. Performance-based assessments have been developed to meet these new assessment needs. They differ from traditional assessments in that they require students to actively demonstrate their skills and knowledge on some type of task while providing them with criteria that designate the expected level of quality for that performance.

This chapter outlined the benefits of using performance-based assessments; it also pointed out ways to avoid some of the problems. This book is designed to help physical educators incorporate performance-based assessments into their instructional formats. By understanding the advantages of using performance-based assessments as well as how to do them, physical educators can incorporate new instruction tools into their programs to both enhance student learning and document student achievement to others.

If physical education is going to survive, changes concerning current practices need to occur to increase our status with other educators, students, parents, and administrators. Programs that are meaningful to students must be developed as a part of this change. Students must be given choices in what they learn and how they demonstrate this learning. Current assessment practices must change, shifting the focus from the *evaluation* of learning to the *enhancement* of it. Many good programs have a difficult time demonstrating that they do meaningful things. Assessment is the key to making positive changes in physical education programs and documenting them.

CHAPTER TWO

What Is Continuous Performance-Based Assessment?

In our concern for the well-being of students, however, we must not make the mistake of lowering our academic standards merely to make school easy. On the contrary, a classroom environment centered on each student's academic well-being must hold those students accountable for the attainment of high academic standards that are both clearly articulated and not negotiable . . . Just trying hard, while critical for success, is not enough. Our classroom assessments should define for students precisely what we expect of them—they must define the truly important achievement targets. (Stiggins 1997, p. vi)

With attention directed toward student achievement, the word *accountability* has become more common, and it is no longer sufficient to say that students learned anything because they simply attended a given class. State officials, school boards, district superintendents, district curriculum specialists, and principals are holding teachers accountable for documenting student learning—making assessment a *necessity*, rather than an *option*.

As discussed in chapter 1, part of the dissatisfaction with physical education actually concerns the assessment process. Many educators feel that traditional forms of assessment (multiple choice, true-false, selected response) measure factual knowledge without requiring students to apply this information. Too often students who score well on selected-response testing items are unable to use this information in a real-world setting. Higher levels of learning—identified in Bloom's Taxonomy as analysis, synthesis, and evaluation—are often not required of students when teachers use traditional forms of assessments to evaluate students. Typical traditional assessments assess recall or factual knowledge but do not ask students to apply this information to other settings. In an attempt to measure higher levels of student learning, many educators proposed new types of assessments. In 1989, Grant Wiggins outlined several alternative types of assessment in an article titled "A True Test: Toward More Authentic and Equitable Assessment" (1989a). Wiggins proposed that students be required to apply information using a more performance-based type of assessment. In this article, he proposed having students do tasks and solve problems similar to what adults do in everyday life. According to Wiggins, testing should be central experiences in learning, giving students an opportunity to showcase their learning in areas that we want students to be competent in.

With traditional testing formats, teachers typically don't do much with assessment results other than use them to calculate student grades. Students are held accountable for knowledge on a test; once that is completed,

teachers move on to the next topic. With too many educators, student competence or mastery of material is less of an issue than covering a given quantity of material. Traditional forms of assessment typically measure the amount of content knowledge or facts students have learned. With Wiggins' proposed assessments, students complete real-world tasks, which require them to know facts and understand concepts well enough to apply them. These assessments are **formative**, meaning students worked many days on a project or performance and were given multiple opportunities to revisit and improve it, thus giving students multiple chances to document learning. The culminating event or performance was probably a task familiar to those in the field and represented mastery of a body of knowledge. In his article, Wiggins proposed a more performance-based form of assessment. Noted assessment authority Richard Stiggins observed, "Performance assessments can be based on observations of process while skills are being demonstrated, or on the evaluation of products created" (1997, 77).

Wiggins and McTighe (1998) identified three basic types of assessment: quiz and test items, academic **prompts**, and performance tasks and projects (see figure 2.1). Types of assessments can be placed on a continuum. On the left are objective tests, those types that have a single correct answer (e.g., true or false, multiple choice, matching) with lots of teacher control; on the right lie those assessments that evaluate learning while giving students much choice in how they wish to demonstrate mastery or competence. The right side of this continuum contains **performance-based assessments**, which often incorporate human

Recall of knowledge			Application of knowledge	
Selected response			Constructed response	
True-false, multiple choice, matching	Fill-in-the-blank	Short answer essay	Open response	Performance-based assessments
Demonstration of knowledge competence			Demonstration of skill	

Figure 2.1 Types of assessment can be placed on a continuum.

judgment in the evaluation process. Not only do they assess student learning, they are also designed to increase student interest and prepare students for life after school. Obviously, teachers must provide parameters and guidelines for those assessments on the right, but students have a great deal of input and freedom in how they choose to address the final product and performance. Part III of this book gives numerous examples of performance-based assessments and demonstrates how these can be woven throughout a unit of instruction to measure learning.

Characteristics of Performance-Based Assessment

Performance-based assessments are typically open-ended, complex, and authentic. They are used in units that are long enough to allow in-depth student learning. Although they require more time to administer, they can be combined with instruction to enhance student performance. Performance-based assessments give teachers new ways to look at student achievement. Figure 2.2 illustrates characteristics typically associated with performance-based assessment in physical education (Lund 1997).

Performance-based assessments satisfy many of the changes that were identified in the reports calling for educational reform. The next section is designed to clarify for you,

the reader, the characteristics of performance-based assessment. Since they are considered key components, a thorough understanding of them will be helpful as you begin to develop your own tasks.

Worthwhile Tasks

Looking at what an expert in the field does on a regular basis is an excellent source of ideas for performance-based assessment. In physical education, performance-based assessments can include game play, a dance or gymnastics routine, or competitions such as track or swimming meets (for other examples, see figure 2.3). Several professions associated with physical activity (i.e., radio announcers, officials, people reviewing and critiquing dance concerts, newspaper writers, coaches) also must demonstrate knowledge and understanding of various aspects of performance.

Any of the physical education experts (i.e., those who use the information taught in physical education in their professions, such as sports reporters, announcers, officials, and coaches) can provide wonderful possibilities for performance-based assessments. Teachers can create engaging assessments for students to evaluate learning using nontraditional formats (see figure 2.4).

Higher-Level Thinking and Complex Learning

Performance-based assessments typically require students to take facts and use them in a meaningful way. Higher-level thinking skills are used in many facets of physical education. Performance-based assessments force

Characteristics of Performance-Based Assessments

- Require the presentation of worthwhile or meaningful tasks that are designed to be representative of performance in the field
- Emphasize higher-level thinking and more complex learning
- Articulate criteria in advance so that students know how they will be evaluated
- Embed assessments so firmly in the curriculum that they are practically indistinguishable from instruction
- Expect students to present their work publicly when possible
- Involve the examination of the process as well as the products of learning

Figure 2.2 Performance-based assessments require a different approach to teaching than do traditional assessment practices.

Examples of Performance-Based Assessments

- Announcing an in-class ball game
- Creating a script for announcing an imaginary game
- Officiating during game play
- Writing a critique of a dance performance of peers or of a video shown in class
- Reporting on a class tournament for the school newspaper or morning announcements
- Coaching a team during a sport or activity unit

Figure 2.3 Performance-based assessments often represent tasks that a professional in the field would perform.

Figure 2.4   Announcing a game in class requires students to demonstrate many different types of knowledge about a game.

students to use higher-level thinking skills such as analysis, synthesis, and evaluation. Consider the many complex decisions regarding choice of skill and strategy made during game play or during gamelike situations. Coaches and teachers analyze performance of game skills by comparing them with a standard of excellent performance. When students are required to use information, teachers can better determine student understanding. It is one thing to know facts or information about a topic; it is quite another thing to create a product or performance that uses this information. Forcing students to apply factual knowledge will sometimes reveal incomplete learning or misunderstanding of a concept or topic. Identifying the five components of health-related fitness on a written test uses a lower level of thinking skills than a student project that requires students to evaluate their personal fitness levels and develop programs that target areas needing improvement. The latter assessment requires students to analyze information and create a plan, which is far more challenging, while at the same time more meaningful.

Articulate Criteria in Advance

Too often teachers give students assignments without explaining the details of what they expect. Students complete assignments on a trial-and-error basis, hoping that they guess correctly about what the teacher intends for them to do. With performance-based assess-

ments, students are given the **rubric** that is used for evaluation of the assessment. (Chapter 3 explains in depth how to develop a rubric.) When teachers write down what they expect of students, teachers develop clearer pictures of expectations concerning the assessment, which then helps *students* understand what exactly is expected of them. Writing criteria frequently causes teachers to go back to the assessment and revise part of it. (*Note:* This step occurs before giving the assessment to students.) Providing students with criteria helps demystify the assessment, allowing them to focus on important components and factors while completing the assessment. Showing students examples of past student performances or products also helps convey teacher expectations for the assessment.

Criteria Firmly Embedded in the Curriculum

Some physical education teachers say that they don't assess students because it takes too much time. Because performance-based assessments have an instructional component, learning and assessing can work simultaneously. For instance, when doing a dance unit, students might choreograph a dance sequence to indicate student understanding of certain dance concepts and principles. When students do this choreography, they learn about shape, effort, flow, levels, and so forth. The dance they present is then evaluated through the use of a rubric that teachers developed for assessment. Because students have the criteria, they can self-assess or peer-assess as they complete the assignment. Teachers can provide additional feedback while coaching students on criteria and explain expectations to students as they complete the project. The criteria given to students are those that the teacher uses to evaluate the final product. The learning task and assessment become seamless and impossible to separate. Various instructional styles such as practice, reciprocal, or self-check incorporate assessment and instruction. By having criteria of correct performance, students have an opportunity to see the criteria listed, which is beneficial for visual learners. The reciprocal teaching style requires students to analyze the performance of a partner and compare the performance of a classmate or partner with the criteria given by the teacher. The recipient of the feedback benefits from having someone watch his or her performance individually while the person giving feedback has an opportunity to see what these criteria look like while someone else is performing.

Present Student Work Publicly When Possible

When people perform for an audience, the audience holds them accountable for a good performance. Given the overt nature of physical education, often game play and other athletic activities are done with others watching, so this characteristic is familiar to physical educators. An audience should be determined for written work whenever possible as well. A brochure done for parents' night about a healthy heart has far stronger accountability than one done for the teacher (see figure 2.5). This brochure was handed out during parents' night as students explained how the heart functioned and guided adults through an obstacle course designed to simulate the different parts of the circulatory system. Sharing such written assignments with others is also an excellent way for students to show off their hard work. Group dance performances or gymnastics routines can also be presented for others, and game play is public as well.

Wiggins (1989) notes that even when an audience is simulated, there is an element of authenticity. Obviously for a dance performance, a real audience is preferred; however, videotapes of student dance performances that are done for

Figure 2.5 This student-made healthy heart brochure containing information from a fitness unit was distributed to adults at a school open house.

an imaginary situation or audience have an element of authenticity as well. The audience designated determines the focus of the project or performance. A dance choreographed for high school basketball entertainment is different from one created for a stage performance.

Process and Product of Learning Are Both Important

The process of learning is very important in performance-based assessment. How students complete an assessment is just as important as the final product with performance-based assessments. When assessments are scored, the process used by students must be included in the criteria, as this is an important part of the learning process. For example, in adventure education, teamwork and cooperation are key elements of the process. Adventure education assessments require students to identify the processes used while solving problems given to them by the teacher. Students not demonstrating teamwork and cooperation "fail" the assessment even though they may complete the task. Since shortcutting a process merely to obtain an identified product negates the strength and value of a performance-based assessment, process is included in the evaluation of performance-based assessments.

Types of Performance-Based Assessments

A variety of performance-based assessments can be used to evaluate student learning. We have identified 10 of our favorites that we believe are the most common types of performance-based assessment. This section introduces and describes them for you. Chapters 5 and 6 provide additional information on open response questions and using student portfolios. Part III of this book provides many examples of these performance-based assessments so that you can see how they are implemented during an activity unit.

Traditional testing formats, such as skill tests or selected-response written tests, do have their place in physical education. When measuring factual knowledge or skills in a closed environment, they are an efficient and effective way to do so. This book does not downplay their importance, but many other sources and books explain them in detail. Since the focus of this book is performance-based assessment, they are not covered or explained in this text.

Teacher Observations

Many teachers use observations to make assessments about student learning. While watching skill practice, teachers make judgments about the quality of student performances and usually provide feedback to students. By writing out the evaluations being done, teachers have concrete ways to document student learning, thus formalizing the observation. Beginning teachers often make the mistake of only watching a few members of the class. As such, when they focus on the most skilled students, they assume students learned the lessons taught. Based on their observations, they assume that students have learned the skill and move on to more difficult skills or activities. If other members of the class had not accomplished the easier tasks, they would be trying to do activities for which they had no chance for success. By doing purposeful teacher evaluations and focusing on

a variety of students with varying ability levels, teachers can determine which students are learning and which need additional instruction.

When teachers systematically target students to be observed and then rotate these observations so that every student is evaluated, these observations can be used to calculate student grades. It is helpful for teachers to bring these observations to parent-teacher conferences; they help teachers explain to adults what their children accomplished in the class. Such documentations are also helpful when teachers talk to others about the success of a program and the students' development of skills, as they have concrete proof of achievement.

Peer Observations

Peers are often good resources for evaluation. Checklists or other rubrics can be developed that provide feedback or evaluation for classmates. **Peer observations** give students their own personal teacher or fitness trainer doing an evaluation of performance (see figure 2.6). The observation can become part of student portfolios, either demonstrating competency in doing the evaluation (i.e., knowing what

Figure 2.6   Peer evaluation can assess higher levels of learning, as students are r_____ evaluate the performance _____ acteristics of skilled perfo___
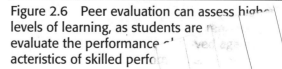

correct performance looks like) or mastery of some skill as verified by a classmate. Teachers might actually have students develop a checklist for observation to check understanding of game play elements, critical elements of a skill, and so on. Some caveats are offered here. First, students must be taught how to do these assessments and know which criteria are important. Too often teachers assume students know how to do peer assessments when actually they do not. Second, for an assessment to be beneficial, it must be done accurately and objectively. Teachers must encourage students to evaluate performances as honestly as possible, reminding them that the purpose of assessment is to provide genuine feedback to improve performance.

Self-Observations

As adults, we rarely have someone around to provide feedback on performance. Teaching students to do **self-observations** can be helpful both for improving immediate performance and also as a skill necessary for adults. Again, it is imperative that teachers educate students about this process and not just assume that students know what they are doing. Specific criteria for the assessment are necessary to provide guidance to students as they move toward being self-sufficient learners. Chapter 3 explains to the reader how to select criteria for assessment.

Game Play and Modified Game Play

Game play is a performance-based evaluation done while students are engaged in playing a sport or activity. Various aspects of game play can be evaluated—psychomotor skills, knowledge of rules, use of strategy, teamwork—each depending on the purpose of the assessment and the criteria contained in the rubric or scoring guide. Game play is very complex. To improve performance, students, regardless of their ability, must understand in which areas they are the most competent and which areas require further learning or practice. By evaluating several aspects of game play, the teacher has a true picture of which concepts students understand well enough to use in game play. Since many teachers want students to be able to play a game when they teach a sporting activity, evaluation of students while they are engaged in game play is a valuable learning tool, regardless of the skill

level of the student. Small-sided games (one-on-one, two-on-two, etc.) also present excellent assessment opportunities. Many sports now have tournaments that are growing in popularity that involve these smaller teams (e.g., volleyball, basketball, soccer). Although the strategy used for these smaller teams is somewhat different, they provide excellent opportunities to evaluate students in physical education.

Role-Plays

Role-plays are simply scenarios developed by teachers to assess some components of physical education or physical activity (see figure 2.7). They are especially valuable for examin-

---

Examples of Role-Plays

- A discussion between a coach and a player. The player doesn't feel that he or she is receiving a fair amount of playing time.
- A discussion between a coach and player. The coach has decided to cut the player from the squad.
- Two friends on rival swim teams meet in a local restaurant after the competition between their teams. One person was beaten by the other in a race, and the winner qualified for state.
- An interview with a coach who knows the game was won by cheating.
- A discussion between two students. One was spotting the other and laughing and fooling around. The student being spotted fell and is now paralyzed.
- A discussion between two dancers who are trying out for the dance team. How much help and feedback should be given to each dancer? The one receiving it might make the squad and the one giving it might not.
- A Native American decides to talk with his or her coach about the difficulty in playing for a team whose mascot is derogatory.
- An interview with a referee after he or she booted a player from a game because of a display of poor sportsmanship.
- An interview with a referee who allowed an overly physical player to continue play, and eventually that player hurt another player.
- An interview with a coach who allows players to continue to play even though the coach knows the players are hurt and could be seriously injured if they continue. The coach feels the team cannot win without these players.

Figure 2.7 Role-plays can put students into situations commonly encountered in physical education for assessment of affective domain learning.

ing some of the **affective domain** components, especially those connected with being sensitive to diverse learners, promoting teamwork and cooperation, creating a safe, nourishing environment, and so on. Through role-playing, teachers can present students with a challenging, real-world problem and evaluate decisions made while the scenario develops. Role-plays may be live, videotaped, or written out. Students can work individually or in small groups to develop a solution to the problem presented. Role-plays can be used as components for student portfolios. Chapter 8 contains examples of this type of assessment.

Event Tasks

Event tasks are performance tasks that can be completed within a single class period or less (NASPE 1995) and usually include psychomotor activity in physical education (see figure 2.8).

Game play, dance compositions, or gymnastics routines are all examples of event tasks. Having students create a novel game using certain pieces of equipment would determine if students know the elements of game play. Requiring certain manipulative or locomotor skills would allow the teacher to evaluate those in an applied setting. **Adventure education event tasks** could evaluate problem-solving, cooperation, and team-building skills. Event tasks are popular assessment options for physical education. (For a sample event task rubric, see figure 2.9.)

Interviews

In certain situations, teachers might choose to **interview** students to evaluate knowledge. Explaining the reasoning behind choosing a game play strategy might reveal to a teacher whether a student really understands when a particular strategy is best implemented. After

---

Equipment needed:

- Beach ball
- One 100-foot rope

Activity is suitable for 8-12 participants.

Statement of problem

Students at a local school in Indiana do not have a beach ball. The students at a Kentucky school are willing to share a beach ball, but there is no bridge nearby that crosses the Ohio River. Students have to work together to get the ball across the river using only the ropes that have been strung across the "river" (approximate distance of 45 feet). It is very important that the ball not fall into the river because the current will carry it away and no one will have a beach ball.

Give students five to seven minutes of planning time to come up with a solution. Students can plan together how to move the ball from one side of the river to the other, but actual implementation takes place as follows:

The two groups of students are placed about 40-45 feet apart. Draw lines on the ground or place tape on pavement or gym floor to mark the "banks" of the river. The rope is doubled, placed on the ground, and lying across the river between the two groups of students. The beach ball is on the "Kentucky" side. Students must figure out a plan to move the ball from one side to the other without the ball falling into the river, and of course no students are allowed in the "river."

Possible solutions

1. Spread the ropes wide enough to make tracks for the ball to roll across to the other side. Students will have to elevate the ropes on one side, hold the ropes taut, and roll the ball slowly across.

2. Students can tie the ball to the rope in some manner and make a conveyor belt.

3. There may be other solutions. Students are pretty ingenious.

Assessment is measuring cooperation and whether students get input from all members of the group. Ideas must be shared and group members must be accepting of all viable solutions. Comments like, "That's a stupid idea" are inappropriate. No one student should be the boss; rather students should all have suggestions, ideas, and contributions. Rubric criteria should address cooperative attitudes and acceptance of ideas from others.

Figure 2.8   Example of an event task.

Beach Ball Traverse, created by Margaret Pentecost, University of Louisville.

Distinguished ("Let's Do Mount Everest Next")

Members of the group brainstorm before beginning to solve the problem so that everyone's voice is heard before starting to move. Members of the group not responding initially are solicited for their ideas and opinions. It is difficult to determine a leader because the group is working in harmony and as a team. Positive and supportive comments come from all members of the group leading to an enthusiastic and positive climate. At the conclusion of the exercise all members of the group have a sense that they contributed to the solution.

Proficient ("Pike's Peak, Here We Come")

All members of the group are encouraged to give their ideas. Positive and supportive comments come from various members of the group, and everyone receives at least one compliment. Group members have a sense that a team effort led to the final outcome or solution.

Satisfactory ("Together We Can Make It")

Group members solve the problem through trial and error. Several different students assume leadership roles as the problem unfolds. Opinions of group members are accepted. Students cooperate with each other to gain a solution.

Unsatisfactory ("Backyard Adventurers")

One or two students assume leadership roles and solve the problem without input from other members of the group. Derogatory comments are heard (e.g., "That's a stupid idea"). Ideas from some students are rejected without exploring their merit. Students may or may not successfully complete the task.

Figure 2.9   Event task rubric for evaluating Beach Ball Traverse.

game play, a student might do a self-analysis of personal game play or an assessment of game play as related to other members of the team (i.e., teamwork or elements of fair play). Obviously, an in-depth interview would not be an appropriate method of assessment for a class of 50, but in situations where a short interview might be appropriate, interviews are an excellent form of assessment. Interviews can be used when a teacher wishes to sample student knowledge rather than assess every individual in class. Information gained through the interview can be used to plan subsequent lessons. This assessment option also benefits students for whom English is a second language, for those with learning disabilities, and for those with writing deficiencies. Higher levels of analysis and synthesis might be revealed through an interview that would not be possible for some students.

Essays

Essays as performance assessments are not the typical compositions one writes for English classes. Essays must have a purpose and an audience and must address that performance tasks are open-ended, complex, and authentic. These written compositions are typically used to evaluate cognitive knowledge. Figure 2.10 illustrates examples of essays that could be used for physical education, along with what specifically to assess.

In all of the mentioned examples, students are given a realistic task, an audience is identified, and a product is created. The tasks are open-ended, giving students a variety of ways to answer them. While writing the rubric, teachers must remember to accommodate the breadth of responses, allowing student creativity while at the same time focusing students on the objectives of the assessment. Chapter 3 provides additional suggestions for writing rubrics.

Open Response Questions

Open response questions give teachers additional written alternatives for assessing how students use or apply knowledge outside the world of the gymnasium classroom. Although at first glance they resemble an essay question, a key difference is that an open response question can usually begin with the words "it depends." In other words, the answer tends to depend on the situation and there are several ways to respond to the question correctly. With open response questions students are presented with a real-world scenario or problem and given an opportunity to solve it. They require complex or higher-order thinking to respond because students usually analyze something (e.g., compare and contrast),

Examples of Essay Topics (With Assessment Rationale)

- Write a speech to be given at a school board meeting outlining the benefits of physical education (to assess student knowledge of the benefits of physical education).
- Create a brochure to be handed out to parents during an open house, back-to-school night explaining some concept learned in class (see figure 2.5).
- Write a dialogue between James Naismith (the inventor of basketball) and Luther Gulick (his teacher, who made the assignment that led to the creation of the sport) explaining what a good game should include (to assess student knowledge of the components and elements of games).
- Create the broadcast dialogue for a sport announcer during an inning of the World Series or any sport or championship game (to assess knowledge of rules, depth of understanding for strategy, etc.).
- Create a pregame interview with a famous coach discussing the strategy to be used for the upcoming game (to assess understanding of game play strategy and when it is best used).
- Have students write a review or critique of a dance performance (either an in-class presentation or a video of a dance performance) for the local newspaper (to assess knowledge of the elements of dance choreography and performance).
- Write a letter to a dance department or a coach outlining your skills and how they could fit in and benefit that program so that person could recruit you as a dancer or as a player for the team (self-assessment of performance skills).

Figure 2.10   Essays can demonstrate student ability to apply knowledge of a sport or activity in a creative format.

propose a solution for a scenario, or solve a problem. Because open response questions are a relatively new form of assessment for many physical education teachers, they are explained with greater detail in chapter 5 of this book.

Journals

Journal writing provides an excellent opportunity for teachers to look at affective domain components of student learning. By providing students with a specific question or focus, teachers might determine when a student struggles to learn new skills, feels competence during instruction, feels a sense of teamwork or fair play occurring during class, and so on. In addition to affective domain evaluation, teachers might use journals to self-assess certain skills. The assessment of personal abilities could also include cognitive knowledge by requiring students to write the critical elements of a skill and indicating which of these are most important for optimal performance. Students could also indicate the skills that were problematic, which ultimately helps teachers plan future lessons.

When having students write about feelings, a teacher should not evaluate these for quality of thought. When that is done, students stop being honest because it adversely affects grades. A teacher can hold students accountable for completion of the journal entry, use of correct spelling, and demonstration of cognitive content, but it is not advisable to evaluate and grade actual feelings.

Student Projects

Student projects generally require a fair amount of time to complete and may involve work outside of the regularly scheduled class. Most projects call for students to create some type of concrete product, which can be submitted for evaluation. Students utilize knowledge gained in class and apply this to a real-world setting (for examples, see figure 2.11).

Because student projects require time and effort outside of the actual class, they extend the time students are associated with physical education material. Students are usually willing to spend the extra time necessary to complete the assessment because the projects are engaging and interesting. These projects utilize higher levels of thinking by creating new products, analyzing a situation or performance, or making an evaluation or determination about something.

Student Performances

Student performances are often used as culminating events in performance-based assessment. In this situation, the instruction of the unit is geared toward giving students the skills necessary to complete the performance. Using the objectives for the unit, teachers design the parameters for the **culminating performance** before beginning a unit, and all instruction for that unit is geared toward having students successfully complete this task. Examples of culminating events include gymnastics routines performed for the class gymnastics meet, a dance choreographed

---

Examples of Student Projects

- Students choreograph a dance and film it for a video. This piece demonstrates student knowledge of various elements of dance design along with concepts of level, shape, and so on.
- Students create a piece of equipment designed to exercise a muscle group or body part (e.g., abdominal muscles, upper body, quadriceps).
- Students research a playground or childhood game (e.g., four square, jacks, tether ball, hop scotch) to learn the history and rules to then teach children from a neighboring elementary school how to play this game. Products include summary of history, rule sheets, any artifacts used for teaching, a video of game play, and so on.
- Student shadows an adult for a day (preferably in a career the student hopes to pursue) and develops ways to increase this person's level of activity. The goal would be to have at least 30 minutes of moderate activity during a normal workday.

Figure 2.11　Many student projects are developed from the challenges faced by people in the field of physical education and sport.

by a group of students over the course of several weeks, training for a cross country-type run, or a synchronized swimming performance that requires several weeks to learn.

Students are often required to use higher-level thinking skills to complete these performances and learn new skills that push them to higher levels of achievement. Instruction for the unit is geared toward providing students with the skills and information necessary for students' success on this culminating performance. Student performances are labor intensive both for the teacher and for the students, but they frequently yield a product that makes students very proud.

Student Logs

Teachers might require students to keep track of practice trials or time spent doing various activities. A **student log** is a method of recording these practice sessions. It can be used to record both in-class or out-of-class activities. Some teachers have an instant activity posted when students enter the gymnasium for class. If charts or recording sheets are available, then students can record their scores for the day. Higher scores could be the result of better skill, or they could be the result of getting to class quickly and having more time to practice. The net result either way is an increased opportunity to respond. When the same skill or activity is repeated for several days in a row, students can document any improvement. When teachers do not see improvement, it indicates that the student was either making errors or demonstrating a lack of effort. Teachers can provide additional attention or instruction to those needing help.

Logs can also be used to document practice or activity out of class. For example, if a student were lacking flexibility during a gym-

nastics unit, the teacher could prescribe exercises to improve the areas needing work. The log is an excellent method of documenting the extra work completed; it is also a motivator and reminder for the student to stretch. When the student's flexibility shows improvement during class, then the teacher can conclude that the logs were appropriate. Lack of improvement would signal a failure to complete the tasks designated or that the wrong tasks had been prescribed. Student logs can be used for documenting various types of physical education homework, practice, or activities outside the scheduled physical education class, thus indicating students' learning and effort.

Portfolios

Portfolios are collections of materials or artifacts that, when considered collectively, demonstrate student competence or mastery of some subject area. Development of fitness and the accompanying knowledge requires several types of information to demonstrate student competence. Portfolios are an excellent way for students to gather the evidence and display it in a meaningful manner. Figure 2.12 shows a list of possible artifacts that might be required for a fitness portfolio.

There are two types of portfolios. **Working portfolios** are places where students can gather diverse information that demonstrates mastery of learning objectives. Working portfolios might contain a potpourri of student work and multiple examples of achievement in a given area. Artifacts in a working portfolio might be evaluated before they're placed in there; however, a teacher would not evaluate this entire collection of student work. **Evaluation portfolios** are turned in for teacher assessment.

Possible Artifacts for a Fitness Portfolio

- Research paper comparing various training techniques
- Log of cardiovascular workouts
- Analysis of cardiovascular workouts (indicating which type is most effective), optimal training schedule, and intensity variations (caused by working out on different surfaces or terrains)
- Lifting log
- Pre- and post-training body fat composition measurements
- Pictures taken during a local road race
- Discussion of pacing strategy for a 10 K road race
- Training program based on an analysis or testing of fitness components
- Analysis of a health spa or fitness facility to determine which gives the most for dollars spent per visit
- Interview questions for a personal trainer
- Graphs noting improvements in strength and flexibility measurements
- Charts depicting muscles used during workouts and stretching

---

Figure 2.12   A fitness unit might encompass a variety of student learning that can be evaluated holistically with a fitness portfolio.

Although the artifacts are the same for both the working and evaluation portfolios, evaluation portfolios limit the number of items that can be submitted for evaluation, which forces students to select those items that best represent student competence on a specific criteria. By making the student be selective, teachers have fewer pieces to evaluate, which saves the teacher much time during the evaluation of the portfolio. With evaluation portfolios, teachers determine a specific set of criteria on which students must demonstrate competence, although students can select the actual pieces they use to exemplify and meet the criteria. Students usually write **narratives** to accompany the portfolio, which walk the reader through the materials and explain why various pieces were chosen to demonstrate competence on those specific criteria. Some portfolios require several specific pieces, whereas others give students total choice in the selection process. Portfolios have become popular ways to evaluate student learning and are discussed in depth in chapter 6 of this text.

How Performance-Based Assessments Change Instruction

The use of performance-based assessments represents a philosophical shift in instructional formats as well as in the types of assessments used. The term *assessment* has become synonymous with *evaluation,* which to many implies a grade. Performance-based assessments encourage teachers to give multiple opportunities to demonstrate learning—which is actually closer to real life. This shift requires teachers to do things slightly differently; it requires them to move from evaluating a student to *coaching* a student so that they reach a given level of excellence. These changes in teaching philosophy are explained in the next section.

Formative Versus Summative

In real life, people often have multiple chances to demonstrate competence without penalty. How many of you reading this book passed your lifesaving exam the first time you took it? If you didn't, it did not mean you could never become a lifeguard. It just meant that more work was necessary before you met the criteria for being a lifeguard. In much the same way, performance-based assessments allow students multiple opportunities to reach the criteria or standard of excellence set by the teacher.

When students make errors on **summative assessments**, they have no chance to correct these to improve performance. The tests have primarily an evaluative quality: When students do poorly on those assessments, there is no second chance. Formative assessments, on the other hand, allow students multiple opportunities to demonstrate competence. When students do poorly on one day, they can practice and have a second chance for success at a later date.

Assessments should point out areas of incomplete learning to students and teachers. They provide evidence that there is room for improvement. Unfortunately, with summative tests, this information arrives too late to be of value to either the teacher or student. Because the unit is over, reteaching and clarification of misunderstandings do not occur. Formative assessments, on the other hand, are given throughout instruction. They may be formal (e.g., game play assessments scored using a rubric), or they may be informal (e.g., teacher observations or verbal interactions with students). Formative assessments are typically given more than once, which allows students additional chances to demonstrate mastery of the materials and content.

When several students do poorly on an assessment, the teacher should go back and try to discover the problem. If students had inadequate background to perform the tasks or comprehend the information, the teacher can develop a way for those students to do remedial work to obtain mastery. If all students had difficulty meeting the target, the material was either too difficult or the instruction failed to help students learn. The teacher in this instance either needed to allot more time for the unit or teach fewer skills in greater depth. This concept is true for any type of learning; it does not matter whether it involves the cognitive domain or psychomotor skills. One of the criticisms of the American educational system is that it is a mile wide and an inch deep. If we decrease the breadth of coverage, greater depth of understanding and enhanced performance are possible. The widespread practice of middle and high school physical education teachers' presenting activities in short units is detrimental to the learning process. These short units simply do not give students adequate time to master the skills and knowledge necessary for meaningful activity or game play. Chapter 8 provides a greater discussion of this topic.

There is evidence that the use of formative assessment improves learning, and low-achieving students benefit the most (Black and Wiliam 1998). Formative assessment provides information that teachers use to adapt instruction for meeting student needs as instruction progresses, rather than at the completion of the teaching unit. In every study reviewed by Black and Wiliam (1998), formative assessments produced significant learning gains in the classroom. According to many studies, student learning increases substantially when a teacher is selective of what students should know and be able to do, focuses instruction on that information, and gives feedback regularly through formative assessment.

Teacher Becomes a Coach

The role of the teacher in performance-based assessment is different from the evaluator role (or gatekeeper role) that teachers play with the traditional assessments. In traditional assessment settings, too often teachers are the hose and students the sponges that soak up knowledge. With performance-based assessments, teachers are no longer the only source of student knowledge. The teacher is a coach who brings out optimal performance from students rather than someone standing before a group giving information to students and then testing them on this material. The word *assessment* comes from the French word *assidere*, which means to sit beside (Herman, Aschbacher, and Winters 1992). Teachers and students work together with performance-based assessments to enhance student learning. These assessments allow students to demonstrate *application* of knowledge rather than regurgitation of facts. Performance continues to improve during the assessment process as a result of the support given by the teacher.

Feedback Improves

Assessment should provide feedback to students and teachers and then evaluate the degree to which students use this information to improve their performance (Wiggins 1998a). Because formative assessments are given during instruction, they provide feedback to both students and teachers about possible gaps in learning. After formative assessments, teachers can go back to material that students just didn't get and teach it in another manner. Students have feedback about their performance and can self-correct any errors. Once students understand where they are in relation to where they should be headed, improvement is more likely.

When you mention the word *assessment*, all kinds of notions are conjured up, most of them negative. For teachers, assessments are typically associated with determining student grades. For students, feelings of dread arise as they think about preparing for a test—the more significant the test, the greater the negative feelings. "The aim of assessment is to educate and improve student performance, not just audit it" (Wiggins 1998a, 707). When teachers and students realize that assessments help improve learning rather than just evaluate it, the negative notions of assessment dissipate.

Assessments Are Progressively More Difficult

Along with advocating the use of new forms of assessment to document student learning, we believe that when assessment is used to inform students and teachers about student progress, the assessment must be progressive in nature, as are the learning activities. **Progressive assessment** is a term we use to describe a process whereby students progress from the performance and assessment of simple to more complex skills—in increasingly complex situations and settings. The assessments also increase in complexity to reflect the progressive nature of the learning activity or required performance. For instance, in the

early stages of learning new skills, the focus may be on learning and demonstrating the correct critical performance elements or correct form in a controlled or closed setting. The assessment for this stage of learning would focus on the student demonstration of the skill in a controlled situation, such as bumping a direct, softly tossed ball from a partner. An observation checklist of the critical performance cues in sequential order could be the assessment and scoring guide. The observation checklist could be used by peers or the teacher to check student performance or by the students themselves while they view a videotaped self-performance. The next learning activity or assessment may focus on the following: The students receive a ball tossed directly to them by a partner; next, they pass the ball in a high arc back to the partner who is 15 feet away so that they can easily set the ball with an overhead setting pattern. The assessment may be a criterion-referenced assessment in which the student is expected to accomplish the task using correct form 8 out of 10 times before going on to another task. The student or peer records a score on the record form provided. If the unit goal is to have students demonstrate and apply learned skills and strategies in tournament games near the end of the unit, then an appropriate pro-

The following is an example of how a checkpoint assessment could be implemented in a badminton unit in which the unit goal focuses on demonstrating the ability to successfully play in a singles and doubles badminton tournament. The teacher introduces the short and long serves within the first two days of the unit. Serving is a complicated skill that must be performed with accuracy on a consistent basis because it is impossible to score in badminton unless you can serve successfully. The teacher provides 10 minutes of warm-up practice time at the beginning of class each day, during which time students serve 10 long and 10 short serves on an official court. Students record the number of successful serves out of 10 for each serve. Students gather data across the unit and graph serve percentage data for daily checkpoints. Students or peers could also collect data about serve placement and returns to further inform them about their serving progress. If the data indicate that no progress is being made or that the student is regressing in performance, then the teacher can plan an intervention for the student, such as a peer observation of the serve's critical elements via a check sheet or rating scale, or videotaping the student's serve for self-analysis. During this process students perform without undue pressure because they are not graded on the assessment. They know that it is conducted to simply help their performance. The assessment is integrated with learning activities, as it is a part of the daily practice activity.

gressive assessment may be to keep statistics of how each student performs and applies the skills and strategies in a game-like situation. This might involve having either teachers or students design an appropriate game statistics form that can easily be used during game play. On the form, the teacher might count the number of attempted bumps, those that were accurate passes and those that were errors, so that the student could determine a percentage of accurate passes. These game performance statistics could be kept over time so that the students could see if they were improving in performance in these game situations. Chapters 7, 8, and 9 provide many examples that use this assessment philosophy.

To truly reflect the progressive nature of the skill performance, most progressive assessments must be authentic or performed in as real-to-life situations as possible. Because progressive, continuous assessments are repeated, they can track student performance on a particular skill, strategy, or skill combination across trials and time (days to weeks). That way, the students and the teacher can monitor progress and intervene if necessary before the student gets too far behind. These assessments are referred to as **progress checkpoints** or simply **checkpoints** (Graham et al. 1998; Lambert 1999).

When assessment is progressive, it can be very motivating to students because they are able to see and keep track of their skill development and progress in the performance of transitional skills toward established goals throughout the unit. The teacher may identify specific progress checkpoints throughout the unit of instruction or semester so that students may see how they are progressing toward goals. As stated earlier, progressively more complex assessments must be planned before beginning instruction for the unit. The final (or culminating) performance, product assessment, or experience should require students to apply knowledge and skills in an *authentic* final performance or product, which demonstrates the achievement of the unit goals and movement toward target standards.

Learning and Progress Seen Through Multiple Lenses

In much the same way as it takes several situations to know a person's ability and poten-

tial, multiple assessments are needed in school to get a clear picture of student abilities and potential. This is a strength of continuous assessment: Students are evaluated through the use of many lenses numerous times so that a full and complete picture of this person's skills is possible.

By looking at this composite of assessments, the teacher has a better idea of what each student has achieved during the unit. Also important to note is that no test is comprehensive enough to cover all the material in a course. Tests merely sample representative information of the material teachers want students to know. Using several types of assessments serves to verify student learning. Many teachers use written tests to measure cognitive ability in a sport such as volleyball. Instead, if the teacher required students to officiate games of classmates, observed knowledge of rules, play selection, and strategy during game play, and had students analyze a skill to help a classmate improve performance, a better, more complete picture of student cognitive knowledge would emerge.

A single assessment form is not sufficient to measure the complex material contained in a physical education unit. Performance-based assessments allow teachers to evaluate the many types of learning involved with an activity or unit. By doing several types of assessments, thus creating a total picture of that student's abilities, one gets the complete and total idea of what the student has learned and accomplished. Just as the blind men who were describing the elephant had many different ideas about what an elephant looked like, by providing multiple looks at student achievement teachers have a more accurate idea about the big picture concerning student competence.

Advantages of Performance-Based Assessment

By now, many of you are beginning to notice that many of the things physical educators do during a unit can easily be turned into performance-based assessments. We enjoy reading the work of Grant Wiggins because when he needed an example to clarify a point, he usually used some type of physical activity because it is so overt and performance based. By making a few modifications, writing out criteria for the performance, and gradually including performance-based assessments throughout a unit, you can begin to transform your assessment practices into being more performance-based.

Performance-based assessments provide several instructional advantages in physical education. Although they do not have to be the only types of assessment used, they can greatly increase the effectiveness of an evaluation system. This section considers nine advantages of using performance-based assessments.

Direct Observations of Student Work

Direct observation of student skill and knowledge in the actual setting is a powerful way to measure student knowledge and the ability to apply it. Traditional assessments are designed to measure student learning indirectly. For example, when students take a test over tennis rules, the teacher assumes that the test is measuring the degree to which a student knows the rules governing a tennis game. If the questions asked are valid, then this is a reasonable assumption. However, a student might know the rules of tennis for a written test but not be able to apply them during a game.

Performance-based assessments allow teachers to assess areas of learning that traditional assessments do not. Actually, many traditional assessments do not really measure a teacher's final learning objectives. For example, at the secondary level, a physical educator's goal is usually to teach a student how to play a game or do an activity. Skill tests may evaluate discrete skills in a fairly closed (unchanging) environment, but they do not evaluate a student's ability to use these skills and put it "all together" during game play. Game play also involves decisions about which skill to use, requiring students to evaluate a complex environment. Skill tests are merely an approximation of what a student must be able to do. Although skill tests do represent a first step in learning, they usually are not the teacher's ultimate goal for the unit.

I remember my frustration while teaching activity units; I felt like I was not assessing my ultimate objective, that of getting students to play the game. Students would score well on skill tests but then were unable to use these skills during game play. A game play assessment would have evaluated these skills and showed me that missing link between skill acquisition and game play. Unfortunately, when I first began teaching, I didn't feel that assessments of students during game play were objective and therefore acceptable, so I did not use them with my classes. Performance-based assessments allow teachers to access information not available through traditional testing. Chapter 3, covering rubrics, contains assessments that allow teachers to directly evaluate the actual learning objective of game play competence. Assessments must measure how well students met the teacher's goals or targets for the unit. When a teacher's goals include game play or some type of performance, performance-based assessments are an excellent way to determine whether students have reached them.

Good Instructional Alignment

Put simply, **instructional alignment** means that teachers test what they teach. Cohen's research revealed the power of instructional alignment strategies (Cohen 1987). Teachers in his study demonstrated a significant difference in learning using instructional alignment. While using instructional alignment, teachers decide on a target, then test what they teach. On the surface, this concept seems to be a logical way to teach. In practice, not all teachers use this strategy. With performance-based assessment, the assessment is sometimes the instructional task. Students know exactly what is expected of them and are given multiple opportunities to meet pre-announced teacher expectations and criteria. Since instruction and assessment are working together in performance-based assessments, instructional alignment tends to be high and student learning enhanced.

Interesting Assessments

Since performance-based assessments usually involve real-world tasks, students tend to find them more engaging and challenging. Rather than study just enough to get a good grade on a test, students spend many hours engaged with their projects, often looking at sources other than teachers or textbooks for additional information. When an assessment simulates what a person in the field might do, students have several role models to emulate (e.g., announcing a game like Harry Carey, doing basketball analysis like Pat Summit, or dancing like John Travolta or Irene Cara). When some type of product or performance results, students accomplish something they can be proud of.

Instructional Feedback

Because they have a formative component, performance-based assessments provide quality feedback to students throughout the assessment. Since students have the rubric that is used to judge the final product, they can self-assess and peer-assess as they move through the assessment, comparing themselves and others with the criteria given. The purpose of assessment should be to enhance learning. The primary reason to assess should be to give feedback to the student about his or her progress. The second reason for doing assessments is to provide information to the teacher that can be used to shape instruction. Instead of assessment being done at the end of the assessment, learning is enhanced when it occurs throughout the instructional process.

Measures Multiple Objectives and Concepts

Today, physical education teachers must make every minute count. Physical education is squeezed into an instructional curriculum loaded with classes that students were not required to take 10 years ago. Teachers often complain that it takes too much time to assess. Because performance-based assessments are linked with instruction, the two can be accomplished simultaneously. Game play can provide assessment opportunities as teachers evaluate skill, strategy, knowledge of rules, and affective domain attributes. Oftentimes physical education teachers can work with other teachers to do an assessment that displays competency for multiple areas. Written assessments could evaluate learning in both English and physical education, and fitness assessments could also address biology content knowledge. Assessments involving other subject areas can be completed outside the gym, which maximizes time available for activity.

Formalized Observations

Today's accountability systems require formal proof of learning, but unstructured observations fail to provide this. Performance-based assessments formalize the observation process, giving you specific items to assess. Observations are more systematic, forcing teachers to evaluate the same criteria and elements for every student. Instead of a teacher just observing a game and giving verbal feedback, a formal evaluation of some aspect of performance can be done. By formalizing the observation procedure, teachers can improve instruction and demonstrate achievement of student learning objectives to parents and administrators.

Active Student Learning

William Glasser once said, "We learn 10% of what we read, 20% of what we hear, 30% of what we see, 50% of what we see and hear, 70% of what we experience with others, 80% of what we experience personally, and 95% of what we teach someone else." Traditional testing formats involve teachers lecturing and students taking tests. Performance-based assessments empower students, giving them freedom to make choices about the direction learning should take. Whether assessments are written or whether they involve psychomotor skills, performance-based assessments should encourage students to go outside the confines of the class for additional learning. By taking an active role in the learning process, students take ownership in the process and are more likely to retain knowledge. Giving students ownership of their learning process can also be a powerful motivator in teaching, as students perceive that they are given a choice for learning. Also, because students share the vision of what achievement should look like—and there are no surprises or excuses—students are more likely to experience success. Not only do the lessons have a longer lasting effect, they may lead students to other projects and activities. Instead of the assessment being the end or culmination of learning, it could be the beginning of a newly found interest area.

Higher-Order Thinking Skills

One of the challenges for educators has been to increase critical-thinking skills for students.

These skills are important for success as an adult and must be nurtured and developed throughout a school career. Performance-based assessments are designed to utilize higher-order thinking skills such as analysis, synthesis, and evaluation. The more opportunities students are given to practice these skills, the more proficient students are at using them. Some examples of using higher-order thinking skills are a scouting assignment, where students analyze the skills and playing habits of future opponents in a badminton tournament, or creating a dance or play for an upcoming performance or game.

Enjoyable for Students

Because assessments are challenging and emulate real-world experiences, students find them interesting and engaging. Time on task tends to be high in class, and students are willing to spend additional time outside of class to complete them. Students have a strong sense of satisfaction and pride when they consider their accomplishments. The product or performance provides a tangible, concrete demonstration of student achievement.

What to Avoid When Using Performance-Based Assessments

Despite the many positive benefits performance-based assessments bring to the evaluation arena, several concerns have emerged about their use. Performance-based assessments are relatively new to the assessment scene, and procedures for using them are still evolving. As teachers continue to expand the use of performance-based assessments, the following issues should be kept in mind. After explaining possible difficulties, we have provided possible solutions to the dilemmas we identify.

Concerns About Reliability and Validity

Reliability and **validity** are always of concern, regardless of the type of test used. Traditional tests require a teacher to make an inference about student competence by sam-

pling a body of knowledge. Skill tests measure student ability to perform components and skills that are used during game play. When a student does well on these, the assumption is made that students can play a game at a level designated by the teacher. Reliability can be high as evaluators have specific criteria to observe when scoring the test. With performance-based assessments, teachers make direct observations of the skills they are trying to teach. When the performance-based assessment requires students to play a game, validity is high as the assessment represents a direct observation of desired student behavior. However, validity can be problematic when the wrong criteria are used for evaluating the assessment. Therefore, care must be exercised when creating scoring guides for performance-based assessments. This problem is addressed in greater detail in chapter 3.

Reliability can be problematic in the scoring of performance-based assessments because an evaluator's judgment is required as he or she determines whether specified criteria have been met. With training in performance-based assessments, an evaluator's reliability can be high. As with all forms of assessment, performance-based assessments must address validity and reliability concerns. With care, both issues can be successfully resolved.

Failing to Set Criteria for an Assessment

When you create a performance-based assessment, the criteria used to judge it must be determined. When there are no criteria, there is no way to evaluate the task or project; therefore, it is not an assessment. A common error of teachers who use performance-based assessments is to create a task but then fail to establish expectations or standards for student performance. Unless there is a stated standard by which to evaluate an assessment, the "assessment" is merely an instructional task, or in other words, a pseudo-assessment. If teachers look at what they want students to know and be able to do (i.e., the essential questions), criteria for evaluation should emerge.

Setting the standard for assessment criteria the first time is difficult because teachers are unsure of what they can expect from students. The important thing is that teachers attempt to determine a level of quality expected from students. It is not enough for students to go through the motions and just complete the assessment; they must understand that a level of excellence is expected. Once a teacher has done an assessment the first time, student work can help shape future criteria and standards. Chapter 3 on rubrics contains more discussion on this topic.

Teaching to the Test

There has been an explosion of testing over the past several years. In some states testing has high-stakes accountability, ranging from giving cash awards to schools and teachers to closing schools with substandard performance. Given the importance placed on these tests, teachers have narrowed curriculum, focusing on those areas that are included on "The Test." **Teaching to the test** has assumed a negative connotation because some think that when teachers instruct students with the sole purpose of passing a test, important concepts are no longer taught. This concern has been expressed over state-mandated achievement tests, which in some states include physical education.

Performance-based assessments are often designed so that the teacher teaches to the test. Wiggins (1989a) points out that if the test is worthwhile, teaching to the test is not a bad thing. For instance, if the test represents some type of culminating performance in which students are expected to "put it all together" to indicate mastery of a content area, then teaching to the test allows students to be successful in achieving the overall unit objective. Wiggins (1989a) also notes that no one complains when a coach teaches to the test. Game play in a sport unit or successful negotiation of an adventure education course makes teaching to the test a worthwhile educational endeavor.

Assessment Is Time Consuming

Performance-based assessments requiring students to create a product or complete a project entail more time for teachers to develop and evaluate than many other types of assessments. For this reason, teachers must make careful choices when deciding to have students do certain types of performance-based assessments. The assessment should be a worthy task, and it should be the best method for assessing how well students achieved the teacher's goals. When selecting the assessment, the time required to complete it should be a worthwhile investment in learning. If a program's goals can be adequately assessed using other assessment techniques, then teachers should consider using these methods. Teachers must utilize available time as efficiently as possible, which includes making wise choices about selection of assessments.

Portfolios That Do Not Distinguish Between Levels of Excellence

Portfolios have become popular performance-based assessments. A colleague of mine recently complained that "all the portfolios looked alike." Care must be taken to build individuality into portfolio assessments. Portfolios allow students the opportunity to document mastery of a content area. Teachers can require students to submit various pieces of evidence but then allow students to self-select other pieces. A narrative explaining the importance of these pieces should also be included. By purposefully requiring individual pieces, teachers encourage students to develop a unique portfolio that documents their competence. These individualized portfolios can discriminate between levels of mastery for various students.

Parents Completing the Assessment

Making students do nonactivity-based assessments in class uses precious class time; a huge factor considering the limited amount of time available for physical education activity. When work is done at home, parental help is a possibility. Although this problem is not unique to performance-based assessments, it can surface more often given the complexity of some performance-based assessments and the need to do outside work to complete them. Having an assessment that is not completed by the student and using in-class time to complete a nonactivity assessment become a huge dilemma for physical education teachers. Building safeguards into assessments completed outside of class such as an in-class assessment to verify student learning could avoid this problem. The in-class piece could address another dimension of the assessment, thus using multiple sources to document learning. Requiring students to add an oral component to the assessment that explained the process used to complete the task could also address this issue. Having students complete all work in class and running the risk of having students get outside assistance is a trade-off. With a little planning, the issue can be resolved and student learning can be maximized.

Focusing Assessment on Irrelevant Content

Performance-based assessments should be open-ended, complex, and authentic. As teachers create performance assessments, they must keep them open enough to allow for multiple interpretations or products to satisfy the requirements for the assessment and evaluation. On the other hand, a task that is too open might be approached using a pathway that failed to demonstrate understanding of the intended content (see figure 2.13). Teachers must exercise caution in writing performance-based assessments: They must focus the assessments on the desired learning yet leave them open enough to be answered in a variety of ways.

Giving Assessments of Performance Rather Than Performance-Based Assessments

Given the overt nature of physical education tasks, some people feel that all assessments are

"performance-based" assessments. By definition, performance-based assessments are complex and measure higher-order thinking skills (Herman, Aschbacher, and Winters 1992). Although skill tests, fitness tests, and results of a race or timed event are examples of assessments by performance, they do not meet the criteria of being complex nor do they require the use of higher-order thinking skills. For these reasons, they should not be considered performance-based assessments. Performance-based assessments measure big-picture learning. They are culminating events that allow students to demonstrate learning in an extensive unit of study. The term *performance-based assessment* is one associated with these newer approaches to evaluating student performance and should not be confused with traditional assessments of performance.

Difficulty Creating "Authentic" Assessments

The word *authentic* is troublesome to some, especially to those who define authentic assessments differently from performance-based assessments. A convention session presenter once tried to make a distinction between a task that was authentic and one that was not by explaining that if a forehand tennis skill test were administered using a ball machine, it would not be authentic; however, if a teacher or another student were hitting tennis balls to

Figure 2.13   If performance-based assessments aren't focused on a specific subject or on specific content, then desired student learning might not be present—thus, it cannot be assessed.

the person being tested, the assessment would then be authentic. If one looks at characteristics of performance-based assessment, then one would conclude that a skill test would not qualify as a performance-based assessment because it did not meet the criteria of complexity. However, rather than spending time arguing about what is authentic and what is not, we suggest trying to make assessments as real to life as possible and not worry about semantics.

Multiple Chances to Get It Right

Some educators see assessment in a purely evaluative light: Students have one chance to prove that they have learned the required material. Because of its formative nature, performance-based assessments give students multiple chances to succeed. Several game play assessments are done during a tournament with the best performance used to determine the grade. Errors made during a game in the early stages of learning should not be held against the student; improvement with experience is expected. When dancers make errors while taping their dance video, they can refilm it. Rewrites are allowed when written work misses the mark. Those educators who use assessment only to evaluate students must recognize, that in the real world, people often have multiple chances to demonstrate proficiency. Athletes compete in many athletic contests, dancers put on several shows, and skaters perform in more than one competition. Giving students multiple opportunities to achieve success is more of a real-world experience than is one-shot evaluation.

Conclusion

Performance-based assessment offers a new set of options for physical education teachers who provide alternative methods for evaluating student progress. This form of assessment gives teachers the opportunity to access student learning in an applied setting where students often demonstrate competence doing real-world or authentic tasks. Given the nature of our subject, these assessment techniques have been embraced by many physical educators. Physical education tends to be very performance based, so creating assessments for physical education is sometimes easier than creating them for other areas.

Performance-based assessments can range from students' emulating the performances of sports and activity professionals such as announcers, sports writers, dance reviewers, coaches, and choreographers, to actually playing games or performing dance production pieces. When teachers use performance-based assessments, the role of the teacher shifts from that of a gatekeeper or evaluator to that of a coach interested in improving student knowledge and skills. Instructional alignment tends to be high as teachers are assessing what they teach, with all lessons focused on having students meet instructional goals. Because assessments are formative, students have multiple opportunities to meet the criteria that teachers relay to them prior to beginning the assessment.

As with any form of assessment, care must be taken to create both valid and reliable assessments. Performance-based assessments are time consuming to develop, time consuming for students to complete, and time consuming for the teacher to score. Teachers must write criteria for these assessments that distinguish between levels of learning. All of this requires much of a teacher's time and energy.

We have seen the positive changes in student learning with performance-based assessments, which is why we endorse them. Students become interested in learning rather than just doing enough to pass the test. Students who have been on the academic fringes become enthusiastic learners. With performance-based assessments, students know what is expected of them and work hard to meet the expectations and challenges set forth by the teachers. Assessment is woven throughout the learning process, which takes the pressure off teachers to get evaluations done during the last days of a unit. We have multiple lenses by which to evaluate student learning, which gives us a far better idea of what students really know and can do. These lenses also provide many opportunities for us to adjust our teaching content as lessons progress.

Now that you have had an introduction to performance-based assessments, the following chapters in this book provide greater detail as to how to create them and incorporate them into your curriculum. We suggest that teachers gradually introduce them into their curriculums to avoid feeling overwhelmed while making changes. We hope that you are starting to see the potential for learning that performance-based assessments provide and are ready to start using them in your program.

PART

II

Components of Performance-Based Assessment

Part II explains the nuts and bolts of performance-based assessment. For instance, rubrics are quite important to assessment, so we have dedicated an entire chapter that explains how to create them. We have also included a chapter of hints and ideas that we think are helpful as you develop various performance-based assessments for your classes; two types are discussed in detail. Equally as important, open response questions are being used more frequently in education. Traditionally, they have not been used much in physical education, but because certain states are adopting this test format for state-wide assessments, we thought it best to explain them in depth. Portfolios, too, are gaining widespread acceptance and use in physical education. A chapter dedicated to portfolios illustrates the potential this form of assessment has in physical education.

The final chapters in this section walk you through the planning process that we believe should be followed when developing performance-based assessments. The examples we provide demonstrate the use of our five-step plan for assessment, which also demonstrates the integration of learning and assessment in the instructional process.

CHAPTER THREE

Rubrics

We as teachers make judgments about students all the time. Since these judgments are based on criteria, whether we can articulate them or not, we have only two choices: we can either make our criteria crystal clear to students, or we can make them guess. (Arter 1996, p. vi-2:2)

Today much of what comes from Japan is of high quality and quite sophisticated. Before World War II, the Japanese were known for producing cheap, low-tech products that would not last long if given much use. Much of this change is attributed to Edward Deming who established high standards of quality for manufactured products. Goods produced that did not meet these standards were not marketed. Standards for quality were the driving force behind Deming's Total Quality Management (TQM) system. Workers knew and understood these standards and criteria before the manufacturing of a product began.

Rubrics attempt to do for education what Deming did for the Japanese economy—

inform students (workers) about standards of excellence before learning (production) begins and then encourage achievement of them to demonstrate mastery of content (manufacture a quality product). Deming knew that quality couldn't be inspected into a product after it had been manufactured. Standards for quality had to be defined and established before the manufacturing process began, and the resulting product must exemplify these standards. Informing students of the criteria used to evaluate student work could implement a process in education parallel to the TQM system.

The Japanese revolution has created a remarkable transformation of the Japanese economy. Perhaps if higher standards were a guiding force in today's American educational system, then a similar revolution—this one in learning—might be on education's horizon.

What Is a Rubric?

Given the rather short time that performance-based assessments have been around, terminology concerning various aspects of it are still evolving. Criteria for judging student performance have been called *scoring criteria, scoring guidelines, rubrics,* and *scoring rubrics* (Herman, Aschbacher, and Winters 1996). In this book, we use the term *rubric* to mean the criteria used for judging student performance.

Rubrics are guidelines by which a product is judged (Wiggins 1996). These guidelines make public what is judged and in some cases explain the standards for acceptable performance (Herman, Aschbacher, and Winters 1996). There is general agreement that the term *rubric* has its origins in the Latin language, but different people identify different origins for the word. Some authors (Wiggins 1996; Popham 1997) claim that the term *rubric* derives from the Latin word meaning *red*. The set of instructions for a law or liturgical service, typically written in red, was a rubric. Thus, a rubric provided guidelines for "lawfully" judging a performance. Another source (Marzano, Pickering, and McTighe 1993) places the roots of the word *rubric* in the Latin term *rubrica terra,* referring to the practice centuries ago of indicating the importance of something by marking it with red earth. Like the red earth in the past, rubrics point out what is significant or important in learning and assessment.

Clear **criteria** are essential in performance-based assessments so that student work can be judged consistently (Arter 1996). In education, rubrics include the criteria used to inform students about desired standards and levels of quality. They are the vehicles by which a teacher can guide students and improve performance. Unlike the single correct answers found with selected response questions (i.e., multiple choice, true-false, matching), performance-based assessments require a professional judgment by the evaluator about the quality of student work. Rubrics indicate the criteria a person scoring performance-based assessments should use when doing evaluations. While performance-based assessments require teachers to evaluate student performance, they can, at the same time, provide specific feedback to students on how to improve performance. Coaches often provide specific feedback to their athletes who are trying to improve. Effective coaches have a vision of what an optimal performance looks like and give appropriate feedback to athletes, using specific criteria to correct errors and enhance performance. Rubrics articulate these specific criteria, describing to students what good performance should look like. Just as specific cues are necessary to improve athletic performance, specific criteria are vital to improving student performance in physical education. When both teachers and students have a clear vision of what an ideal performance should look like, mastery of desired criteria is much more likely to occur. The specific criteria found in rubrics help students understand what they must do to achieve mastery of content.

Writing a rubric is probably the most difficult part of creating assessments. A later section of this chapter (pages 54 through 58) guides you through the process. At professional conventions (e.g., state, regional, national conferences) teachers sometimes show assessments that they use with their classes. These "assessments" are actually pseudo-assessments because they have no rubric attached and fail to define a level of quality or performance that they expect from students. They may be excellent tasks for promoting student learning, but without a rubric, they do not provide a means for assessing the performance. In chapter 2 we said that performance-based assessments had two parts, a task or exercise for students to do and the criteria by which to judge the performance. Without a standard of evaluation, "assessments" are nothing more than instructional tasks.

Deciding explicitly what to expect of students requires a large amount of professional knowledge. Given the range of achievement possible from students the same age, making this determination is difficult. Books on developmental levels of children might provide helpful guidelines for student achievement.

▶ Gabbard, C., B. LeBlanc, and S. Lowy. 1994. Physical Education for Children: Building the Foundation (Second Ed.). Prentice-Hall, Inc. Englewood Cliffs, NJ.

▶ Gallahue, D., J.C. Ozman, and J. Ozman. 1997. Understanding Motor Development (Fourth Ed.). WCB/McGraw-Hill.

▶ Graham, G., S. Holt-Hale, and M. Parker. 2001. Children Moving: A Reflective Approach to Teaching Physical Education. (Fifth Ed.) Mayfield Publishing Company, Mountain View, CA.

▶ Kirchner, G., and G. Fishburne. 1995. Physical Education for Elementary School Children (Ninth Ed.). WCB Brown & Benchmark Publishers. Madison, WI.

▶ Nichols, B. 1994. Moving and Learning: The Elementary School Physical Education (Third Ed.). Mosby, St. Louis, MO.

▶ Pangrazi, R. 2001. Dynamic Physical Education for Elementary School Children (13th Ed.). Allyn and Bacon, Boston, MA.

Moving Into the Future (NASPE 1995) also provides benchmarks for the grades K-12. Middle school children can vary developmentally as much as three years above or below chronological age (Pangrazi 2001). A student's prior experience also greatly influences what teachers can expect. For example, if you teach in an area where soccer is popular, expect to have students in the same class who play on traveling or competitive teams along with those who have played very sparingly.

Performance criteria can improve instruction if properly designed (Arter 1996). They point teachers to excellent performance and can provide guidelines for what students should know and be able to do. Lessons with specific criteria tend to be more focused than lessons that wander around a topic or fail to provide clear tasks that lead to skill improvement or student learning.

In reality, teachers make judgments about students all day, every day when they look at student performance and decide whether the student can really perform a given dance or execute a skill sequence. Even though teachers make judgments of quality all the time, they fail to write down the criteria or standards that they use while making these. Criteria are there whether we acknowledge them or not; a rubric simply makes the criteria public. Creating a rubric requires that a teacher put down in writing the criteria by which the performance is judged.

The most useful feedback given to students provides guidance about strengths and weaknesses and how the weaknesses can be improved. Criteria should be stated in specific, measurable terms so that students know exactly what they must do to meet them. When teachers share these criteria with students before beginning an assessment, students know what is required of them in advance. Just as workers understand what a quality product looks like when the TQM system is used, rubrics make students aware of standards for excellence in education. When students understand teacher expectations, performance is enhanced (Lazzaro 1996).

Criteria for Rubrics

Descriptors, traits, or **characteristics** are all terms used to indicate the elements contained in a rubric to define excellence (Herman, Aschbacher, and Winters 1992; Wiggins 1998). They reflect the elements of good performance and become the source for the criteria that are used to judge the performance. Teachers can evaluate student performance from a variety of perspectives. The following section discusses the various types of criteria teachers can use to evaluate student performance.

According to the literature, there are three different types of criteria that teachers might use to determine grades: product, process, and progress (Guskey 1996b). **Product criteria** simply refer to what students produce. These could refer to a concrete artifact such as a project, like a pamphlet or brochure. In physical education, product criteria frequently are stated in terms of student performance. A student might be expected to play a game, create a dance, or do a dance routine. Both student performance and projects are examples of products.

Merely stating student performance outcomes in terms of *products* says nothing about a student using correct form. When physical educators require students to use correct form, they are talking about another type of criteria, **process criteria**. In physical education, process criteria are those critical elements necessary for correct performance. Classroom teachers use the term *process criteria* a little differently. Classroom process criteria generally refer to effort, class participation, or homework—in other words, the *processes* that students use to learn (Guskey 1996b). Although some physical education teachers may take these factors into consideration when calculating a grade, the term *process criteria* in physical education generally refers to the quality of physical performance. Physical education teachers often evaluate process criteria when they use self-check or peer evaluation techniques or when they insist on students having correct form during performance.

Guskey (1996a) reports that teachers also use a third type of criteria, **progress criteria**, to determine student achievement. Progress criteria do not look at the students' current level of achievement, but rather at how much they have improved or progressed on a learning curve. To measure progress criteria, teachers must administer assessments more than once.

Types of Rubrics

The type of rubric chosen for an assessment depends on the task being evaluated and the needs of the assessor. Some rubrics such as analytic rubrics or holistic rubrics are very complex and require much time to generate. Checklists are the easiest rubrics to create. Scores from point system rubrics are easy

to convert to letter grades or percentages. Selecting the appropriate scoring system is an important part of the assessment process. The following discussion is designed to introduce teachers to five different types of rubrics and explain when each is most effectively used.

Checklists

A checklist is a list of characteristics or behaviors that are basically scored as yes-no ratings (Herman, Aschbacher, and Winters 1992). With a checklist, a list of characteristics regarding a performance or product is written, and the scorer decides whether the trait is present or not. Checklists can be useful ways to evaluate the critical elements or process criteria of motor skills because it is not necessary to evaluate a level of quality. Teachers or scorers are only concerned about whether the student demonstrates the characteristic. Figures 3.1 and 3.2 show examples of checklists. Figure 3.1 shows a checklist for appropriate sport behavior during games. In this example, the teacher is only concerned whether the student has demonstrated

Yes	No	
_____	_____	Plays within the rules of the game.
_____	_____	Does not argue with others.
_____	_____	Shares in team responsibilities.
_____	_____	Gives others a chance according to the rules.
_____	_____	Follows the instructions of the coach.
_____	_____	Respects the other team's efforts.
_____	_____	Offers encouragement to teammates.
_____	_____	Accepts the calls of officials.
_____	_____	Accepts the outcome of the game, regardless of a win or loss.

Figure 3.1   A checklist rubric is designed to note the presence of a given characteristic or trait.

In many cases teachers should use multiple types of criteria to judge the same performance. Once, while teaching a tennis class, the first set of lessons spent a lot of time evaluating correct form on the serve. Students were videotaped, analyzed by peers, analyzed by the teacher, and by then end of that section, their form was wonderful. When we moved into a product assessment, requiring them to serve the ball into the proper court, I forgot to add the process criteria. The result was the toss-and-dink serve that is used by people with limited tennis experience. Because you are not supposed to change the rules midway into the assessment, I let students get by with that serve. Experience has taught me to specify all criteria that I expect to see and never to assume anything!

_____	I play within the rules of the game.
_____	I don't argue with others.
_____	I share with team responsibilities, before, during, and after the game.
_____	I give others a chance according to the rules.
_____	I follow instructions given by the coach.
_____	I respect the efforts of others, even those of opponents.
_____	I offer encouragement and support to teammates.
_____	I accept the calls of officials and don't draw attention to myself after a call is made.
_____	I accept the outcome of the game, regardless of a win or loss.

Figure 3.2 Self-administered checklists can be useful tools for providing feedback on desired student learning.

these behaviors during play, while making no determination of the degree to which the trait is present. Instead of indicating yes or no, checklists may also list the traits and provide a place to check whether or not the behavior is present. Figure 3.2 is an example of a checklist that students can administer to themselves.

Teachers use journals to determine student reactions and feelings to different tasks or activities. A checklist could be used to indicate the presence of various points without making a judgment about the quality of the response. Students are scored on whether they have included specific criteria on an entry or met standards of writing elements. Judging the quality of journal entries content can be problematic, as students will begin writing what they believe teachers want to hear rather than expressing their genuine feelings. Because checklists contain the desired characteristics, they provide students with guidelines for successful completion of the assessments without requiring a judgment of the extent to which the characteristic is present.

Checklists generally contain more traits or descriptors than usually found in other types of scoring guides. This detail is helpful for students first learning to perform a motor skill or another activity. Although teachers must provide enough characteristics to be diagnostic, they should not include so many that the checklist becomes cum-

bersome or difficult to use. When too many characteristics are included, the key elements of performance may be neglected because the scorer focuses on less important characteristics of performance. Students can use checklists to analyze skills while doing peer assessments or self-assessments. When this is done, teachers must show students how to do the assessments. Students must understand explicitly what the various terms on the checklist mean.

Point System Rubrics

Point system rubrics are very similar to checklists except that they award points for the various criteria on the list. As with checklists, the scorer is not required to make a judgment of quality. If the characteristic is present, the student is awarded a set number of points. As with checklists, point systems offer students feedback, as they can quickly see whether they were awarded points for a given dimension or trait. Point systems also tend to have more descriptors than an analytic or holistic rubric, which can be helpful to student learning by providing feedback. An advantage of using a point system scoring guide is that teachers can add up points earned and convert this score into a grade. When a teacher wants to place greater emphasis on a certain trait or dimension, more points can be awarded for it (that is, it's given more weight). Figure 3.3 illustrates an example of a point system rubric. A caution is offered when you use point systems: If several traits are listed under the main characteristic, then either every element must be present to earn points for the category or the teacher must assign points for the various subcomponents, which when added, equal the total points allotted for that section. Figure 3.3 illustrates this concept.

Analytic Rubrics

Unlike the point system or checklist rubrics, analytic rubrics require a scorer's judgment to determine the degree of quality for the trait or dimension included, thus providing more diagnostic detail than the previously mentioned scoring systems. Checklists and point systems indicate only whether a trait was definitely present. With an analytic rubric, the scorer evaluates the strength or weakness of a trait. Because each dimension is scored independently of the others in the rubric, students can easily see areas on which they must improve.

Fitness Portfolio

_____ Fitness evaluation (15 points)

    _____ Abdominal strength (2 points)

    _____ Pacer or other test of aerobic endurance (4 points)

    _____ Flexed-arm hang/pull-ups/push-ups (2 points)

    _____ Sit-and-reach (2 points)

    _____ Body fat (2 points)

        _____ Triceps

        _____ Calf

    _____ Resting heart rate (1 point)

    _____ Height (1 point)

    _____ Weight (1 point)

_____ Fitness plan (25 points)

    _____ Calculate target heart rate (2 points)

    _____ Calculate body mass index (2 points)

    _____ Needs analysis (5 points)

    _____ Proposed workout plan (16 points)

        _____ Warm-up and recording chart (3 points + 1 point for chart)

        _____ Strength workout and recording chart (3 points + 1 point for chart)

        _____ Flexibility program and recording chart (3 points + 1 point for chart)

        _____ Aerobic program and recording chart (3 points + 1 point for chart)

_____ Nutritional analysis (15 points)

    _____ Food record sheet for one week (5 points)

    _____ Analysis of food intake according to basic food groups (3 points)

    _____ Average caloric consumption per day (2 points)

    _____ Proposed nutritional action plan (5 points)

_____ Results (45 points)

    _____ Completed workout charts (10 points)

    _____ Weekly journal entries for exercise and nutrition (10 points)

    _____ Analysis of fitness improvements (10 points)

    _____ Discussion of results regarding nutrition (5 points)

    _____ Analysis of fitness and nutritional products (10 points)

Student's choice of visiting a local finess center and evaluating its services, offerings, and so on or doing two of the following:

    _____ Food label analysis for five favorite foods (5 points)

    _____ Food analysis for favorite fast-food meal (5 points)

    _____ Analysis of a commercial diet plan (student's choice) (5 points)

    _____ Video analysis of weightlifting technique for two stations (5 points)

    _____ Analysis of value for a popular piece of fitness equipment advertised to public (5 points)

Figure 3.3   When assigning points to broad categories in a point system rubric, teachers must also indicate the number of points that the subcategories receive.

There are two types of analytic rubrics—quantitative and qualitative. **Quantitative analytic rubrics** (also called **numerical analytic rubrics)** require the scorer to give a numerical score (e.g., three out of four) for each trait evaluated. Quantitative rubrics are similar to checklists because the traits are listed, but they differ in that these traits are evaluated for quality (see figure 3.4). With a checklist, the trait must be fully present in order to credit the student work. The rudimentary presence of a characteristic can be noted with an analytic rubric. Because analytic rubrics require a decision about the degree of quality for each trait listed, they require more time to score than checklists or point systems.

Words that give a verbal indication of the degree of quality—such as *never, sometimes,* *usually,* or *always*—should be included with the numerical score so that the numbers have meaning or are grounded. These verbal indicators give the scorer an idea about the level or quality of performance that each number represents. Without these, reliability would be low because a scorer might shift the expectations associated with different numbers as the evaluation process occurs. Also, verbal indicators help ensure consistency when more than one person is doing the scoring.

Qualitative analytic rubrics provide verbal descriptions for each level of the various traits to be evaluated. Descriptions of a quality are written for various levels of each trait or characteristic (see figure 3.5). The evaluator can

Game Play Assessment for Doubles Tennis

The student:	Never 1	Sometimes 2	Frequently 3	Always 4
1. Uses correct form on the forehand.	1	2	3	4
2. Uses correct form on the backhand.	1	2	3	4
3. Uses correct form on the lob.	1	2	3	4
4. Uses correct form on the volley.	1	2	3	4
5. Uses correct form on the first serve, making solid contact.	1	2	3	4
6. Second serve when needed is good and "in."	1	2	3	4
7. Uses shots at appropriate times.	1	2	3	4
8. Places shots rather than just returning them.	1	2	3	4
9. Moves into position quickly and prepares to play the ball.	1	2	3	4
10. Returns to base position after making a play.	1	2	3	4
11. Approaches the net for offensive play.	1	2	3	4
12. Covers the entire court with partner.	1	2	3	4
13. Communicates with partner.	1	2	3	4
14. Hits shots to open spots on opponents court.	1	2	3	4
15. Play between partners is balanced and even.	1	2	3	4
16. Recognizes good performance from partner and opponents.	1	2	3	4
17. Calls shots correctly.	1	2	3	4
18. Knowledge of rules is evident.	1	2	3	4

Figure 3.4 Quantitative analytic rubrics are useful for providing feedback to students and assessing student ability to utilize discrete sport or activity skills in an applied setting.

Shot Execution

4 Executes all shots taught with good form, using them at appropriate times. Footwork is correct. Student knows in advance which shot to use and begins preparation for that shot while moving into position. Can read spin. Shot is unhurried.

3 Utilizes most shots taught with good form, usually using them at appropriate times. Feet are set when making the shot.

2 Uses several of the shots taught, yet not always at the appropriate time. Some form breaks are apparent; however, the form is mostly correct. Student arrives in position to play the ball just in time.

1 Relies on one or two shots for the entire game. Incorrect form causes shots to be misplaced or ineffective. Student is not in position when shot is attempted.

Court Movement

4 Moves around, covering all parts of the court and consistently attempts to return to home position. Feet appear to be in constant motion, and weight is on the balls of the feet to move quickly. Is in position to play all shots. Always anticipates where the opponent will place the next shot and moves into position to play it.

3 Covers court, usually attempting to return to home position. Weight is on the balls of the feet to move quickly. Is usually in position to play shots and can anticipate opponent's shot.

2 Covers court, but is occasionally out of position. Weight shifts to the balls of the feet delaying arrival to the ball to make the shot. Student attempts to return to home position but may not always get there. Some attempt to anticipate opponent's return shot.

1 Moves to play the ball after the ball comes over the net and then remains there. Parts of the court remain uncovered at times. Weight is usually back on the heels, slowing the ability to respond to the shot. Tends to reach to play the ball rather than being in position.

Service

4 Always uses correct form while executing the serve. Serve is placed in the corners of the opponent's service area. The first serve is powerful and occasional aces result. Second serve when necessary is always in and is also very strong.

3 Usually uses correct form while executing the serve. The first serve is very strong, usually ending within the service area. The second serve usually lands in.

2 Demonstrates several elements of correct form while executing the serve, although does commit some errors. The second serve is consistent and usually lands in. May not use a full swing on the second serve—the serve is more of a "punch" shot.

1 First serve is usually not in. Little difference between first and second serve with regard to power. May not use a full swing for either serve.

Rules

4 Shows evidence of thoroughly knowing and applying rules. Partners rotate up and back for service. Can play a tiebreaker without instruction. Can answer any question when asked.

3 Shows evidence of usually knowing and applying rules. Serving order and rotation are correct. Can answer most questions when asked.

2 Shows some evidence of knowing rules. Serving order and rotation are correct. May have a few errors. Struggles with some questions.

1 Is unfamiliar with rules. Depends on opponents or partner for instruction. Is unsure of serving order and rotation. Struggles with most questions.

(continued)

Figure 3.5   Qualitative analytic rubrics provide verbal descriptions of teacher expectations and are useful for providing formative feedback about several elements important to playing a game or performing well.

Strategy

4   Demonstrates much evidence of strategy against an opponent. Hits shots to the open places on the court. Uses lob and volley shots to gain an offensive advantage. Tries to anticipate opponent's shots, moving into position to play them. Communicates well with partner. Consistently works with partner to cover the court. Serving order and rotation benefits own team. Court positions are based on his or her team's strengths. Hits to opponent's weaknesses.

3   Demonstrates evidence of strategy against an opponent. Usually hits shots to the open places on the court. Communicates with partner, cooperating to cover the court. Uses lob and volley shots to gain an advantage.

2   Uses some strategy against the opponent. Attempts to hit the open places on the court. Some communication with partner. Some evidence of working with partner to cover the court.

1   Hits shots directly back to the opponent so that they are easy to return. Does not talk to partner. At times, both players go after the ball. Little evidence of teamwork or cooperation.

Fair Play

4   Consistently recognizes good play by others. Congratulates opponents for a good game regardless of the game's outcome. Works well with partner to cover the court at all times. Shows strong evidence of cooperation and teamwork. Does not try to play the entire court alone. Calls all shots honestly and fairly.

3   Usually recognizes good play by others. Works with partner to cover the court most of the time. Shows evidence of cooperation and teamwork. Does not try to play the entire court alone. Calls shots honestly and fairly.

2   Occasionally recognizes good play by others. Shows some evidence of working with partner to cover the court. May dominate court play from time to time. Calls shots honestly and fairly.

1   Rarely talks with others. Is not working as a team with partner. Complains consistently about line calls made by the opponent. Makes incorrect calls in his or her favor.

Figure 3.5   *(continued)*

decide which statement or level best describes the student's work relative to that trait.

Describing levels of quality with a descriptive statement for each of the various traits is a laborious task. The difficult part is determining various levels of performance and then writing descriptions of these that point out differences between each level. Several rubrics are presented in chapters 7, 8, and 9 of this book. Those, along with the ones in this chapter provide teachers with a blueprint from which to begin writing. Adapting someone else's ideas is easier than creating an entire rubric. A book written by Marzano, Pickering, and McTighe (1993) contains several rubrics written for a variety of nonphysical education products or student work. Resources such as this book can provide ideas for descriptive terminology necessary to write qualitative rubrics.

When deciding whether to use a quantitative or qualitative analytic rubric, consider that numbers are easier for people to remember than verbal descriptions. Also, because quantitative analytic rubrics produce numbers, these can be added to produce scores that are easily converted into grades. On the other hand, qualitative rubrics when well written, provide the scorer with accurate descriptions of the desired quality for a given level, making it fairly apparent how to evaluate the performance or product. They are easier to interpret than are quantitative analytic rubrics (Herman, Aschbacher, and Winters 1992). Descriptive words help improve the consistency of scoring. Note the descriptions given in figure 3.5. Qualitative rubrics also can provide students with clear descriptions that directly enhance learning.

We prefer to use quantitative rubrics when evaluating game play. Action is usually fast paced in game play, and teachers don't have time to refer back to qualitative statements when they have not used the rubric much in the past. The scoring criteria are also easier to remember, and a few more descriptors or traits can be included than one would normally use with a qualitative rubric. We use qualitative rubrics while evaluating written performance-based assessments when we have the luxury of time to refer back to the criteria in the rubric if questions arise.

Level 4: Student executes all shots taught with correct form, using them at appropriate times. Seems to anticipate shots, moving into position and playing the ball in an unhurried manner. Has a powerful first serve, resulting in occasional aces. Second serve, when necessary, is strong and well placed. Clearly knows the rules and can answer any question. Utilizes strategy to win points by hitting to the opponent's weaknesses. Uses lob and volley shots when needed to gain an offensive advantage. Works well with partner to cover the entire court and does not try to play alone. Recognizes good play by opponents and partner. Calls all shots honestly and fairly.

Level 3: Student executes all shots taught, usually with correct form and at appropriate times. Is frequently in position to play shots and can anticipate opponents' shots. Uses correct form on the serve, resulting in a strong, well-placed shot. Second serve, when necessary, is usually in. Student shows evidence of knowing rules, applying them appropriately. Uses strategy to defeat an opponent, hitting shots to open places on the court to gain an advantage. Recognizes good play by opponents and partner. Play between partners is equal. Shots are called honestly and fairly.

Level 2: Uses all shots taught but not necessarily at the appropriate time. Shots have some form breaks. Player arrives in position with enough time to play the ball. Student covers court but is occasionally out of position. Attempts to return to base/home position but does not always get there. First serve is adequate but not strong. Second serve is more of a punch shot. Student shows evidence of knowing the rules but may make errors. Knows serving order and rotation. Attempts to hit the ball to open places on the court. Some evidence of communicating with partner and working together to cover the court. Occasionally recognizes good play of partner and opponents. May occasionally try to play the entire court without utilizing partner. Calls shots honestly and fairly.

Level 1: Student relies on one or two shots for the entire game. Incorrect form causes shots to be misplaced or ineffective. Student is not in position when attempting shots, reaching for the ball rather than moving into position. First serve is usually not in. Little difference between power in first and second serve. May not use a full swing for either serve. Student is unfamiliar with rules, depending on opponents or partner for help. Hits shots directly back to opponents. Little communication and teamwork with partner, resulting in both players going after the ball. Is not working as a team with partner. Complains consistently about line calls made by the opponent. Makes incorrect calls in his or her favor.

Figure 3.6   Holistic rubrics are useful for summative evaluation of student performance and for determining student grades.

Holistic Rubrics

Holistic rubrics are paragraphs written to describe various levels of performance. Several different dimensions and traits are included in each paragraph (see figure 3.6). A scorer assigns a single score based on the overall quality of the product or performance rather than evaluating the merit of each trait. Whereas analytic rubrics require a separate evaluation for each dimension, holistic rubrics require scorers to decide which level best describes the overall quality of the student work or performance. Because the scorer makes only one decision about the quality of the student product or performance, holistic rubrics are faster to use. Holistic rubrics are also useful for assigning grades because a single overall score is given. The descriptions in the level and the number of levels used can correspond with a teacher's grading scale.

Holistic rubrics are often used for summative (final) evaluations or for large-scale testing (e.g., state-level tests). In both instances, students are not expected to improve performance, so they do not need the diagnostic detail that an analytic rubric provides. Teachers can begin to develop a holistic rubric by combining the traits of a given level for the analytic rubric into a paragraph. Holistic rubrics tend to have fewer traits; they use only major characteristics to determine the quality of the product or performance. Therefore, when you convert traits from an analytic rubric into holistic rubrics, some adjustments must be made. Because holistic rubrics assess overall student performance, strengths and weaknesses of the individual traits are not readily diagnosed. Holistic rubrics give limited feedback to students, which is why they are more likely to be used for summative assessments. Holistic rubrics are less diagnostic for students, which can pose problems with student self-assessment.

Holistic scoring can sacrifice validity and reliability for efficiency (Wiggins 1996). Problems with validity arise when two students get the same score for different reasons. Because the product or performance is considered as an entity, students don't know specifically why they were given a certain score. The reasons for rating the product or performance at that level are not always apparent with holistic rubrics because several dimensions contribute to the final rating scale or score. With an analytic rubric, one can see a score for each characteristic or dimension; they don't blend together and students can tell exactly how the characteristic was evaluated.

Because various traits are combined into a single level, holistic rubrics tend to provide less diagnostic feedback than do analytic rubrics. To counteract this concern, a teacher might use a marker to highlight the characteristics that make a performance or product a particular level. Or, a teacher may highlight those characteristics that were at a higher level than the overall work received when scoring a written product or performance using a holistic rubric.

Validity and reliability can also be threatened on a holistic rubric when evaluators weigh traits differently. For instance, on a game play assessment the first scorer might highlight skill execution while the second scorer considers strategy and court position most important. Because student work is considered an entity, training on holistic rubrics is less complex. However, unless scorers are trained to know which dimensions or criteria are most important, one scorer might emphasize one or two traits that have relatively little importance to another scorer, thus threatening validity and reliability. Similarly, when any hierarchy of traits exists, it must be indicated in the rubric.

Sometimes student responses fall between levels, having characteristics from each of two levels in the same piece of student work or performance. When this occurs, those traits considered most important determine the level at which to score the product or performance. This issue should be addressed when training those scoring student work. Another possible solution would be to allow scores of 1.5, 2.5, or 3.5 to indicate the presence of characteristics from more than one level.

Some teachers prefer holistic rubrics because they are more conducive to determining a student grade or because some teachers like evaluating the work as an entity rather than considering different components individually. Accurate analytic or holistic rubrics both distinguish between levels of student performance. When you use a rubric to score student performances or products, levels of achievement or student understanding should be distinct and obvious. Analytic rubrics are slower to use for scoring than are holistic rubrics because a decision is required for each dimension or trait. A rule of thumb is to use analytic rubrics during instruction (i.e., formative assessment) because they give diagnostic information. Holistic rubrics are best used if projects or performances from many students must be scored or if the assessment represents a final product or performance for an activity unit.

Generalized and Task-Specific Rubrics

Most teachers write rubrics specifically for a single performance-based assessment—a task-specific rubric. Another approach for creating rubrics is writing one that addresses broader concepts, which can be used for more than one performance-based assessment—a generalized rubric. The following section explains these two types of rubrics and the benefits for selecting either one.

Generalized rubrics are universal rubrics used to assess a variety of performances. Generalized rubrics are popular with statewide assessments that evaluate a broad concept such as writing ability. They tend to look at the big picture rather than give specifics relative to the assessment task. Generalized rubrics use more general descriptors or traits rather than criteria specific to a single task (see figure 3.7). A generalized rubric for gymnastics would focus on characteristics relative to amplitude, elegance, lightness, and rhythm that are important in every gymnastics routine, regardless of whether it is performed on the floor or a piece of apparatus. A **game play rubric** might look at skill execution, strategy, shot placement, and court movement, which are elements common to most games.

One advantage of using a generalized rubric is that a person creating an assessment does not have to develop a rubric for every assessment task. Creating rubrics is a time-consuming, labor-intensive process. Because generalized rubrics can be used to score multiple tasks, the assessor can eliminate this step when creating assessments. Second, training is not necessary for each task even when several members of a physical education department or district are scoring the same assessment tasks, assuming initial training on the rubric

Base/Home Position

Level 4: Consistently returns to base/home between skill attempts. Feet are constantly moving even when ball or projectile is not on his/her side of the net. Is always in position whether making a play or supporting teammate.

Level 3: Frequently returns to base/home position between skill attempts. Keeps feet moving so as to position self to make a play or support teammate. May occasionally be out of position.

Level 2: Returns to base/home position between skill attempts. Often is in correct position to make a play or support teammate. Occasionally stops on court or field.

Level 1: Occasionally returns to base/home position between skill attempts.

Adjusts to the Movement of Others

Level 4: Consistently adjusts to movement of other players either offensively or defensively. Is aware of changes and moves made by an opponent. Anticipates opponent's movements. Weight is always forward and on the balls of the feet, making player ready to move.

Level 3: Frequently adjusts to movement of other players either offensively or defensively. Is aware of changes and moves made by an opponent. Weight is usually forward, making player ready to move.

Level 2: Makes adjustments to movement of other players either offensively or defensively. Weight is often forward, making player ready to move.

Level 1: Tends to wait to move until after opponent has completed shot or play. Slow in reacting to movement of teammates or opponents.

Appropriate Choices

Level 4: Consistently makes appropriate choices about what to do with a ball or projectile. No hesitation or latency is apparent when getting ready to make a play. Decision about how to make the play is based on response from opponent and seems to be automatic. Seems to anticipate opponent's response.

Level 3: Frequently makes appropriate choices about what to do with a ball or projectile. Decision on how to play the ball or projectile made well before the object arrives, making response deliberate. Little hesitation or latency on the response.

Level 2: Makes appropriate choices about what to do with a ball or projectile. Decision on how to play the ball or projectile is made shortly before the object arrives, making player appear to scramble at times.

Level 1: Makes a play on the ball or projectile, but it may not be appropriate considering court position, position of the opponent, or game strategy. May have some hesitation or delay in play or shot selection.

Skill Execution

Level 4: Consistently uses correct form while executing and performing a skill. Movement is smooth, seemingly effortless, and deliberate. Is in position before making the play and shows follow-through when appropriate.

Level 3: Frequently uses correct form while executing and performing a skill. Movement is smooth and deliberate. Positioning is correct before making the play, and player follows through when appropriate.

Level 2: Uses correct form much of the time while executing and performing a skill. Occasionally has to rush to position to make the play.

Level 1: Student movment approximates the appropriate skill, but movement is hesitant or choppy. Form breaks are apparent.

Support

Level 4: Consistently provides support off the ball or projectile, positioning self to receive it when a teammate has the object. Player positioning reflects the use of sound strategy, being in an optimal position to make the subsequent play.

Level 3: Frequently provides support off the ball or projectile, positioning self to receive it when a teammate has the object. Use of strategy is apparent.

Level 2: Attempts to provide support off the ball or projectile when a teammate has the object. May occasionally find self in a nonadvantageous position.

Level 1: Fails to position self to receive a pass or provide support to a teammate. Frequently is behind the play rather than in a position to enhance current play status.

(continued)

Figure 3.7 This generalized game play rubric could apply to several different invasion games.

Cover

Level 4: Consistently provides defensive help for a player making a play on the ball or projectile, or moving toward the ball or projectile. Teammate is able to make an appropriate play, as opponent is unable to interrupt. Provides support by creating a player advantage (e.g., three-on-two, two-on-one) for teammate. Teammate is successful with intended play because of this support.

Level 3: Frequently provides defensive help for a player making a play on the ball or projectile, or moving toward the ball or projectile. Support for teammate is apparent and facilitates the play. Teammate is usually able to make intended play because of this support.

Level 2: Attempts to provide defensive help for a player making a play on the ball or projectile, or moving toward the ball or projectile. Support for teammate is noticeable.

Level 1: May attempt to provide defensive help for a player making a play on the ball or projectile, or moving the ball or projectile, but actually impedes the play or progress. Positioning is not timely and may be inappropriate.

Guard/Mark an Opponent

Level 4: Consistently covers the opponent, making it impossible for teammates to pass to the player. Maintains a position between an opponent and the goal when in control of the ball. If the guarded opponent has the ball, the player is then in position to intercept any passes attempted. Maintains a wide base of support, a low center of gravity for balance, and a rapid movement in any direction. Focuses on opponent's midsection to better stay with the opponent.

Level 3: Frequently is in position to cover player being marked to prevent a pass or score. Maintains a wide base of support to move in any direction, keeping a lowered center of gravity. Usually maintains defensive position, staying with the opponent.

Level 2: Attempts to cover the player being marked to prevent a pass or score. When loses position on player being marked, attempts to regain it.

Level 1: Is often behind the opponent, unable to intercept a pass or keep player from scoring. May know correct position, but opponent is usually able to move quickly, putting the person guarding the opponent out of position.

Figure 3.7   (*continued*)

occurred. Once people have had training on generalized rubrics, they can use them to evaluate several different assessments. Reliability tends to be lower at first for generalized rubrics, but once a person has had training on scoring using a generalized rubric, reliability increases (Arter 1996).

Generalized rubrics consider important tasks for the subject area or field. A person creating a generalized rubric looks for important skills that these tasks have in common. From these skills, relevant and explicit criteria are identified. The generalized rubric for game play in figure 3.7 uses the performance criteria for game play, as identified by Griffin, Mitchell, and Oslin (1997). From the seven categories identified for game analysis, an analytic rubric was developed that describes levels of performance for each of these areas. The components are important in many games, especially those classified as invasion and court games. Reliable and valid criteria generalize across tasks.

Because generalized rubrics tend to look at broad concepts they may go beyond the scope of your assessment. Every characteristic or dimension does not have to be scored every time when you use a generalized rubric. What is scored depends on the purpose of the assessment. With generalized rubrics, dimensions can be either emphasized or downplayed, according to assessment needs, as long as this is communicated with all people scoring the task.

Task-specific rubrics, which contain criteria unique to the assessment, are created for individual assessment tasks. Figure 3.5 is an example of a task-specific, qualitative, analytic rubric. They are generally easier to create than generalized rubrics because you can focus on a specific activity area or sport rather than consider characteristics that are universal to several activities or sports.

Task-specific rubrics tend to have higher reliability than do generalized rubrics because they address a single task. However, when multiple people are used to score assessments, raters must be trained on each task-specific rubric, which can be a time-consuming process.

Task-specific rubrics can often be modified with little effort to apply to another sport. Figure 3.8 illustrates how this can be done, by modifying of a tennis rubric for badminton. When a task-specific rubric is preferred, the teacher might create a rubric that combines characteristics from a generalized rubric with characteristics specific to a task or assessment. The broad criteria that generalize across performance could form the basis for the rubric, requiring the teacher to only add criteria specific to the assessment being used. This approach saves teachers time and results in a solid rubric for the assessment.

Selecting Criteria

Criteria need to distinguish between useful indicators and genuine criteria (Wiggins 1998a). Deciding how many or what criteria to include is similar to making a salad—you have to determine which are the essential ingredients and which elements are the extras, but not necessary. When writing a rubric, include all essential elements and hold the extras. Criteria for effective rubrics should do the following:

▶ Include all important components and aspects of performance

▶ Avoid details that are insignificant

▶ Be written in language that the user understands (this may involve separate rubrics for scorers and students)

▶ Take into account any contextual variable that may affect performance

▶ Link to instructional objectives

▶ Reflect best practice or professional opinion

▶ Address every task and component of the assessment

Consulting resources can help avoid problems with validity created when rubrics address incorrect criteria. Criteria used for a rubric should be derived logically from an analysis of what students must know and be able to do to demonstrate competence.

Expert opinion, rather than personal preference, should be used to determine criteria. While determining criteria, one must be aware of teacher bias and avoid selecting criteria that are not important.

When creating rubrics, the trick is to include all of the essential criteria without getting bogged down in detail. Not having all the important criteria also creates an invalid rubric. During a pilot of the rubric, if a student meets all the criteria specified and still has a substandard performance, the criteria are inappropriate.

When several people use the same rubric, a brainstorming session helps determine the list of criteria to be included. Consulting colleagues for their opinions about essential elements may help you decide what to include as criteria, thus avoiding omission of key criteria. Generating a list of many items and asking someone with content knowledge to rank the top 10 may be yet another way to generate the list of criteria used for the rubric. When writing rubrics, you shouldn't include the trivial or leave out the important. A rubric must represent a balance between too little and too much. Too much detail can cause confusion for scorers because they have too many points to consider and lose sight of what the final overall performance or product should entail. On the other hand, too little detail can make the evaluation of student work difficult or even impossible.

How to Create Rubrics

As stated earlier, writing rubrics is one of the most difficult parts of creating performance-based assessments. Throughout our years of teaching and working with students, we have found that there are seven basic steps to writing analytic or holistic rubrics. These include the following:

1. Envision the desired student performance on the assessment.
2. Determine the criteria.
3. Pilot the assessment.
4. Write levels for the rubric.
5. Create a rubric for students.
6. Administer the assessment.
7. Revise the rubric.

A teacher told students to develop a tri-fold brochure advertising a tennis camp to show their content knowledge in tennis. The students in one of the groups really got excited about the project and decided to meet over the weekend to make it really nice. Unfortunately, they did not have access to a computer and ended up printing the information and hand drawing some of the diagrams. When they handed the brochure to the teacher, students with less content knowledge got higher scores because they were able to use computers from home, color printers, and so on. Although the content of the handwritten brochure was superior, the teacher gave other students more credit, despite the fact that she had never stated that the brochure had to be done on the computer.

From	To
Tennis (Doubles)	Badminton (Doubles)
The student:	The student:
1. Uses correct form on the forehand.	1. Uses correct form on forehand shots.
2. Uses correct form on the backhand.	2. Uses correct form on backhand shots or around the head shots.
3. Uses correct form on the lob.	3. Uses clear shots before moving to the net to gain offensive position and advantage.
4. Uses correct form on the volley.	4. Uses correct form on change of pace, such as the drop, smash, underhand drop (hairpin), and so on, making it difficult to determine which shot the player is using.
5. Uses correct form on the serve, making solid contact.	5. Uses correct form on serves.
6. Second serve when needed is good and in.	6. Uses both short and long serves when appropriate, placing them on the court where the opponent is not standing.
7. Uses shots at appropriate times.	7. Uses shots at appropriate times.
8. Places shots rather than just returning them.	8. Places shots rather than just returning them.
9. Moves into position quickly and prepares to play the ball.	9. Moves into position quickly and prepares to play the bird.
10. Returns to ready position after making a play.	10. Returns to ready position after making a play.
11. Approaches the net for offensive play.	11. Uses a variety of shots to alter the pace of the game and add deception.
12. Covers the entire court with partner.	12. Covers the entire court with partner.
13. Communicates with partner.	13. Communicates with partner.
14. Watches opponent and hits shots to open spots on opponent's court.	14. Watches opponent and hits shots to open spots on opponent's court.
15. Play between partners is balanced and even.	15. Play between partners is balanced and even.
16. Recognizes good performance from partner and opponents.	16. Recognizes good performance from partner and opponents.
17. Calls shots correctly.	17. Calls shots correctly.
18. Knowledge of rules is evident.	18. Knowledge of rules is evident.

Figure 3.8   In some cases an existing task-specific rubric can be modified for a similar sport by changing the skills being evaluated.

The complexity of the assessment determines whether you need a rubric for both students or if only one is necessary. With complex assessments, two versions of the rubric are necessary. Both will contain assessment criteria, but you will need to write a separate one for the scorers, which lists items that they should look for to document student learning. If students are given this information, they will have the information you are seeking to assess. See the discussion on transparency in this chapter (p. 60).

The first questions to consider when writing an assessment are, "What am I assessing?" and "Why do I want to assess that?" These questions probably require you to go back to your instructional goals. When these questions are not addressed, assessments do not align with the curriculum. Although this appears to be a rather simple and logical step, too frequently it is not done. People creating performance-based assessments are sometimes guilty of not aligning curriculum and assessment. In an attempt to be "authentic" and "real world," an assessment germane to the subject area is created first, then the teacher looks for the standard or objective that it could assess. The result is a fun, nifty assessment that doesn't address or evaluate the desired content.

Although most rubrics are written for assessments that align with your objectives, in some instances, rubrics are written apart from an actual assessment task. We recently have begun developing a rubric to evaluate behaviors that we consider appropriate for physical education majors. Although there is no real task, the rubric will still evaluate our objectives for the dispositions we wish to see demonstrated by students majoring in physical education. Similarly, teachers might create a rubric for which there is no definitive task. This scenario is similar to developing a generalized rubric. Regardless of the purpose, the steps to follow for writing a rubric are similar. These steps are explained in the next section.

Step One

An idea of what you expect students to be able to do on this assessment should emerge when you consider the instructional goals and the assessments used to measure student learning relative to these goals. Teachers must decide what they will accept as evidence that students have met their instructional goals or objectives. By looking at your goal for instruction, you determine how best to assess it.

The first step, regardless of the type of rubric you will write, is to develop a mental picture of the student performance or behavior that you expect to occur. If working as a team to develop the rubric, spend some time discussing the student performance in an attempt to clarify the vision for all members of the writing team. If working by yourself to develop the rubric, try discussing your ideas with other colleagues. You may wish to open the topic up in an Internet chat room. Having a clear picture of what you expect will make subsequent steps much easier.

Step Two

After envisioning desired student performance, teachers must capture these ideas in writing. Too often teachers have mental expectations regarding an assessment, but fail to articulate these for students. When teachers fail to write down their criteria, a guessing game results in which students try to read the teacher's mind to determine what their performance must be to satisfy expectations. Begin by brainstorming several words that could become descriptors or traits for your rubric. When used, these words give a clear explanation of your goals and objectives. Next, write down short sentences or phrases for these dimensions that would indicate student competency, thus showing that they have met your expectations.

When developing a rubric, one must determine ideal, acceptable, and unacceptable performance. This task directs teachers to desired traits or characteristics. Although the intent at this point is not to develop **levels**, considering unacceptable performance can provide valuable insight on characteristics teachers wish to include in the rubric. When you consider what you don't want students to do, you can clarify what you do expect.

A question arises here: "How many characteristics should you include?" The type of rubric being created along with the complexity of the assessment helps answer this question. Obviously, simpler assessments require less complex rubrics. Checklists or point system rubrics have greater detail because they usually are used to assess narrower concepts or smaller ideas and projects. Because they only require a decision about whether a student has satisfied the criteria and are relatively faster to use while scoring, greater detail can be included. With an analytic or holistic rubric, too many criteria may create an unreliable assessment. When scoring an assessment with too many things to consider, the evaluation process may be slowed down considerably to the point that it is inaccurate, or an assessor may actually forget to consider some of the criteria. When writing qualitative or holistic rubrics, I typically focus on no more than four to six characteristics. When writing a quantitative analytic rubric, I try to keep the list of characteristics around 15.

After you have developed a list of descriptors or phrases that help describe ideal student performance, take a look at the entire list and see which items fit together. By grouping similar criteria and phrases, a list of descriptors for your rubric will emerge. Some elements collapse nicely with others on your list. This may not be your final list, so be open to change.

Step Three

The next step in developing your rubric is to pilot it. Criteria explain the rules that are in effect as students complete the task, and they should increase the quality of student performance. For a pilot, criteria may simply be a list of important items that students need to consider when doing the assessment. Even though the scoring guide is rudimentary, it can provide useful information as students complete the assessment. One of the key components of performance-based assessment is to give students the criteria with the assessment to help guide their decisions as they respond to the assessment task. It is critical that, when doing the pilot, students should have some type of scoring guide or criteria to reference. If teachers are developing checklists or point system scoring guides, the pilot will help determine if the correct descriptors were chosen. When a teacher is creating an analytic or holistic rubric, levels of excellence must be developed during step four. Writing

levels without some student work to serve as benchmarks is difficult. A teacher might consider scoring student work using a checklist or point system scoring guide (these are easier to write and don't require levels of performance) for the pilot and then using student work generated during the pilot to develop levels for quantitative or holistic rubrics.

Because giving an assessment is a lot of work, some teachers may wish to use the task to measure student achievement. If this is the case, we suggest that the first time the assessment or rubric is utilized, make an assignment with less at stake (relative to a student grade) rather than an assessment that will have a major impact on a grade.

Step Four

Effective rubrics facilitate the evaluation and scoring process by differentiating levels of aptitude and performance. After looking at many performances or analyzing many student products, the person writing a rubric has a solid idea about what is acceptable and what is not.

A teacher might ask, "What does an excellent product or performance look like?" "A poor product or performance?" "What are the characteristics that distinguish levels of performance?" Teachers must determine how "good" is "good enough" to meet their expectations for student performance before determining which criteria to include. Unfortunately, this step is one that too many teachers fail to take when creating performance-based assessments. If teachers don't specify a level of quality, they fail to differentiate between acceptable and unacceptable student performance, making any type of student response acceptable. Piloting performance-based assessments and their rubrics will provide teachers with a performance or product to examine when writing levels of performance for the rubric. Videotapes of student activity and game play may also be sources for writing levels of student performance.

The actual scoring rubric emerges from the student products or performances resulting from the pilot. When teachers have a product or performance that they think is appropriate, they should look for characteristics to describe it. Sometimes teachers can't identify the evaluation criteria distinctly before looking at student work, but they can recognize these characteristics when they see them. By noting what skilled players do (and hence, what less skilled players do not do), teachers can observe different levels of student performance as they "emerge from the work" and become apparent.

Levels for a rubric should do the following:

▶ Distinguish between the best possible performance and the least successful

▶ Use descriptors that provide a true distinction between performance levels

▶ Explain to students what is expected rather than dwelling on omissions

▶ Focus on quality, not quantity

▶ Avoid comparison words such as *more than, better, worse,* and so on.

One of the purposes of assessment is to improve student performance. When looking at a truly excellent performance, the characteristics that make it different from others help write the rubric levels. Weak descriptors don't give a student insight into quality of performance or clarify scoring. Rubrics must clearly point out and differentiate between levels of performance and degree of understanding.

Some students may have a naïve or simplistic understanding of something rather than a sophisticated one. Students with a naïve understanding of a concept tend to simplify it, rather than addressing higher levels and more sophisticated factors. Some students know a lot of facts, but they don't understand a concept or see the big picture (Wiggins 1998a). An effective rubric differentiates between a sophisticated and naïve understanding of the material.

Rubrics can also predict and anticipate errors, or they can uncover misunderstanding and alert scorers to these mistakes. Students might know a given offensive strategy, but they may not really understand when to use it most effectively in game play. Students might know the critical elements of an overhand throwing motion, but may not see the connections between it and other similar movement patterns and skills, such as a tennis or volleyball serve.

Step Five

Because the actual rubric is written for the person (usually the teacher) scoring the performance-based assessment, another rubric for students may need to be written that gives them a clear understanding of what they are required do without revealing the information you are trying to assess. You may write this for your students, or you can let your students write one themselves. Often the student discussion required to create a student rubric clarifies teacher expectations and requirements for the assessment. When students put criteria into their own words, they are more likely to internalize them, really understanding their meaning. Through student discussions, teachers can also be alerted about any misunderstandings that students might have regarding the requirements of the assessment before they begin their work. This step is not indicating that students should actually develop the rubric for a complex task. This should be the job of a person who has in-depth content knowledge.

Step Six

The next step in developing and perfecting a rubric is for teachers to administer the assessment to students. The student rubric should be attached to the assessment so that students can self-assess or peer-assess as they complete the assessment. Whether students are being evaluated on game play, choreographing dance routines, or creating some sort of written product, self-assessment and peer assessment are helpful learning tools in the instructional process.

Step Seven

Rubrics evolve over time. Teachers should not expect to create the perfect rubric on their first attempt. Even after teachers have written what they consider to be a finished product, they still should continue revisiting rubrics and their criteria to refine and improve them. Rubrics should be considered works in progress and as such, should have the word "draft" written on them. Continual attempts to improve their quality are worthwhile uses of teacher time.

Special Considerations to Address When Creating Rubrics

As stated earlier, probably one of the most difficult parts of developing performance-based assessments is writing the rubrics. Validity, reliability, transparency, and subjectivity are all points that must be addressed to create a quality rubric. Because evaluating an assessment with a rubric involves professional judgment every time the scorer completes the evaluation, assessment people are especially cautious about validity, reliability, and subjectivity. Because part of any assessment is to evaluate student knowledge, those creating the rubrics must make sure that the rubric (in the writer's attempt to be clear) does not solve the problem described in the assessment for the student. Without attention to the items previously listed, the quality and value of the assessment can be jeopardized. The following section addresses these points individually.

Validity

Because performance-based assessments are frequently direct observations of student ability (i.e., a teacher would assess a student while playing a tennis game), some types of validity are of relatively little concern. **Content validity** (how well test items represent the total content of that which the teacher wishes to measure), **predictive validity** (a test indicates future performance), and **concurrent validity** (measures a small sample of items that represent the total content measured) are less important when an actual performance is evaluated. Of greatest concern when writing rubrics is **construct validity** (determines whether the teacher is actually measuring what is intended to be measured).

When an assessment is valid, it measures what it purports to measure. With objective tests, inference of competence or mastery of learning is made through the questions asked. For example, objective assessments can determine how well a student knows rules for gymnastics officiating. A performance-based assessment might require a student to score routines during an intraclass meet. Because students are actually required to evaluate the gymnastics routines, no inference about student competence is necessary because the student is actually demonstrating the ability to do something. In this case, validity problems are most likely to arise if the rubric looks at the wrong characteristics. If the right characteristics, skills, or traits are not used, the test does not measure what it is intended to measure. Construct validity is more likely to be a concern when the teacher does not include the correct traits in the rubric. For instance, if the rubric evaluated whether a student had on the correct clothing and ignored gymnastics ability or how well the routine flowed from one element to the next, the criteria would point the scorer to the wrong components, thus leading to invalid conclusions about student mastery of the desired content and learning.

A second validity problem arising from the rubric occurs when several characteristics are listed in the rubric, some of which are more important than others are. If the person creating the rubric does not indicate that some characteristics should carry more weight, a person scoring the rubric could unknowingly do an incorrect evaluation by overemphasizing a less important trait. Similarly, game play rubrics might be invalid if teachers emphasize correct form or number of touches made by the student while failing to consider use of strategy or various aspects of fair play. If someone performs well on each of the criteria and cannot put them together to play a game or perform an activity, then the criteria are not evaluating the right things. The judgments one makes about student learning can be invalid when the wrong dimensions are emphasized. When determining criteria for an assessment, be sure to indicate if some are more important than others so that both students and those scoring the assessments are clear on the rank of importance.

Reliability

When an assessment is reliable, it consistently produces the same results. What that means is that when several people are scoring a performance or product, scores from each evaluator should be similar. One way to instill reliability is to use criteria to score performance-based assessments that are clear and complete. The more clear and simple the rubric, the greater the reliability (Wiggins 1996). Another way to instill reliability is to train scorers to use the rubrics reliably (Fredrickson and Collins 1989). When several people use the same assessment rubric, training is essential for objective scoring to help scorers understand and clarify assessment criteria. As scorers are trained on judging the criteria, in a sense, this calibrates the criteria, ensuring that all are interpreting the standard in the same way. With proper training, evaluations using performance assessments can produce scores with reliability similar to that of standardized test scores.

Rubrics typically reward quantity of work instead of quality of work (Wiggins 1996). It is easy to count events as they occur, and there is little judgment concerning the number of times something happens. A rubric that counts events is likely to be reliable, but it is not necessarily valid. Many years ago when we were coaching gymnastics, beginner routines were required to have four superior moves. Some gymnasts did have the four superiors, but their skills while executing them were poor. Additionally, the transitions between moves were also not very good. If the number of superior moves was the only criteria for judging excellence in the gymnastics routine, reliability would have been high, but the score given to the routine would not reflect the quality of performance.

Similarly, intra-rater reliability problems occur when the criteria used by the scorer shift. This change of criteria is referred to as *drift*. That is, the scorer moves away from the original criteria established for grading to another set as the evaluation process continues. Elements of the student performance that were not acceptable on the early performances or products may be allowed on the later ones.

In a sense, performances or products receive a given grade because of *when* they were graded rather than for the actual content or quality because the criteria used for evaluation shifted during the scoring of papers or performances.

A valid rubric prevents the problem of drift because the scorer has something concrete to reference when a question arises as to how to evaluate a product or performance. The order in which student work is scored should not matter. This means that each student is evaluated fairly and consistently, which is one of the goals of evaluation and assessment.

Transparency

Assessment rubrics need to have enough detail or **transparency,** so that people doing the scoring can do so reliably. This level of detail often includes putting some of the answers in the scoring guide. For example, if teachers were writing dance assessments, elements of good choreography would be included in the scoring guides. However, because part of the information the teacher wanted to assess involved students' knowledge of the elements of good choreography, giving students the same rubric as that given the evaluators would be counterproductive.

Criteria for assessments must be transparent, or clear enough, to students so that they can assess themselves and others with roughly the same reliability achieved by the actual test evaluators (Fredrickson and Collins 1989). Although transparency is important for an effective rubric, it can also cause problems with written assessments (Cunningham 1998). When there is too much detail, students know exactly what they must do to meet the criteria for the assessment without going through the desired thought and critical thinking processes as intended by the teacher.

A beginning teacher recently required students to teach others in the class a sport skill. She was using the assignment as an indicator of student knowledge of process criteria (e.g., critical elements) of the sport skills taught in class. Her rubric was based not on content but on effective teaching behaviors—a practical plan, informative visual aid, appropriate questions, checking for understanding. Although the assessment could have been an effective way to evaluate student learning, since the rubric focused on effective teaching practices and student presentation skills, student knowledge of the sport was not assessed.

To avoid problems with transparency, a teacher should create a separate scoring guide for students when the scorer's rubric contains too much information. The student rubric outlines key criteria explaining teacher expectations, but it does not contain the detail found in the scorer's rubric. Letting students know how an assessment is evaluated is a key part of performance-based assessment. However, the scoring guide cannot be so thorough that students are not required to demonstrate desired competencies and skills while completing the assessment.

Subjectivity

Degree of **subjectivity** refers to the amount of judgment used in assigning a score to a student's test performance. Subjective tests require judgment, analysis, and reflection on the part of the scorer before the assessment can be evaluated (Fredrickson and Collins 1989). By their nature, performance-based assessments require a certain amount of subjectivity to score. Despite their subjectivity, performance-based tasks make assessment more credible than traditional assessments because these tasks relate to real-world demands. Performance-based assessments allow teachers direct access to certain aspects of student knowledge. Because a professional judgment about the quality of performance is required, subjectivity does enter into the evaluation.

Subjective evaluations, such as those used for performance-based assessment, have been criticized by measurement specialists for not being valid and reliable (Hensley et al. 1987). The issues of validity and reliability stem, in part, from lack of training. With proper training, "there is no reason that subjective evaluation cannot be valid, reliable, efficient, and as objective as possible" (61). Gymnastics judging is very subjective, but training about criteria makes scorers reliable. A gymnastics judge's score is subjective but credible. A gymnastics judge is required to make a series of judgments concerning several specified elements. The fact that a panel of judges can end up being within an acceptable range of one another (the range varies depending on the score) is a testimony that training can make the scorers reliable when judging physical performance (figure 3.9). A critical point to remember here is that the people making these decisions have credible subject matter expertise. As such,

Figure 3.9 With training, people can use professional judgment to evaluate performance-based assessments in a valid and reliable manner.

this subjectivity actually involves making decisions based on professional judgment. Therefore, the term *professional judgment* is more accurate than *subjectivity* to describe evaluation of performance-based assessments.

Teachers constantly use professional judgment when they do any type of evaluation. With traditional tests, professional judgment enters in before the scoring begins: While determining what is to be assessed, when writing questions to sample knowledge of the material learned, and while deciding on the best answers for these questions. Thus, professional judgment is involved with both traditional assessment and performance assessments, we simple tend to downplay the professional judgment used in creating traditional tests.

Rubric Hints and Guidelines

Writing rubrics can be difficult, even for the veteran who has written many of them. We admit that some of our rubrics have been less than perfect when we began writing them, but we have learned from our mistakes. We offer the following ideas to help you avoid some of the problems we've experienced as you begin your road to learning how to write rubrics.

Use Samples of Student Work

One characteristic of performance-based assessments is that they can be answered using a variety of approaches. Conveying this acceptable variety through a rubric may be difficult. **Exemplars** or anchors are samples of student work, which demonstrate an acceptable or unacceptable performance. Exemplars help explain why a particular score was assigned (Fredrickson and Collins 1989). When evaluators can compare the piece being evaluated with another product or performance, it is easier to determine an appropriate score. The term *anchor* is also used to represent student work, giving the evaluators something to "ground," or base, their evaluations on. With examples of work or performance at the various levels, the scorer has concrete examples with which to compare other student work.

Some of the out-of-the-box thinking that teachers wish to encourage can be demonstrated through student work or exemplars. Rubrics using a single anchor, on the other hand, can stifle creativity (Wiggins 1996). Through the use of several diverse anchors and exemplars, creativity in performance-based assessment can easily be encouraged. Samples of diverse or divergent models of excellence show scorers possible acceptable answers. Because one of the advantages of using performance-based assessment is to encourage students to reach higher levels of thinking or to think creatively, allowing diversity in the response is an essential component. Exemplars can also be used for student performance. Videotapes of performance could be exemplars of student performance. Consider the wide variety of acceptable dance pieces that could be used to satisfy a choreography assessment. Videotaped examples of the various acceptable dance forms could help judges understand the scope of acceptable performance.

A caveat is offered here: Using an exemplar at the top level could limit future student products or performance unless that exemplar was truly exceptional. Teachers should use anchors for the highest level only if they fully

exemplify exceptional quality. When teachers use an excellent paper to illustrate the top level of the rubric, this in essence, creates a norm-referenced rubric. If Michael Jordan or Rebecca Lobo were in a physical education teacher's basketball class, then either might be used to anchor that top level. Short of that talent level, teachers should indicate that what they are showing represents good quality, but higher levels of performance are possible. Some assessment people disagree with that philosophy. We feel that exemplars should show students what is possible, but not limit their potential for excellence.

Give Rubrics With the Assessment

A key characteristic of performance-based assessment is to give students criteria that evaluate the assessment when the task is presented. Sharing rubrics with students when an assessment is given helps them understand teacher expectations for the task. Student achievement is greater when they know expectations and criteria before beginning the task (Lazzaro 1996).

When students have the criteria used to judge an assessment, they can self-assess or peer-assess the product before turning it in to the teacher for evaluation. Self-assessment is an important life skill, which performance-based assessments can encourage. Performance-based assessments frequently require a lot of time to create and evaluate. When the level of quality is increased through self-assessment, teacher time is saved because better products or performances, which are usually easier and quicker to assess, result. Also, students can refer to the rubric for feedback rather than seeking clarification from the teacher, which is another time-saver for the teacher. Some teachers do not give a rubric with performance-based assessments. This practice can decrease clarity about the assessment and limit student performance. Even if the rubric is rudimentary, it should be presented with the assessment.

Have Students Create Some Rubrics

When dealing with simple assessments or those that don't have a significant impact on the student, having students write their own rubric is an excellent part of the learning experience. Students are more likely to understand important criteria when they discuss and develop the rubric. Discussing and clarifying an existing rubric (sometimes referred to as unpacking the rubric) is an excellent instructional strategy for de-mystifying a rubric. When discussing rubrics with students, the level of quality expected can be clarified. You might also consider having students write checklists for sport skills as an assessment technique. Students could use their own scoring guide to self-assess or peer-evaluate and determine the accuracy of their list. These lists could actually become another assessment as you evaluate the list to check for knowledge of these sport skills.

Despite these positive reasons for having students write rubrics, when dealing with complex performance-based assessments, students should not write the accompanying rubrics. A multitude of factors must be considered when designing rubrics. Students do not have the sophistication about or necessary understanding of the material being evaluated to create a rubric for a major assessment. Also, using the wrong criteria can jeopardize the validity of the assessment. If an assessment is major, it should be valid.

Teachers with high levels of subject matter expertise sometimes struggle with deciding which dimensions to include and where to set the standard. When teachers allow students to write their own rubrics, they are in a sense passing the buck on identifying criteria and setting levels of achievement. A teacher should not bypass the responsibility of providing expert judgment regarding evaluation of an assessment. With complex assessments, teachers should write these scoring guides themselves and interpret them for students.

Allow for Multiple Correct Answers

Often in traditional assessment, questions are designed so that the responses are either right or wrong. With performance-based assessment, there are multiple ways to address assessments, and one is not more correct than another. Frequently a response could begin with the words "it depends." As such, the rubric must allow for this variation and the teacher must be willing to accept alternative interpretations and performances that are within the scope of guidelines and criteria established. When rubrics are written in broad terms, they allow for this range of acceptable student responses.

Sometimes a teacher's biases or limited experience can constrain a response. When a teacher fails to consider the potential breadth of an assessment, the range of acceptable responses is curtailed or narrowed. Brainstorming with a colleague to explore alternative responses may help ensure that the rubric allows for potential diversity of acceptable answers. Piloting an assessment and the accompanying rubric also helps point out varied ways that students can address the assessment. This pilot administration also can provide some anchors or exemplars to direct scorers to what constitutes an acceptable answer when the assessment is used again.

Rubrics should never mandate the process, format, method, or approach that students are to use to complete the assessment (Wiggins 1998a). Allowing students to make choices about those areas forces students to think critically while formulating a response. Further, when students address an assessment in a variety of ways, student thinking is enhanced and responses show greater insight into student knowledge and understanding.

This is not to say that whatever a student writes is correct. Teachers must set their boundaries making sure that students understand that there is a range of acceptable answers and that not just anything will be accepted.

Do Not Assume Frequency Is the Sole Indicator of Quality

Sometimes teachers score strengths and weaknesses that are easy to see and count. One reason they rely on quantity to distinguish between levels of performance is that quantity is much more reliable to score than quality because it is easier to count something than to judge it. Using frequency to determine levels of difficulty while writing rubrics is much easier than developing verbal descriptions for each level—for example, during game play, the top-level student serves four aces, the level below requires three aces, and so on. Too often, when frequency is included as a criterion in a rubric, the issue of quality of the response is not addressed.

Frequency should not be used to determine the level of performance unless frequency improves the quality of the response. Frequency is not necessarily a determinant of quality and therefore should not be used as the sole factor in evaluating student performance or a product. If during game play a student has the majority of the responses, this does not make him or her a better player. You must consider other factors such as teamwork and quality of the response (i.e., correct form, employing strategy) to determine how well the student plays. When writing a rubric, select criteria that relate most directly to the purpose and nature of the task. A rubric should look for the quality of a response, not just at how many times a student does something.

When a teacher merely wants a student to identify a certain number of characteristics, a more traditional test does this and is faster and easier to score. On a traditional test, a student might be required to identify four of the five fitness components. If teachers want students to apply knowledge purposefully, a performance assessment with a scoring guide that addresses the quality of a response is a better option. For example, a student develops a fitness plan based on results of a recent fitness test; results of the test are correctly interpreted and the areas targeted for improvement are accurate. The plan proposed by the student targets those areas needing improvement and should, if followed, lead to positive results. Although students must include all fitness components in the assessment, the focus is on using these components rather than just listing them.

Limit the Scope of the Assessment

Sometimes assessments ask questions that are very broad, resulting in a rubric that is too long and cumbersome to use. Reliability is also a problem with assessments that are too broad or open because the range of acceptable responses becomes virtually limitless and quite complicated to use. When a question becomes broad or vague, desired student content may not be assessed because students may use areas other than those that the teacher intended to satisfy the assignment and subsequent assessment. Writing the accompanying rubric would be impossible.

Teachers creating assessments must limit them so that the rubric captures the range of correct responses. When the rubric becomes complex to the point of becoming cumbersome, you should reexamine the assessment to determine if its scope can be narrowed while still assessing the appropriate content. Usually the assessment task must be changed prior to narrowing the rubric.

Consider the Levels of Difficulty

Students should be given credit for attempting more difficult tasks. For example, in diving, the judges' scores are multiplied by a difficulty factor. An easier dive has to be more correct to receive the same score as a more difficult one. More difficult tasks can be encouraged if a rubric is written to give this additional credit. Beginning volleyball players will be more likely to attempt spikes, running the risk of putting the ball into the net, if a level of difficulty is rewarded. Students willing to tackle greater challenges rather than taking a safer or easier route should be rewarded.

Avoid Comparison Words

Rubrics need to distinguish between levels of quality. A clearly written rubric increases reliability because characteristics of performance are noted for each level, independent of the other levels. Rubrics that provide rich, detailed descriptions of criteria are easiest to use for scoring.

Because writing clear descriptions of levels of student performance is difficult and time-consuming, some people developing scoring guides resort to using comparison words such as *better, more than,* and so on as they develop various levels of performance. Teachers should avoid using language that makes comparisons between different levels. Descriptive words that have stand-alone meaning and are independent of other descriptors or levels help clarify a rubric, thus facilitating its use. Words such as *rarely, sometimes, frequently,* and *extensively* are far more descriptive and paint a better picture of desired student performance than do comparison words. Also, validity tends to decrease and reliability increases when words of comparison are used (Wiggins 1996). A reliable rubric with low validity is of little value.

Determine the Number of Levels to Write

Teachers frequently want to know how many levels to include in a rubric. This answer can be decided when they consider the purpose of the assessment. When a teacher merely needs to distinguish between acceptable and unacceptable performance, then only two levels are required. Even if more levels are desired, teachers might start with two levels, *acceptable* and *not acceptable*, and then use more samples of student work to provide more characteristics and additional differences and similarities for other levels.

When you are is doing a written assessment or product, one technique for determining levels is to sort the work into piles. Sometimes the quality of the work allows the piles to emerge naturally. Other times the number of piles created depends in part, upon how many levels you need to create. For example, when grading A through F, five piles are necessary with a sixth pile being used as a no-response category. Teachers must address each level used when writing a rubric. The more levels written, the smaller the difference between levels. Because distinguishing between levels becomes more difficult with more levels, reliability decreases (Wiggins 1996; Herman, Aschbacher, and Winters 1992).

When outside requirements do not dictate the number of levels necessary for a rubric (e.g., five categories for grades), as a minimum a rubric should have at least three levels: one to indicate desired student performance, a second to indicate the cut score (below this would not be acceptable or passing), and the third level that describes unacceptable student performance. The authors actually recommend creating four levels so that a level above desired or expected student performance is available to recognize exceptional student work or performance. This level should represent the ultimate performance (e.g., Tiger Woods, Annika Sorenstam), something only 1 to 2% of the students whom you teach over a lifetime will ever achieve. If an exceptional student level is written, those students going beyond teacher expectations can be rewarded for their efforts. With this ultimate level, a ceiling effect is avoided because students can go beyond class expectations. Sometimes student achievement is stymied because they don't realize potential levels of performance. By writing the ultimate

level, teachers encourage students to raise their expectations and broaden their horizons.

Even if students never reach this level, they have a sense of what is attainable and "out there". The level below this is actually the expected performance. If grades were a consideration, the level below "ultimate" would be an A.

Writing an even number of levels forces more care in judging (Wiggins 1996). Sometimes with an odd number of levels, teachers tend to score the product or performance toward the middle. Writing a rubric with an even number of levels forces evaluators to make decisions about the quality of the work or performance.

Although most authors recommend writing rubrics in terms of what students can do, errors can also indicate level of performance. For instance, when playing volleyball, a novice typically reaches for the ball, rather than moving into position (behind the ball, facing the target). Including this characteristic of novice performance in a volleyball rubric would make a valuable clarification for the person scoring the performance; however, it should be written in terms that describe student performance, rather than stating what students cannot do.

Adjust the Rubric After the Assessment Has Been Scored, Not During

Despite all the care taken while writing a rubric, sometimes when a teacher begins using a rubric to score an assessment, it becomes painfully obvious that omissions and errors have been made. Although the rubric can be improved, a teacher must continue evaluating student work using the criteria given to the student with the assessment. A great deal of care should be exercised when creating rubrics so that they cover every dimension to be evaluated. Teachers must also realize that students should not be penalized for problems inherent with the rubric. It could end up that student grades are much higher than deserved because of a poorly written rubric. For example, if a teacher neglected to include change of levels or direction as criteria on a dance choreography assessment, criteria relative to these areas should not be used as factors in grading. Problems with rubrics accentuate the need to pilot a scoring guide before using it for a major student grade. We have been guilty of writing rubrics that miss the mark. When this happens we swallow our pride and revise the assessment and rubric for the next use.

On the other hand, during an extended unit, teachers might begin with a basic rubric and, as student skill level increases, increase the difficulty of the rubric as well. These changes are acceptable as long as students are informed of the new criteria prior to beginning the next round of assessments. For example, in a dance unit, the rubric for the first piece might emphasize change of levels, pathways, and direction. The final dance choreographed for the culminating event should be much more complex, as teacher expectations for student learning increase. Changing expectations or demands on student mastery of content is permissible, as long as these changes or new rubrics are given to students before beginning the assessment task.

Conclusion

Rubrics make public the criteria used to evaluate student performance. When criteria are made public, students know what teachers expect and are more likely to meet these expectations. Rubrics enhance student learning; they focus students toward the desired outcomes. They help remove the mystery that too often surrounds assessment. Rubrics are helpful for teachers, as well, because they force teachers to really define their expectations for achievement before beginning the assessment. Frequently after a rubric is written, teachers return to the assessment and provide additional detail or instruction that improves student performance when the assessment is used. Creating a scoring guide forces teachers to think through the assessment process and, to some extent, streamline it.

There are several different types of rubrics that teachers can use to remove the veils that too frequently cover up evaluation expectations. I admit that sometimes I get pressed for time and give performance-based assessments that are not accompanied by a rubric. Student performance on these is consistently below my expectations. When I give the rubric, student work is measurably better. When I show exemplars, the results amaze me.

Why don't you give your students a similar opportunity to shine? You might not create the perfect rubric or select the optimal type of scoring guide the first time an assessment is used. However, teachers must also remember that it is much easier to edit an existing rubric than create one from scratch. As such, they are encouraged to take the first step, beginning to shape criteria into a rubric, knowing that through revision and reuse, a meaningful, worthwhile means of scoring student achievement emerges.

CHAPTER FOUR

Developing Performance-Based Assessments

Good teaching is inseparable from good assessing. (Wiggins 1996, v-6:8)

We have identified many types of performance-based assessments in this book but have not given much insider information about their development. The purpose of this chapter is to provide some hints that we have found useful regarding the development and implementation of various types of performance-based physical education assessments. The assessments we cover in this chapter include observation (teacher, peer, and self), game play and modified game play, role play, event tasks, interviews, essays, journals, student projects, and student logs. Two other types of performance-based assessments, open response questions and portfolios, are covered in greater detail in chapters 5 and 6.

Observations

Because so much of physical education learning involves overt skill performance, observation is one of the best assessment tools available. Teachers, peers, and students themselves can observe skills and provide assessments of performance designed to improve learning. Although teachers typically make up these observational tools, several activity subject books (e.g., tennis, golf, social dance, and weightlifting) are excellent sources for developing these tools. Table 4.1 lists books that include skill sheets that can be duplicated and used for observational assessments.

Table 4.1   Sources for Skill Sheets

Title	Author	Publisher
Advanced Golf: Steps to Success	Owens and Bunker	Human Kinetics
Advanced Swimming: Steps to Success	Thomas	Human Kinetics
Alpine Skiing: Steps to Success	Yacenda	Human Kinetics
Archery: Steps to Success	Haywood and Lewis	Human Kinetics
Australian Football: Steps to Success	Jaques	Human Kinetics
Badminton: Steps to Success	Grice	Human Kinetics
Basketball: Steps to Success	Wissell	Human Kinetics
Bowling: Steps to Success	Strickland	Human Kinetics
Fencing: Steps to Success	Cheris	Human Kinetics
Field Hockey: Steps to Success	Anders and Myers	Human Kinetics
Golf: Steps to Success	Owens and Bunker	Human Kinetics
Ice Skating: Steps to Success	Kunzle-Watson and DeArmond	Human Kinetics
Netball: Steps to Success	Shakespear	Human Kinetics
Nordic Skiing: Steps to Success	Guillon	Human Kinetics
Racquetball: Steps to Success	Kittleson	Human Kinetics
The Physical Education Handbook	Schmottlach and McManama	Allyn and Bacon
Rugby: Steps to Success	Biscombe and Drewett	Human Kinetics
Self-Defense: Steps to Success	Nelson	Human Kinetics
Soccer: Steps to Sucess	Luxbacher	Human Kinetics
Social Dance: Steps to Success	Wright	Human Kinetics
Softball: Steps to Success	Potter and Brockmeyer	Human Kinetics
Sport and Recreation Activities	Mood, Musker, and Rink	WCB McGraw-Hill
Squash: Steps to Success	Yarrow	Human Kinetics
Swimming: Steps to Success	Thomas	Human Kinetics
Table Tennis: Steps to Success	Hodges	Human Kinetics
Teaching Cues for Basic Sport Skills for Elementary and Middle School Students	Fronske and Wilson	Pearson Education, Benjamin Publishing
Teaching Cues for Sport Skills	Fronske	Allyn and Bacon
Team Handball: Steps to Success	Clanton and Dwight	Human Kinetics
Tennis: Steps to Success	Brown	Human Kinetics
Volleyball: Steps to Success	Viera and Ferguson	Human Kinetics
Weight Training: Steps to Success	Baechle and Groves	Human Kinetics

For teachers who wish to develop their own observational assessments, critical elements and extensions used to teach the various skills are excellent components to include on the assessments. Including the critical elements and extensions on observation forms ensures that students receive congruent feedback from the observational assessment. The following sections provide ideas for using teacher-, peer-, and self-observation assessments.

Teacher Observation

Because most of the learning in physical education involves overt student behaviors, teacher observation is probably one of the most widely used assessment practices in physical education. Teachers give students a task to perform, then watch them to see how well they are performing. Teachers can use observation both to enhance and document student learning when they formalize the process by writing down the items they want students to demonstrate.

During initial skill practice and development, teachers usually provide oral feedback to students. To transform oral feedback to a more concrete form of assessment, teachers can record student performance in terms of process (form) or product. Even at this early stage of skill development, assessments are useful for the teaching-learning process. I typically give students some type of task at the conclusion of the lesson, then circulate and record the number of correct skill responses I observe while watching various students. Sometimes I have students self-record their best score or performance on the attendance sheet. A teacher can use a simple and low-tech recording process, such as writing on a clipboard, or a more complex technology like a hand-held computer. When teachers evaluate process, the first step is to decide what indicators of performance they wish students to demonstrate. The second step is to write down the indicators or criteria by which to judge student performance. When recording product-type scores, teachers should still require good form for the skill attempt to count.

There are several advantages of actually recording student performance rather than just providing oral feedback. By writing down the criteria, teachers become more focused on the quality of performance they expect from students. Also, knowing what students can do is useful information for planning subsequent lessons. By doing these more formalized assessments daily, teachers can document or verify learning or improvement to students, parents, or administrators. And because the observation becomes more systematic when written, teachers can ensure that all students are learning. Some students learn to avoid performing in physical education. Typically, these students are not highly skilled and usually are not successful with skill attempts. To avoid the embarrassment of not performing well in front of peers, the students avoid responding whenever possible. Siedentop and Tannehill (2000) refer to these students as **competent bystanders**. They are not behavior problems, but they also are not learning and acquiring the skills. Some of these students are very clever with their nonresponses, and teachers never notice them.

When a drill or skill is repeated for several days, teachers have an opportunity to observe learning and improvement by selecting target students and recording their performance on these tasks. The teacher might select two lower-skilled students, two with average skills, and two others with higher skill levels to get a feel for performance of students at various levels of skill. These observations become the checkpoints referred to in chapter 8.

Teachers can also systematically observe different students each day during these teacher observations to assess how well students are performing. By looking at six to eight students per day, a teacher can verify learning for every member of an entire class during an instructional unit. Results of the observation can be shared via written feedback to students after class. Teachers can use the results of their observations when planning future lessons.

Teachers may also use observations to group students by ability for instruction or feedback. If a teacher wanted to mix abilities within a group (as for forming a team or

While doing a research project, I observed students with more skill than most of the class and those with less skill. The teacher had identified a young lady as my target student who she felt had a lower level of skill. As it turned out, the target student was actually a competent bystander. In a three-week volleyball unit, she touched the ball 41 times. Competent bystanders are just as the name implies—competent at not responding to an activity without drawing teacher's attention to their patterns of nonresponse. By systematically doing teacher observations, I saw that competent bystanders become very obvious, very quickly. If teachers are aware of these competent bystanders, then they can consciously monitor student performance on a regular basis and encourage the student to begin participating.

practice group), teacher observations provide essential information for forming the group. Sometimes grouping students of like ability is a wise instructional strategy. When students are not as skilled as others, they can benefit from smaller group instruction. Higher-skilled students might be given a game to play that challenges their level of skill development while lower-skilled students who are having similar problems performing the skill receive instruction from the teacher in a more closed environment.

Although we use teacher observations to verify learning and to provide feedback for our students and ourselves, some teachers use these assessments for grading purposes. Students are notified that they will be randomly observed throughout the unit and that these observations will be factored into the final student grade. Students don't know who will be observed on a given day, so all students are encouraged to perform at high levels because their performances may be evaluated for grading purposes. Students are not given observational results until every member of the class has been observed and the observational cycle begins again. This keeps students from knowing who has been targeted for the grading observation for the day and helps ensure on-task behavior. Because students eventually see the results, this assessment also provides feedback on performance. When teacher observations are included in the grading system, teachers should observe students at multiple times during the unit to make sure that the student hasn't been evaluated on an atypical day—for example, when a student didn't feel well or was with an extremely low-skilled or high-skilled partner. Multiple observations over time allow the teacher to gain a more accurate picture of student performance.

Peer Observations

Peer observations are also excellent ways to do assessments that inform students about their performance. Many teachers have more students in class than they can provide individual feedback to on a regular basis. Peer observations are excellent ways to increase student feedback by making each student a teacher for his or her peer.

To create a peer observation instrument, teachers must again decide what they want students to know and be able to do, then create a set of criteria for assessing that. Peer observations are especially useful when first learning a skill. During initial learning phases, it is critical that students have quality practice and don't learn errors that must be corrected at a later date. After initial instruction, the teacher can distribute a list of criteria that should be present in the skill. Too often teachers merely distribute this list without demonstrating or explaining to students how to use it. Students being observed must understand that the purpose of the observation is to encourage correct practice and is not meant to be punitive or for grade calculations. All feedback they receive from the peer is intended to help improve performance. Students giving the feedback must understand that the purpose of their assessment is to enhance student learning. They are trying to get their partner(s) to perform skills correctly so that improved skill performance will result.

In addition, students doing the observations must also be taught what good performance looks like so that they are not giving incorrect feedback. When creating worksheets for peer evaluations, teachers must remember that they are usually dealing with novice performers. When teachers develop an assessment format and students are taught to observe certain phases of performance using a set protocol, they become more skilled at assessing the performance of others. Additional practice on different skills following the same observation protocol further increases student accuracy.

Having the correct cues is critical to this type of assessment; therefore, teachers should list the cues they wish students to use. Because it is easier to assess using the protocol described earlier, teachers should list the cues in the order that they are assessed, starting from the feet and moving up the body. We suggest that students be taught to look at the following components of skill performance in the order listed:

1. Stance

2. Preparatory position or action

3. Execution

4. Follow-through

Teachers can organize the cues under these categories. Since beginners are not capable of observing too many things at once, teachers should limit the cues being observed to five or fewer and allow multiple opportunities to view the performance of others. We encourage teachers to do several observations with students so that students learn what to look at, as well as how to look at it. They can compare results of their observations with those of the teacher. This training helps the observation be more reliable.

If paper or printing is problematic, teachers could create erasable forms by laminating the form or covering it with clear contact paper. By giving students erasable markers, a teacher could collect the forms after a class and, before erasing them, note what students had written. By looking at student observation results, teachers can gain information about the quality of skill performance. By comparing student observation results with teacher observation results, teachers can have an indication about the degree to which students understand what good skill performance looks like.

Beginners have a difficult time seeing all that is happening during a live performance. Videotape, on-line movies, or DVDs allow students many opportunities to observe the same skill. The following is an example of a peer evaluation using videotape. Although this assessment was designed for videotape analysis, a similar assessment could be used to evaluate actual student performance in the gymnasium.

You have just begun a new company designed to improve people's tennis skills. Because of your tennis expertise, people send you videos of the skills that they want to improve, and you provide feedback about their current skill level as well as what they can do to improve their level of play.

You have three people who have submitted videos of their forehands, backhands, and serves. You do the following:

1. Watch the skills at regular speed and evaluate the performance. Using the critical elements presented in class as a resource, write down the critical elements you observe that they are doing correctly or incorrectly. Watch the video once for each person. Do this for all three skills for all three people.

2. Watch the video a second time. This time you are allowed to go frame by frame and see the performance in slow motion. Write down your analysis based on watching performances at this speed. Was your impression the same, or were you able to detect additional cues or errors at the slower speed?

3. Draw a picture (similar to the frames you might see drawn for an animated cartoon) to give your client an idea of what his or her racket head looks like during the swing for each of the three strokes.

4. Using your error correction sheet, design an improvement plan for your client for each of the three strokes submitted to you. Plan a 20-minute stroke warm-up that your client can use to improve his or her game.

5. Send your client the bill!

Although the purpose of the sample assessment is to provide feedback to peers, teachers could evaluate the observer's cognitive knowledge of the skills by changing the format slightly. By assessing students on the accuracy of their cues and the accuracy of their evaluations, teachers can assess students' knowledge of the critical elements as well as their ability to apply it to a real-world scenario. If the same videotape were used for all members of the class, students could be assessed on their ability to evaluate correct and incorrect performance. The teacher then scores these cognitive assessments for accuracy, and they could be used to calculate part of the students' grades for cognitive knowledge. Students could even do this assessment from their homes or in a school computer facility as homework if video clips were loaded onto a computer, put on a Web site, or burned onto a CD-ROM.

We also have used peer observation forms to evaluate affective behavior during game play. By listing the desired behaviors, students have an opportunity to comment on or rate their opponents' positive sport behaviors. Also, by listing these desirable sport behaviors, students are reminded of how you expect them to act during game play. When they know that a teacher is noting student performance, they tend to demonstrate more acceptable game play behaviors. Figure 3.1 in chapter 3 is an example of this type of assessment rubric. Other examples of peer assessment may be found in chapters 2, 3, 6, and 8.

Note: Although peer evaluation can be a positive aspect of your assessment system, we feel very strongly that under no circumstances should peer assessments be factored into a final student grade for the student being assessed. That evaluation is the responsibility of the teacher, and assessments to determine grades should not be delegated to students.

Self-Evaluation

One of the goals of secondary teaching is often to make students self-sufficient learners. During elementary school, students should have developed, according to the National Physical Education Content Standards (NASPE 1995), competency in several physical activities and proficiency in a few. This should be seen as the first step toward developing a physically active lifestyle. As students become adults, we as physical educators hope that they never stop acquiring new skills or improving previously learned ones. Since this goal implies that learning must first take place, students who do not have the opportunity to participate in additional formal classes may ultimately become their own teachers in adulthood. For this reason, self-assessment skills are useful to develop in students.

Self-assessment can occur in a variety of scenarios. Dancers often do self-assessments as they look into the mirrors that surround the practice studio. Videotaping is also an excellent way to do self-assessment. In a crowded physical education class, a video camera could be one of the stations. A student aide could be assigned to do the taping at this station and students could view their performances at a later time. Digital photography also makes self-assessment possible. Students could download pictures or on-line videos from the teacher's computer file, off the Web, or burn them on a CD-ROM to complete analysis at home or in the school computer lab.

Self-assessment may also occur when teachers inform students of possible problems with performance when form is wrong. For example, while teaching a tennis forehand to begin-

ners, I have them stand next to the fence. If they bring their racket back and it hits the fence, they then know they are over-rotating their shoulders, which negatively affects the timing of the swing. I also teach them to listen for that *ping!* sound (instead of a *thud!)* when the ball bounces off the "sweet spot" of the racket.

The list of archery errors found in table 4.2 could help students evaluate process by looking at the product, or where their arrows land after being shot. When you assign them to mark the grouping of their arrows on a target and list possible reasons for the arrow placement, they can do self-assessment of their skills. Students would then try to eliminate those possible errors on subsequent rounds of archery.

Kinesthetic sense is an important part of the learning process. Once students "feel" what a movement is like when it is correct and if they are cued to pay attention to form, they can then detect errors in their own performance, thus demonstrating self-sufficient learning.

Regardless of whether the teacher uses mirrors, videotaping, product cues, or kinesthetic sense, teachers can have students self-assess their own movements or skills by providing a list of proper cues and allowing students the opportunity to honestly evaluate their own skill or performance. Students can also self-evaluate affective domain behavior. Instead of having students fill out a form listing the appropriate behaviors for their opponents, you could have them self-evaluate their own fair play behaviors. By comparing results from their self-assessment with those given by the opponent, students see how their perceptions differed from those of others. This comparison might be an important revelation to the young performer about his or her affective domain behaviors. By writing a reflective paper comparing the results of the two observations, students would have an additional opportunity to assess and potentially improve affective domain learning. See figures 3.1 and 3.2 in chapter 3 for an example of a peer affective domain assessment and a self-administered affective domain assessment, respectively.

Again, as with peer evaluation, students should never be required to self-assess for grading purposes. When teachers want honest

Table 4.2 Archery Errors

Students shoot a round of six arrows and record their placement on the sheet provided. Use the following list of errors from archery to help students determine their form errors to improve their performances.

Common errors causing flight to the left

Hunching the left shoulder
Anchoring away from the face
Throwing the bow arm to the left
Sighting with the left eye
Placing the weight on the heels
Holding the arrow tightly at the nock

Common errors causing the flight to be to the right

Throwing the bow arm to the right
Jerking strings
Turning the head to the right
Placing the weight on the balls of the feet
Tilting the body forward

Common errors causing the flight to be low

Inching forward with the string fingers on release
Dropping the bow arm too soon after release
Using an under-strung bow
Stretching the chin forward to meet the string
Using too high an anchor point

Common errors causing the flight to be too high

Throwing the bow arm after the arrow on release
Lifting the bow arm on release
Lowering the string elbow or hand before or during release
Drawing beyond the anchor point
Tilting the body away from the target with weight on rear foot

appraisals of skills and abilities, these assessments should not be factored into a student's grade.

Game Play and Modified Game Play

When writing objectives for activities or sports, many teachers want students to be able to play a game at a recreational level upon completion of instruction. Skill tests are designed to be approximations of game play ability. The assumption is that if a student can perform a variety of skill tests well, then that student should be a competent player in an actual game. This is not always the case, as many teachers can attest. I can remember skill testing my students on several volleyball skills and requiring them to achieve a certain level of competence before allowing them to play games. Despite their scores on skill tests, they were unable to put these skills together to play a meaningful game of volleyball. The best way to assess student achievement on game play ability is to actually evaluate students during game play.

Small-sided, or modified games, that teach students to use these skills in an increasingly open environment are an essential part of skill development used in game play. These situational or developmental learning activities allow students to apply skills in a controlled gamelike setting that moves them into a more open environment than is typically found on a skill test. Just as the move from skill performance to game play must be progressive, so should the assessment process. Students can play two-on-one and two-on-two games, which allow skill development and evaluation of skills at the same time. Teachers must look at student responses in these increasingly more complex game situations to determine whether students have grasped the concepts necessary for game play. Too often students can recognize what to do in a two-on-one transitional drill, but they are incapable of recognizing that same situation in game play. When teachers continue to assess during these small-sided games, gaps in learning become apparent and teachers know what they must re-teach. These modified games can also be used for summative assessments. In many cases, small-sided games are actually easier to use than a regulation game for assessment purposes.

When assessing game play, I like to develop a list of skills that I feel are essential for being a competent player. These skills become my descriptors for a quantitative analytic rubric. I include some skills, knowledge of rules, game play strategies, as well as some affective domain dispositions when I develop my list of descriptors. The list should capture the important elements of the game without becoming so long that doing the assessment becomes a burden. Usually 12 to 15 is a reasonable number of descriptors to use while evaluating student performance. Unit objectives may provide an appropriate starting point for developing the list of descriptors for the rubric.

Sometimes the actual descriptors are longer than will fit on my evaluation sheet. When this is the case, I use an abbreviated form of the descriptor on the scoring sheet and have the entire element written out on another paper. By doing this, I am sure that I am consistent with my judgment of playing abilities and don't forget the intention of the shorter version found on the score sheet. When letting students evaluate peers, I make sure they understand what is meant by the abbreviated version found on the score sheet. Letting students use these score sheets to assess other

classmates is beneficial because they better understand the assessment process and know what I am looking for when I evaluate them.

Students enjoy comparing their scores to those of the teacher to see where they agree and where they differ. This system is also a convenient way to discuss criteria so that they better understand what teachers are looking for with the assessment. Since assessment should be used to enhance learning, giving students an opportunity to understand the areas on which they are being assessed is an important part of the process.

If you have a dilemma about which items to include on your game play rubric, share these with a colleague and get feedback. This process can help establish validity for the rubric when all people evaluating the criteria are knowledgeable about the game or activity. Another method is to test your rubric as a pilot during some preliminary game play days and see if it discriminates or distinguishes between levels of skill. If your best players are not receiving the highest scores, you need to make some adjustments to your descriptors. Similarly, your poorest players should score the lowest on your rubric. When the results of the evaluation do not differentiate levels of skill, it is an obvious signal that you have missed some important components.

A quantitative analytic rubric can be a little overwhelming when you first begin to assess game play, especially if you are looking at 12 to 15 descriptors. I suggest assessing 3 or 4 descriptors each day as you move between different games and evaluate different students. This plan is especially useful for teachers with large classes. One strategy would be to look at psychomotor skills one day, cognitive abilities another, and affective dispositions a third day. Novice observers might begin to develop their game play observational skills by looking at small-sided or transitional games alluded to earlier. By removing some of the complexity from the game, teachers can assess student performance accurately.

Another hint is that I always do my assessments in pencil, which allows me to change a student's score as game play skills improve. An alternative is to make several copies of your rubric and use a new one for each day's assessment. Since game play can be used as a formative assessment, students should be given the opportunity to improve scores on subsequent days. When you share assessment results with students, they can see what they must work on to improve their skills—yet another way assessment can be used to enhance learning. Sometimes students may question your judgment of their abilities. The better they understand the criteria, the less likely they are to question their assessment results.

When I use separate score sheets on different days, I never average the scores. Theoretically, skills should improve, and students should not be penalized for poor performance when they began instruction. Rather, their final scores and grade should represent the level of achievement at the conclusion of the unit, which is most representative of the degree to which a student has met the unit's learning objectives.

Although quantitative analytic rubrics are superior for assessing game play, other types of rubrics can also be used. Checklists or point system rubrics may be used if you had no desire to evaluate the quality of a descriptor listed. Qualitative analytic rubrics and holistic rubrics, as described in chapter 3, may also be used (see figures 3.5 and 3.6, respectively). I do feel that holistic rubrics are valuable for a final or summative analysis of game play because students are given a single score that represents an overall analysis of game play ability. However, holistic rubrics are less useful for formative evaluation of game play because the student doesn't know the exact reason for being rated or evaluated at a given level of play.

A caution is offered here about adding skills to the list of descriptors developed for game play. I do not assess skills solely during game play; I also use traditional skill tests to assess these skills. On a skill test, students have the opportunity to show you the skill in a fairly closed environment. By the setup used in the test protocol, the student is ensured of having a chance to perform that skill to the best of his or her ability. The skill test is an indicator of students' level of competence relative to that skill. It allows them to demonstrate that skill in a closed environment, thus enhancing the opportunity for correct practice. In game play, the setup for the skill might be less than ideal, resulting in process or form errors while the student attempts to make a play. The student should not be penalized for using poor form while making an attempt during game play.

Another thing that I have discovered is that some students never perform certain skills in game play. When you want an opportunity to assess these skills, you need to create an environment designed for it to happen (e.g., skill tests). Some students are reluctant to spike a ball during volleyball game play or may never have the opportunity to attempt a spike because they were not set up or because another skill (e.g., a dink) was a more appropriate response. If game play were the only place the skill was assessed, the student would consequently receive a zero.

An analogy for this is the pull-up test for strength. I know students have some upper-body strength, even though they cannot do a pull-up. By using other measurement techniques, I can assess upper-body strength. In much the same way, a student might be able to perform a skill in an ideal setting but not in less than ideal conditions. With that in mind, I do include skills on game play because I know my more competent players will attempt them. Students who have the confidence to perform spikes and dinks during game play and who do so with correct form are probably your better players. Because a good rubric should discriminate between skill levels, it makes sense to include skills on a game play assessment because your better players demonstrate them and should use correct form. Remember, assessment should look at student achievement through a variety of lenses. By assessing skills on skill assessments and game play, you have more information about student achievement.

Statistics can also be good indicators of game play performance. You can track game play statistics and note improvement over time to assess student learning. When deciding which statistics to track, select those most important to the level of game play you are trying to teach. Also, make sure that when students record statistics, they know what the statistics mean. Recently I watched a sport education class in which the teacher had the students record "assists." Someone commented that some students didn't have very many assists, which led to the conversation about what an assist was. Don't just assume students know what a game component is—teach them.

Although it is preferable to evaluate during live game play, it also is possible to videotape games and evaluate students at a later time. It requires more of the teacher's time, but it may also be a useful technique for the beginning observer. When the teacher or evaluator misses a play, videotape allows the opportunity to review a play segment more than once. Videotape assessment of game play is also a way to establish reliability. Inter-rater reliability can also be established using videotape when the teacher and another colleague both assign the same scores to students involved in game play.

Grading is obviously easier when using a holistic rubric because a single score results. To determine a final grade for game play, a teacher could use the quantitative analytic rubric for formative assessment. For the final grade, the teacher would develop levels of excellence (as you would do for a qualitative analytic rubric) for each descriptor (i.e., levels one, two, three, and four). Next all the statements of a given level (i.e., level one) for each descriptor would be combined into a paragraph to create a holistic rubric explaining the quality of performance for that level. This same process is followed for each level and the result would be a holistic rubric. The holistic tennis rubric in figure 3.6 was created in this way (see figures 3.5 and 3.6). You have thus created a holistic rubric from the descriptors that you have used to evaluate students throughout the unit.

If you want to stay with the qualitative analytic rubric, you could divide the rubric into psychomotor, cognitive, and affective descriptors and take an average score for each of those areas. If your grading philosophy (see the discussion in chapter 10) is 50% psychomotor, 30% cognitive, and 20% affective, then multiply your average scores by those respective percentages to determine your final grade.

Whatever method you use to calculate a grade, the important thing to remember is that a grade should reflect the degree to which a student has achieved your learning objectives.

Role-Play

Role-playing is another type of performance-based assessment. It is especially useful for assessing affective domain behaviors but can be used for assessing other knowledge as well. When teachers use role-play to assess affective domain behavior, students are given a somewhat touchy or uncomfortable scenario and asked to react to it. It may relate to events that have actually occurred in class. For example, a teacher might create a role-play that centers around discussing what to do with a low-skilled player who was unable to perform the skills necessary for the big game. This role-play would be appropriate before the teacher announces who will be on which team for the class tournament. Group members might be asked to brainstorm ways to increase this person's contribution to the team. A related scenario could be that this lower-skilled person meets with friends after school and is upset over the assignment to play with team members who have an elitist attitude. The person is afraid of being ridiculed and needs to develop a strategy for dealing with the situation. Role-plays allow students to take scenarios and look at them from a variety of perspectives. The first scenario might be made more complex by having the discussion going on and then having the lower-skilled player come into the locker room unannounced. The role-play would continue with this lower-skilled person present giving students an opportunity to address an even touchier situation.

Teachers assign the roles for students to actually play. When assigning roles, teachers must make sure that the student assigned to that role cannot necessarily be identified with that role outside of the class. Middle school students are notorious for teasing classmates. Roles should be selected so that other students cannot "brand" one another and give a source for teasing or embarrassment. Teachers must make sure that students understand that these roles are purely for class purposes and not intended to be continued after the exercise continues. Following the role-play, a debriefing session should follow where students are given the opportunity to express how they felt during the scenario. The debriefing gives students a chance to consider the feelings of others. Teachers use the debriefing to teach lessons important for class purposes. Students might create their own role-play scenarios to discuss a topic given to them by their teacher. They could write the script to portray the topic intended.

Although these role-plays are useful situations for addressing sensitive topics, they also may look at cognitive learning or psychomotor skills as well, depending on how the scenario unfolded. If cognitive or affective knowledge is assessed, then criteria for assessing these should be conveyed to students. When role-plays are used to assess affective domain topics, teachers should avoid assessing content and what was said. They should focus more on participation by all group members and a willingness to let others have an opportunity to speak and give opinions. Checklist or point systems rubrics that give credit to those who participate can be used for evaluation. Again, the objectives for the assessment determine both the nature of the task or role-play as well as what is being evaluated.

Event Tasks

Event tasks are performance tasks that can be completed within a single class period (NASPE 1995) and usually involve psychomotor activity in physical education. A teacher might pose a problem to a group of students and have them design a solution. For example, a teacher might give students some locomotor skills and ask them to combine the skills into a movement combination done to music. Beginning dance choreography assessments that ask students to create a piece showing various elements of dance—such as a change of levels, changes in direction, and symmetrical and asymmetrical balances—might be completed within a single class period. Adventure education event tasks frequently present scenarios requiring students to demonstrate cooperation and problem-solving skills. These often can be completed within a single class.

Event tasks are ways for teachers to check for levels of understanding with certain concepts. Because of the brevity, they are usually more appropriate for formative assessments rather than summative assessments. They provide teachers with feedback on student learning, as students have the opportunity to apply concepts covered in class.

As with all performance-based assessments, students must have the criteria by which the performance is evaluated. Keeping in mind that with performance-based assessment the process is just as important as the product, teachers need a way to determine the process students followed to complete the task. Adventure education event tasks usually feature a debriefing session after the task when the teacher has an opportunity to ask students questions about the process they used to solve the problem. Reflection papers could also be used in the assessment of adventure education tasks to evaluate the process used to solve the problem.

When creating event tasks, a teacher must begin by looking at the objective the event task is designed to assess. By fully evaluating all components of the objective, teachers can design a suitable task to measure student learning on the objective. The type of rubric written for the task depends on the criteria specified in the objective. For example, combining locomotor skills shows a teacher that students were able to perform the skills and move smoothly between the skills, so those elements would appear on a rubric. Requiring students to perform this with music demonstrates student ability to count music and do the locomotor skills with a rhythm. Since the assessment is probably formative, a checklist, point system, or qualitative analytic rubric is appropriate. An adventure education event task occurring at the conclusion of a unit of study could use a holistic rubric that evaluates the level of quality for the process used by students to solve the problem.

Student Performances

These assessments are generally done over several days or maybe even several weeks. They are complex and require students to combine skills and knowledge into a meaningful performance. It is much more difficult for students to do skills in combination than to do them one at a time. Moving from one skill to another adds an element of difficulty to the combination. Doing skills in time to music also adds another dimension of difficulty. When teaching dance or gymnastics units, teachers can instruct students on the elements of choreography so that they know how to combine dance and gymnastics elements into meaningful and interesting compositions or routines. Students can be evaluated on their ability to create the composition, their ability to perform the composition, or their ability to both create and perform, depending on the objectives.

Student performances might also include creating an exercise sequence for a fitness warm up. By identifying the purpose of the warm up, teachers could evaluate student knowledge of some principles of exercise physiology regarding a good warm-up and also the ability to identify which muscles are used for an activity. Aerobic dance movements might also be included in the warm-up, which would imply putting movements to music. As adults, students would find the information needed to create this performance useful. Although student performances are generally live, teachers or students might choose to videotape the presentation for later use.

Depending on the learning objectives established for the unit, teachers often require students to create performances when teaching dance, gymnastics, rope jumping, or synchronized swimming units. These culminating performances provide students with an opportunity to combine the various steps or skills learned in the unit into a final product. Students usually work very hard at creating these pieces and making the final product as finished as possible.

When teachers wish to use some type of performance for their culminating event, they should start small and work toward the final product. A choreography assignment given on the first day of a unit without future instruction or guidance is a daunting task for beginners. Students should not be given the entire project without some lead-ups or tasks that let them practice their choreography skills just as they would practice dance or gymnastics skills. When you assign simple choreography elements, such as combining an asymmetrical balance with two symmetrical balances using a locomotor transition between the three balances, students begin to experiment with movement and gain confidence in their abilities to create dances. By watching other members of their group and class, they begin to learn how to combine movements to create aesthetically appealing products.

As with all performance-based assessments described in this book, teachers must begin with the final objectives in mind then develop a plan that allows students to reach the final goals. Although teachers would obviously not make a choreography assignment to beginners on day one of a six-week unit and tell them to get busy, they should let students know at the beginning of instruction where they intend to head and what students will do at the conclusion of the unit. A teacher might begin by showing videos of students' performances or clips of people performing dances or routines. When students have the end product in mind, the lessons that enable students to learn these skills make more sense to them along the way.

Since this type of performance-based assessment looks at a culminating performance, it is appropriate to use a holistic rubric for the final assessment. See chapter 3 for an explanation of how to create a holistic rubric.

When I give students guidelines and criteria for performance, I find that they often meet or exceed my expectations. I give them a holistic rubric, then spend some class time breaking it apart to look at the elements contained in the paragraph descriptions. Students can thus create their own analytic rubric to use for guidance while creating the performance—they actually are creating a formative self-assessment tool—but still have an idea of how to consider the performance at a more holistic level.

Evaluating student performances takes practice. Teachers should consider videotaping student performance to review so as to ensure accurate assessment of the work. Videotaping is also a good idea because students can observe their own performances and do a self-assessment of the work. It is impossible for the performer to envision how a performance looks to the audience. By videotaping the piece as it is created, students can see how the composition looks to others, and provide themselves with feedback about the quality of their work. They also could critique others' work and provide feedback either as a formative or summative assessment. If evaluating dance choreography, teachers could assign the students the role of dance critic and have them write a review of other students' work. As part of the learning process, students could evaluate performances from past years using the criteria established by the teacher. Such assessments provide students with an opportunity to become familiar with the guidelines that are used to evaluate their own work later on in the unit. Past work could also be shown to give a visual picture to students about the quality expected at the various levels of performance. The videotapes help anchor the criteria to actual performance.

When I create holistic rubrics, four is the minimal number of levels that I write. Because most students never achieve my highest level of performance, I expect that my A students will perform at the level below this (level 3). If students can do everything in level 2, this is a C performance. I do not actually write the paragraph describing a B performance. My B students can do everything described in level 2 and some things in level 3. My D students cannot do everything in level 2 but are above level 1. Level 1 is a description of unsatisfactory performance and a failing grade. When students perform at this level, they have not achieved the learning objectives written for the unit. Students must understand that although there is a lot of latitude with acceptable performance in choreography, there are certain elements that must be present. Teachers may wish to write additional levels to correspond with a grading scale, which is also acceptable.

Journals

Student journals provide an excellent way for teachers to measure student knowledge and understanding of physical education concepts. Teachers should not just require journal writing to repeat information presented in class. Rather, students should be required to put information into their own words and do some type of interpretation or comparison. When students explain a concept in their own words, they are forced to process the information. Learning moves from the recall or knowledge level to a higher level of thinking on Bloom's Taxonomy, such as comprehension and analysis.

When selecting topics or questions for journal writing, teachers again must go back to the purpose of the assessment to determine the desired content. When teachers assess students' ability to remember information presented in class, more traditional assessment methods allow this to happen and require less time to determine student achievement. When teachers look for students to process information at a more complex level of thinking,

questions must be phrased accordingly. Journal writing prompts should ask students to explain things in their own words or relate them to previous learning that requires analysis skills. *Why* and *how* are excellent words to use to probe student learning.

Journal writing allows students to make self-evaluations of progress or learning, provide teachers with insight about student feelings of participating in various physical education sports or activities, or reveal confusion about learning some of the cognitive concepts associated with physical education. Although some teachers allow more of a free-writing format, we have found that when we focus student attention and narrow the topic, the information given to teachers is more relevant to instruction and provides better feedback about levels of student understanding. Our most successful journal entries occur when students are prompted with a question, such as a request to explain a concept or strategy covered in class.

Journals are also excellent ways for teachers to access affective domain information. Some affective domain prompts might include the following:

- **Did you feel successful while practicing today's activities? Explain your answer.**

- **What was the hardest thing that you accomplished today? Why did you think it was more difficult than other tasks or activities?**

- **What practice strategy did you use during today's lesson? Was it successful? Why or why not?**

- **If you were to learn a new skill from someone in this class, whom would you select to teach you? Why did you select this person?**

- **Select one thing that you would change about today's lesson. Why did you choose that event or task? If you could rewrite the script concerning that event, how would it read?**

The reader should note that writing prompts for journal entries should be somewhat complex, thus requiring more than a yes or no response. Questions that probe the student response provide teachers with more information. Frustration or feelings of alienation toward other class members or toward physical activities usually can be detected through journal entries. Teachers may be unaware of events occurring in class that contribute to students' lack of learning or lack of enjoyment concerning the learning process. If teachers expect students to take journal writing seriously, then teachers must read them and let students know the entries have been read. Written comments, smiley faces, and stickers let the students know that their work has been seen. Reading journals is a time-consuming process. For this reason, we suggest that you not require all journals from all classes to be submitted simultaneously. Staggered due dates can make assessment less of a chore for the teacher.

Although teachers might check an affective journal entry for completion of the assignment, length, or coverage of certain topics, student journals should not be graded for content when teachers expect an honest response or entry. One of the quickest ways to shut down student openness is to require students to think or write a certain way. Teachers could assess journal entries concerning student cognitive understanding of a concept covered in class but not for affective domain content.

Student Projects

Student projects are another excellent assessment tool used in performance-based assessment. They typically take several class sessions to complete and require students to take learning to a higher level of performance. Through the use of your available resources, student projects can evolve into meaningful end products while at the same time assess student learning. Students rarely have an opportunity to show their creativity, and student projects allow your creative students to shine. Many times the shy or quiet students are the ones who really perform well on these assessments.

One student project evolved from a concern by a teacher who expressed how students no longer knew about games that children used to play before the advent of Nintendo and computer games (see figure 4.1). For the project, students were required to find the game's history and rules and determine the skills involved. The teacher included such games as jacks, penny boards, croquet, four square, marbles, pickup sticks, hopscotch, darts, horseshoes, and yo-yos. Students then produced a video that showed the game being played and explained the rules and skills involved. Originally, the final project was the video presentation and a written assignment on the rules and history. However, since the high school was located adjacent to an elementary school, the project eventually expanded: High school students taught their games to fourth graders one spring afternoon (see figure 4.1). The schools were located in a low-income area where many students fail to finish high school, so the interaction between the age groups was extremely positive for everyone involved.

A folk dance project could determine how well students interpret instructions for five relatively simple folk dances and then put them to music. Assessing students on their ability to perform the steps correctly involves an accurate interpretation of the instructions and knowledge of dance terminology. Putting

Figure 4.1   Student projects might involve having older students teach games or activities to elementary school students.

the steps to music requires students to listen to the music and count music and steps correctly. A videotape of the final project provides a permanent product of students demonstrating their dance and music skills on tape.

Sport skills can also be assessed through the use of a group project. Students can be assigned to make an instructional tape for younger students (e.g., high school students could make a tape for middle school students), which shows correct form from a variety of angles, errors, ways to correct errors, and the skills' application during game play situations. The tape could evaluate both cognitive and psychomotor skills learning. It also could be a means of measuring affective domain behavior through cooperation and consideration shown to other members of the group.

Another successful project that I have used is for students to develop a magazine. Each member of the group is in charge of some type of editing such as features, cover, artwork, and advertising. Every student in the group is expected to contribute an article and an advertisement (must be an ad about something healthy) to the final project. Students must choose a title for the magazine, and all articles must reflect that title or theme. Given the computer skills of today's students, many creative endeavors will result. Students are required to reflect on their input into the magazine and also about what they learned by doing the publication.

Projects can become excellent learning tools for students as well as a way for assessing student learning. Students should be given some class time to complete tasks that require the efforts of the group. Once a division of labor occurs, individuals in the group working on their own usually can complete several components of these projects. Because several people are usually involved in a project, teachers must have a way to assess individual contributions to the final product. Reflection papers describing an individual's role in the group are one way to find out who did each of the various tasks as well as who provided leadership skills when working as a group. I also have students start with a large amount of money ($10,000) and distribute paychecks to members of the group. The rule is that every member of the group must receive a different sum of money. A justification must be provided as to why certain individuals were paid certain amounts. Another way to determine individual effort is for the teacher to require individual products from each student as well as the final group project. Without some type of assessment of an individual's contribution to the group, some group members usually receive less credit than their efforts deserved while others receive more than they actually earned.

Student Logs

Student logs are excellent ways to show the process involved in learning. Teachers can look at a behavior over time to see how students should show improvement when an adequate amount of effort is expended. Skill practice or physical activity outside of class time is easily demonstrated on logs. These logs can demonstrate student willingness to exhibit a physically active lifestyle, as stated in the NASPE National Physical Education Content Standards (NASPE 1995). Fitness activities can be documented with the use of student logs as well. Many teachers use these logs as one of the artifacts included in student portfolios (see table 4.3). For example, students might document strength training or conditioning for a fitness unit, thus addressing the national standard on achieving and maintaining a health-enhancing level of fitness. Other students might set a goal to participate in a bicycle race or triathlon. Logs could document training miles and demonstrate student ability to condition using sound training principles learned in physical education classes.

Logs of class participation can also be used for assessment. Students can track skill or fitness improvement over time. Some students are unable to do skills initially presented in class and are actually below the normal expectations for students of that age. Logs can help

Table 4.3   Student Log

Date	Activity	Amount of time
3/15	Tennis	1 hour
3/17	Jogging	30 minutes
3/18	Roller blading	30 minutes
3/21	Aerobic dance	1 hour
3/21	Stretching	20 minutes
3/22	Swimming	45 minutes

This student log might be used to document out-of-class activity as part of an assessment for the third content standard, according to the NASPE, or as an artifact for a fitness portfolio.

these students demonstrate progress toward the learning objectives designed by the teacher, thus documenting the learning process.

When a teacher's objective is to document student improvement or participation, logs are an excellent assessment selection. Logs also can be motivational tools for students, as they demonstrate evidence of improvement over time. Student effort is sometimes difficult to demonstrate; logs provide a concrete method for documenting this component.

The scoring criteria used to assess logs depends in part on the teacher's objective. If a teacher merely wants a student to complete the log with no judgment of quality, then a checklist might be used to evaluate the inclusion of various components designated by the teacher. By doing an analytic evaluation of the various components, teachers have an opportunity to evaluate each of the descriptors to determine a level of quality. If participation were one goal, then teachers would want students to demonstrate evidence of regular activity. If improvement were another goal, then the percentage of gain or improvement would be another category to be judged. Teachers must keep in mind the problems with assessing improvement and remember that high-performing athletes show little improvement compared with someone who is just beginning. When multilevels of talent exist in a class, the teacher might develop a dual-assessment system. First, the teacher would establish the criteria to be reached and if these were achieved, students would then not need to demonstrate improvement. Those who were unable to reach the designated criteria might be evaluated on gain or improvement scores. The dual system could be designed to maximize student performance, regardless of entry-level ability.

Conclusion

When thinking about assessment, teachers must continually address two questions: "What do I want students to know and be able to do?" and "What am I willing to accept as evidence that students have met the objectives?" Although we have addressed many types of performance-based assessments, we are by no means recommending that you throw aside all of your current assessment practices to implement performance-based assessments. We recommend that you view assessment in physical education as a recipe. When you use too much

of any one ingredient, the final product is never as you expected. Extra ingredients tend to disrupt the delicate balance of a recipe. Unfortunately, we don't have the ideal recipe for balancing the various types of traditional and performance-based assessments. You as a teacher have to experiment until you have achieved balance and you feel as though your assessment system is really evaluating and documenting desired student learning.

By developing a variety of assessments, teachers have many different lenses by which to observe student learning. Only by using many lenses do teachers really understand the total extent of student learning and achievement. Teachers also should keep in mind that many of the assessments described in this chapter can become artifacts in student portfolios. Even though assessments provide insight into student performance for an activity or concept, when combined with other assessments and put into a portfolio, they give a complete picture of student learning. Portfolios can combine the many assessment lenses you use and help clarify the extent of student learning. Chapter 6 contains much information on portfolio development.

Many times performance-based assessments can have multiple evaluation purposes, depending on what the teacher requires. Adding a reflective component or paper requires students to self-evaluate their role in the process of the assessment as well as their progress in learning. Cognitive components can be evaluated along with psychomotor skills. The criteria used to do the evaluation determine what the teacher expects. In some instances, multiple rubrics can be written for the same assessment task, thus providing additional lenses through which to view the same task.

We have written this chapter to provide you with hints for using the assessments described in this book. Some of our suggestions come as the result of a failed assessment. If you have an assessment that "bombs" or backfires, we encourage you to look for reasons that it didn't work. Some suggestions given in this chapter resulted from successful assessments. They were not as effective as we would have wished the first time they were used. Good assessments usually require several refinements to eliminate the rough edges and work out the snags. We encourage teachers to continue to develop assessments to provide multiple lenses for evaluating student learning and achievement.

CHAPTER FIVE

Open Response Questions

Assessment of student learning should come from educators' keen judgments about what's worth learning, just like in the selection of content . . . We tend to take more care as we decide what to teach than when we make decisions about how we will determine if students developed and learned. (Lambert 1999, 4)

In physical education, the traditional way to assess **cognitive knowledge** or **affective dispositions** is through a written test. When teachers are interested in assessing only comprehension or knowledge, tests with selected responses are usually the best choice. When a teacher wants to determine how well students actually *use* this knowledge, another type of assessment format is necessary. Open response questions give teachers alternatives for assessing student ability to use and apply knowledge outside the world of the gymna-

sium classroom. They are useful for assessing knowledge, understanding, and affective dispositions in performance-based instruction. Using a real-world context, open response questions require students to apply knowledge in a variety of situations. Students are encouraged to think critically as they develop solutions or responses to challenging prompts or scenarios.

There are two advantages of using open response questions. First, when students are forced to look at an unfamiliar situation (one that has not been directly addressed or used as an example in class), teachers can determine whether students really understand information presented as they reprocess it to address the open response question. Second, when students are required to evaluate, create, synthesize, or analyze, they use higher-level thinking skills, often forcing themselves to stretch their cognitive abilities. Teachers can then reward students who demonstrate creativity and insightful thinking, behaviors regarded as useful to adults.

Open Response Questions Versus Essay Questions

Open response questions are actually very different from essay questions. Essay questions require a specific answer, whereas open response questions have multiple solutions. When using essay questions, teachers have definite content they are addressing. An open response question can be answered using several approaches. One approach is not more correct than another; each is acceptable. The words "it depends" are often a good way to begin to respond to an open response question. When the question has one definite cor-

rect answer, it is an essay question, not an open response question. Table 5.1 shows how open response questions differ from essay questions.

Consider the difference between the following two questions:

---

1. Explain what is meant by a man-to-man defense and a zone defense.

2. You are about to play in a regional finals basketball tournament. You know that your opponent has two outstanding guards who score most of the points, while the other three players usually take less than 10 shots per game. Describe a potential way to defense this team, giving your reasons for your choice(s).

Essay question (1) simply asks for two definitions while the open response question (2) requires students to analyze the abilities of their own team while at the same time developing a strategy for the game. With the open response question, students must know both defenses and when they are best used. The better a student understands basketball, the richer the response. A very knowledgeable student might address substitution patterns,

Table 5.1   Open Response Versus Essay Questions

Open Response Questions	Essay Questions
Allow for a variety of solutions	Require a definite solution or answer
Reward creative and insightful thinking	May recognize creative thinking while not rewarding it
Allow integration of subjects and learning from other classes	Reveal student knowledge gained
Incorporate student's personal experiences and prior learning	Focus on knowledge from class
Require much time to score effectively	Usually are scored fairly quickly
Encourage students to expand their thinking	Measure a finite body of knowledge
Require students to apply knowledge and information to the big picture	Measure content and factual knowledge
Reveal levels of student understanding and misunderstanding	May be difficult to determine level of understanding
Format must be learned by students and teachers	Are familiar to students and teachers
Have a real-world context	Do not usually give or explain context
May ask a novel task or situation	May ask previously covered material

ways to avoid fatigue, or when to put various players and teammates into the game (i.e., at the start of a quarter, at the end of the half). The open response question gives greater insight into student understanding of a basketball game. We have found that this type of analysis carries over to game play as students develop strategies for playing different opponents and teams as the result of answering similar open response prompts. Physical activities can be very complex, and when students are encouraged to think critically about various aspects of the game, a whole new dimension is added.

An essay question measures *what students know*; open response questions measure both what students know and also *what they can do with this knowledge*. Just supplying facts, as one would do with essay questions, is not sufficient for answering open response questions. Students must use information from the scenario described in the stem and address the situation presented while solving the problem posed. In other words, an open response question looks at a student's ability to use material you have taught them and apply it in a novel, yet true-to-life scenario.

Characteristics of Open Response Questions

Open response questions provide unique ways for assessing student learning and attitudes. Because open response questions can present a problem or scenario with multiple possible answers, teachers can look at student learning in ways not possible through traditional assessments. Despite their openness, there are some components or key elements that must be included for a well-written open response question. The following section introduces you to open response questions by discussing characteristics that good questions include.

A Real-World Problem or Scenario

Setting the question in a realistic context is an important characteristic of open response questions. Because one purpose of education is to prepare children for life in an adult world, they must be exposed to situations reflective of the adult context. Open response questions reveal how well students really understand certain concepts or skills as they are asked to apply them to real-world scenarios. Providing a real context also alerts students that the information learned in class will be useful as an adult. A teacher wishing to assess knowledge about fitness concepts might write a question requiring students to develop a plan for staying fit throughout the remainder of their high school careers. Instead of merely asking students to list the five components of fitness and principles of training, students would have a practical, real-world context in which to apply this information.

Question Context From a Scenario or Prompt

With an open response question (the section on pages 25 through 26 explains these types), some type of prompt is given to students that determines the situation to which they will apply their knowledge. The prompt will vary according to the type of question asked. As discussed in chapter 2, an audience is established with performance-based assessments, which helps define the context. Developing levels of fitness for a high school student is very different than developing fitness for someone who is getting ready for retirement. If a reading passage were used for the prompt, teachers could have students respond to some controversial statement, thus revealing their knowledge about a given topic. The prompt sets the stage for the student response, often serving to focus and limit the scope of the answer.

The Prompt Is Clearly Linked to a Learning Objective

One of the characteristics of performance-based assessments is that you continually go back to the objective when considering the assessment. Open response questions can assess learner objectives that other forms of assessment do not touch. Many of today's education standards are written in terms of students understanding concepts and applying knowledge (see page 4 in chapter 1 for a list of the National Physical Education Content Standards). Open response questions are designed to accomplish just that. Teachers can assess student understanding at a conceptual level, which is what most standards and objectives strive to attain.

For example, effective game play strategy teaches students to gain an advantage over an opponent. This advantage can be taught when the student learns how to create a two-on-one situation where the student has a teammate with whom to outmaneuver the opponent. There are a variety of ways to create this situation. An open response question would reveal to the teacher whether the student really understood how to create this mismatch rather than just knowing that two-on-one gives a playing advantage.

Higher-Order Thinking Verbs Are Used

Because open response questions require analysis, synthesis, or evaluation, the verb in the objective that describes what students will know and be able to do must require some of these higher-order or critical-thinking skills. Figure 5.1 shows a list of *power verbs* (i.e., those that indicate action or observable performance) that can be utilized in open response prompts (Kemp, as cited in Vickers 1990). When these verbs are used in an open response prompt, they encourage students to think critically. Comparing two entities (e.g., badminton and tennis) demonstrates student ability to analyze. Badminton and tennis are both net games involving rackets, which means that some strategies can be similar for each game. However, the type of object being played (tennis ball versus shuttlecock) greatly affects the type of shots used. Students might evaluate a product or game, giving reasons for or against using or playing it. Open response questions encourage students to use critical-thinking skills as they apply knowledge gained from physical education classes.

analyze	list
compare	prove
contrast	summarize
discuss	trace
criticize	diagram
define	illustrate
describe	prove

Figure 5.1   These power verbs may be helpful when writing open response questions.

More Than One Plausible Answer

Typically, real-world problems can be addressed in a variety of ways. Open response questions exemplify this characteristic in that there are many possible ways to respond to them. Teachers can encourage out-of-the-box thinking and allow students to use their own personal experiences as they generate a response. This is not to say that any answer is correct. Students are required to provide correct information while formulating their answers, and their responses must be plausible. Because students have to justify and defend their responses and explain the logic behind them, teachers can detect incomplete learning and incorrect thinking about topics being assessed.

An Explanation of the Solution Is Required

Providing an answer to the problem or question is not sufficient with open response questions. Students must explain the reasoning used to formulate the answer. Sometimes an answer can appear wrong, but when students explain their reasoning behind the answer, they may have considered additional factors when determining the answer—actually going beyond the intent of the teacher or the question. If Fosbury, the high jumper who revolutionized that event in the 1972 Olympics, had presented his technique for clearing a high bar without explaining his reasoning, a teacher might have marked the response incorrect.

Asking students to develop a stretching routine for an activity or game explaining the benefit of each exercise would reveal student knowledge of the activity (demands or requirements of the game or activity) as well as the benefits derived from the stretches. Teachers could then determine if students know the value of the various stretches well enough to develop a stretching routine for an adult form of that activity. Students can sometimes give a correct or plausible response without really understanding a concept that the assessment measures. In the stretching example, students could simply list exercises that they had done in the past. By requiring an explanation of the process used to develop or arrive at this list, teachers can evaluate whether students know the benefits of the stretches selected. Requiring students to explain the process used to derive an answer gives insight into student learning and understanding. With open response questions, it is not enough for students to just have the content knowledge; they must also support their answer and show their reasoning.

Hidden Student Knowledge May Be Revealed

Open response questions can reveal knowledge and learning that a teacher didn't think to ask from students. Students come from various backgrounds, and open response questions give them the opportunity to use prior learning while responding to the question's prompt. Essay questions generally produce no surprises, as students answer using information and knowledge gained from the class. Students are challenged to synthesize information when answering open response questions, applying it in unique and creative ways.

The Focus Is on Big Ideas, Important Skills, or Key Concepts

Open response questions provide teachers the opportunity to examine student thinking and understanding on key concepts. They provide students with an opportunity to see connections between knowledge and information given in class, and they can see how these concepts interrelate. Open response questions often explore the *how* and *why* of learning rather than focusing on the *what*. As students begin seeing connections between concepts, learning becomes more meaningful and long lasting.

The Situation Presented Is Interesting to Students

Students are subjected to many assessments while in school, many of which are of little or no interest to them. With a topic that students find appealing, a teacher can increase student interest in completing an assessment and perhaps even spark their creative energy (see figure 5.2). Open response questions should

Figure 5.2 Open response questions can address topics that are relevant to students, thus making the assessment more interesting and enjoyable.

On one occasion I was using an open response question with a folk dancing unit. One student pointed out the patterns that were made as class members went around the circle using a right and left grand move. The student had been studying patterns in math class and noted that, as students went around the circle, every other person faced either in or out. From the response, I knew that the student understood his relationship with other members of the class, instead of just knowing what he was to do. The student had a different way of explaining the step and what he was doing, which was actually more insightful than what I had presented to the class. Similar levels of understanding can be demonstrated with questions that deal with game play strategy. Too often students know how to run a play, but they have little sense of where other members of the team are when asked to analyze or explain the strategy.

center on subjects and areas that engage students while at the same time provide challenges for them to complete. When this is done, students are more likely to take the assessment seriously and be motivated to do their best. Letting a student envision getting ready for a vacation in Florida or a hiking trip in the mountains provides a great scenario for answering a fitness question. Dancing on stage for an audience or playing in a highly competitive tennis tournament (Wimbledon anyone?) also provides enticing scenarios for open response questions on these activities.

Interdisciplinary Possibilities

Interdisciplinary learning is important in today's schools. Instead of compartmentalizing knowledge, students are asked to apply it in other areas. Physical education is an excellent way to assess physics or science concepts in an applied setting. Open response questions can require students to address problems through interdisciplinary lenses, applying their knowledge of sport and exercise to other content areas. The gymnasium becomes more meaningful and important in their lives.

Types of Open Response Questions

There are several formats that can be used for open response questions. Question formats include single dimension, scaffolded, multiple independent components, student choice, and those requiring a response to provided information (Dick, Buecker, and Wilson 1999). The more information that teachers require of students, the longer the responses are. Single dimension questions are the easiest for the teacher to create and for the student to answer. When deciding which format of question to use, teachers should consider the information or student knowledge they wish to access. The following section explains the characteristics of these types of open response questions and provides examples of each.

Single Dimension

Single dimension open response questions are straightforward. This format is used when a teacher wants to have an open re-

sponse question that only requires 10 to 15 minutes to answer. Single dimension open response questions usually ask students to draw a conclusion or take a position. Students are then required to support this with explanations, examples, or evidence. Single dimension questions are also useful when students have to explain a phenomenon or describe a procedure. Consider the following example.

Your team has been criticized by opponents for exhibiting unfair play and poor sportsmanship habits. When does behavior stop being a way to support the team and start being an issue of fair play? Explain the reasoning behind your response and provide examples when possible to clarify your answer.

Scaffolded

Scaffolded open response questions contain a sequence of tasks that become increasingly more difficult. While writing these questions, teachers start with the simplest task and move to more complex ones. Each successive question depends on the response given to the previous question, with the context becoming more complex with each question. Success on a given task usually means that students had correctly answered previous parts of the question. The following is an example of a scaffolded open response question:

You see an ad for a new abdominal shaper machine. For just $99, you can flatten your abdominal muscles and look great for the pool.

A. What muscles should an abdominal shaper exercise?

B. Identify several exercises that could also work these muscles with no apparatus involved.

C. You have a strip of rubber tubing. Devise an exercise to work your abdominal muscles.

D. Decide on whether to buy the abdominal shaper. Give the reasoning to support your response.

Multiple Independent Components

Another type of open response question is a **multiple independent component question**, where students are given fairly independent questions that address the same prompt. Multiple independent component questions have at least two parts. Since they are independent components, one response is not dependent upon the next, and one question is not necessarily more complex than a previous one. When creating this type of question, teachers must be careful that the components are of equal difficulty and assess equivalent knowledge.

The Big Game is coming up and you want your team to win the district league title. To do so, you want to improve your softball or baseball batting abilities.

A. Identify several drills that you might use to improve the power of your swing and explain the purpose of each drill.

B. Changing your bat might also be a way to improve your power. What effect would different bats have on batting power, and how would the bat affect the batter's swing?

C. You have popped up to the shortstop during your last eight at bats. Identify and explain possible reasons why and what you might do to correct this problem.

Student Choice

With **student choice open response questions**, students have the option of selecting the topic they wish to address from a list of options provided. Students choose between several selections offered. These questions are more difficult to grade because of the variation of answers. When giving students choices about which stem to answer, teachers must make sure the choices are similar so that answering one is not easier than answering another. When written correctly, a single scoring guide can be used to evaluate any of the student choices.

You have just finished a unit on tennis and wish to learn another sport. You noticed some similarities and differences between the striking patterns found in tennis and those used for another sport.

Select volleyball, badminton, pickleball, or racquetball, then compare and contrast the striking patterns for the two.

Response to Provided Information

With a **response-to-provided-information open response question**, students are given information and then asked to respond using that information. Readings could be used for the prompt (articles about fair play from *Strategies* or *JOPERD* are excellent sources), or some type of graphics or data could be used. Pictures should be shown to illustrate the question since it is a provided information question.

Provided for you are pictures and descriptions of two tennis rackets. Compare the two with each other, then decide which is best for you to buy. Analyze your game play needs, then explain in your answer what advantages your chosen racket specifically has to offer your game. Note in your answer any characteristics that the unchosen racket had to offer and why you deemed the other racket's assets more valuable.

Students would be required to give reasons for their choice based on the information presented. The knowledge accessed here would be a self-analysis of playing ability, knowledge about the various types of striking patterns used in tennis, the mechanical advantages offered by each type of racket, and an explanation of game play strategy, all of which using their personal abilities. If students had developed an affinity to playing tennis as the result of a tennis unit, purchasing a new racket might be a real-world situation for them. If a price tag were also included with the questions about the tennis rackets, students would also make a judgment and a decision: How much will I play tennis in the future, and will I play enough to justify buying a very expensive racket?

If students were responding to an article, teachers must remember to provide students with adequate time to read the article or passage as well as time for writing their responses.

How to Write Open Response Questions

When writing open response questions, the following steps should be addressed. This format is useful for developing any of the types of open response questions previously outlined.

1. Identify the standard or knowledge the teacher wishes to evaluate.

2. Determine a real-world context in which this knowledge would be needed or valued.

3. Write the prompt or scenario to be used for the question.

4. Create the task, telling students what they must do to solve the problem.

5. Write a scoring guide for students, outlining criteria that help them address the question or problem.

6. Write a scoring guide for people who will evaluate the response (i.e., the scorers).

7. Administer the open response question.

8. Revise and improve.

The next section explains these eight steps and offers suggestions for implementing them.

Step One

The first step in creating an open response question is to focus on clearly identifying the content the question addresses. Writing the question becomes easier when you have a clear idea about the content to be addressed. This could be

▶ national, state, or local standards;

▶ goals of the unit being taught; or

▶ several units of study, which can have students compare or evaluate ideas, showing the links or relationships between them.

When looking at your unit objectives, you should determine the best way to assess student learning. Areas that lend themselves to open response questions should be targeted and developed. When multiple approaches or solutions to a problem are possible or when teachers are trying to determine if students can apply facts and knowledge, an open response question may be the most appropriate form of assessment. When the objective is for students to recall facts or information, an open response question would not be necessary or appropriate. Because open response questions require a lot of time to create, teachers should decide whether an open response question is the best way to assess the desired information. Other assessment forms may be more appropriate.

Step Two

Determining the real-world context in which this information would be used is critical for two reasons. First, it helps motivate students to put forth extra effort because they can see a real purpose for answering the question. Devising a strategy for playing in a championship game is much more appealing than simply describing an offensive or defensive strategy. Second, the reason for using a real-world context is to help students see that information learned in class is important not only while in class but also in the world outside of school or later in life. Students tend to remember things better when they can see meaning for the information.

Step Three

Establishing the situation in which the problem or question is to occur is the fun part of writing open response questions. Teachers can create a scenario that has real-world implications while adding a context to the open response question. The prompt should focus on an important problem that students would *want* to find an answer to or a solution for. Background information should be provided that both entices students into answering the question and gives information necessary to frame and provide a context for the question. The scenario given is the "hook" that engages the students. If possible, the scenario should describe something to which students can relate. Sometimes reading passages can provide the prompt. Interesting facts or bits of information may also be incorporated in this portion of the question to help provide the setting or context for the question.

The scenario should be realistic and is only limited to one's own imagination. Here are some possibilities:

- You are trying to get a summer job at a fitness facility. It is a great job that pays well, offers a free membership for employees, and several of your friends are already employed there.

- Your classes this year have really been hard and you have spent a lot of time studying for them. The chocolate ice cream that you eat while studying has put an extra 10 pounds on your body that you wish to lose.

- You have a new friend that likes to play tennis. You would like to be able to play tennis with this person, but your skills need work.

When students personalize the context, they are more likely to see how knowledge relates to their own life. Developing upper-body strength might not seem too important to students. However, when a teacher uses a prompt of "your house is on fire and you are on the second floor," the context makes upper-body strength suddenly become meaningful and important.

Step Four

The next step in creating an open response question is very critical. In this step you describe the actual product that students have to generate to respond to the question.

The directions given should be very clear, explaining in detail what they are expected to do. You explain what the final product or performance will be. Some suggestions include the following:

- ▶ Persuade an audience
- ▶ Analyze a perspective
- ▶ Compare and contrast
- ▶ Make a decision
- ▶ Create a dialogue
- ▶ Construct an interview with a person (on paper)
- ▶ Outline a plan

The list of action verbs in figure 5.1 is helpful for this step as teachers decide the type of task the question involves. Teachers also must determine if they want students to analyze, compare-contrast, synthesize, or judge something. These higher levels of Bloom's Taxonomy require more time to complete, as they require more thought and complex reasoning from students. Teachers must allow adequate time for students if they are to answer the question to the best of their ability.

The task is added to the scenarios given in the third step of question development.

- You are trying to get a summer job at a fitness facility. It is a great job that pays well, offers a free membership for employees, and several of your friends are already employed there. *Prepare a five-minute speech that would convince the owner that you are well qualified for the job.*

- Your classes this year have really been hard and you have spent a lot of time studying for them. The chocolate ice cream that you eat while studying has put an extra 10 pounds on your body that you wish to lose. *Develop an exercise plan that will burn calories and help you get in shape. What eating habits will you adopt?*

- You have a new friend that likes to play tennis. You would like to be able to play tennis with this person, but your skills need work. *Analyze your present skills and abilities and identify the skills you must improve to make you a better player. Develop a practice sequence and schedule for improving your game.*

As you can see, these ideas are quite concrete, and students understand exactly what they are to do. When describing the desired product, teachers should keep in mind what students are capable of doing and the knowledge base they have. When a teacher does not give students information necessary to complete a question, students cannot be expected to respond to the prompt in class with no outside resources.

After writing the task, teachers must determine if it accesses the desired information. Asking students to compare a striking pattern between sports is very different from having them analyze it for possible errors. Having a colleague read the question to give input is helpful in determining if the task really asks for the information sought. Personally completing the question is another way to determine if the question is complete.

Some things to look for include the following (Dick, Buecker, and Wilson 1999):

▶ Have I clearly stated the task?

▶ Will students understand what they must do to complete the question?

▶ Will the verbs chosen require students to perform the desired task?

▶ Could I select another, more appropriate verb?

▶ Have I given students enough time to complete the question?

▶ Have I provided my students with the necessary background information to answer the question?

▶ Is any information I've provided going to mislead students?

The checklist provided in figure 5.3 contains useful items to consider for open response question design.

Checklist for Designing Open Response Questions

Does the question do any of the following:

- Provide students with a real-world setting and problem?
- Use power verbs, thus requiring higher-level thinking?
- Require students to explain processes used while completing the question?
- Require students to explain their reasoning or justify their answer?
- Accept a variety of approaches and solutions for an answer?
- Clearly identify what is required of students?
- Provide sufficient detail to complete the question?
- Use developmentally appropriate language?
- Include a rubric for evaluation?

Figure 5.3   By addressing this list of questions, teachers can evaluate the quality of their open response questions.

Step Five

The rubric created for people who will evaluate the responses should have all the elements presented in the student scoring guide but have much more detail. For results to be reliable, scorers need to understand the full implications of the response. When specific information is required for part of the answer, it should be provided to the scorer. Although the person doing the scoring may have a strong background in the subject, a list of acceptable possibilities should also be given. For instance, a question concerning components of fitness would have the elements listed in the assessor's scoring guide. If the critical elements of a striking pattern were required for the answer, these would be listed in the assessor's scoring guide. If any content knowledge were required in the answer, the scoring guide should convey this information to the evaluator and not assume the scorer has this knowledge. When some elements carry more importance than others, the scorer's rubric should also contain this information.

Step Six

Open response questions should be broad enough that several approaches are acceptable, encouraging students to use their creativity while answering the question. The rubric gives students criteria that are used to evaluate their responses, including a clear explanation of what is expected in a quality student response. A requirement of quality should also be indicated in the scoring guide. Students must know that just any answer is not acceptable.

When writing a scoring guide for students, you should go back to step one, noting what the question was to measure, as this sometimes can provide a list of descriptors and criteria that should be present in the answer. The verbs used in the description of the task also indicate which criteria are necessary. When items are to be identified, it should be reflected in the scoring guide. When a comparison is asked for, the rubric should require students to present and address both sides of the issue. The number of levels contained in the scoring guide depends on the purpose of the question. As a minimum, two levels should be given: a description of an acceptable answer, as well as a description of an unacceptable one.

Step Seven

While administering an open response question in physical education, teachers should make sure that students have an appropriate location to answer the question. When the question is short (such as a single dimension open response question), laps or clipboards in the gymnasium are appropriate. When the question is going to require 45 minutes or more to complete, efforts should be made to move to a classroom or an area that contains seating.

Time may be another factor to consider. Some children need longer than others to complete the response; those requiring more time should have it. Setting up an activity for students to engage in after they have completed the question addresses this concern. Assuming the teacher could monitor the activity as well as supervise those still finishing the question, opportunity to practice skills might be given (e.g., station work). Students might begin a fitness workout after they have completed the question. Teachers do not want to decrease the importance of the question by giving activity options, but they should make provisions for those who finish earlier than others in the class.

Some questions may lend themselves to being completed at home by the student. If the teacher is trying to determine an affective disposition or attitude or is attempting to give students an opportunity to practice answering open response questions, a take-home question might then be a viable option. When allowing students an opportunity to complete the question at home, teachers should consider the complexity of the question, the purpose of the question, and implications for student grades. When teachers do not want students to use outside resources, then the questions should obviously be administered in a controlled and monitored setting. When a question could be completed outside of class without jeopardizing the response, a take-home format may be a viable option to consider.

Step Eight

With any performance-based assessment, revision and improvement are standard procedures. Every time the question is used, it probably has been changed, hopefully for the better. Teachers should continually be on the lookout for improvements that can be made. Student responses may actually trigger some beneficial changes. Here are some questions that should be asked when constructing a question:

▶ Does this question satisfy my learning objective?

▶ What does this question tell me about student learning?

▶ Does this question reflect what I want students to know and be able to do as a result of my teaching?

▶ Does my rubric focus the student response on targeted knowledge?

▶ Is the real-world application relevant to physical education?

▶ Do students have the necessary content to answer this question?

▶ How much time do students need to answer this question?

▶ Do my students have all the skills necessary to complete the question?

▶ Do my students have the necessary resources to answer this question?

Usually, numerous revisions are necessary before a question is truly of the quality a teacher wishes to reach.

Suggestions for Using Open Response Questions

Open response questions provide students with a means of accessing information that is difficult to access with other types of assessments. Because it is a relatively new form of assessment for many teachers, the following suggestions are offered to help teachers incorporate them into their assessment plans:

▶ Start slowly and keep it simple.

▶ Use open response questions for measuring understanding of major concepts.

▶ Consider teacher time when using open response questions.

▶ Consider student time when assigning open response questions.

▶ Be sure to give students a rubric when you give the question.

▶ Avoid indistinct questions.

▶ Avoid transparency with the rubric.

▶ Create questions that can be completed in a reasonable time frame.

▶ Pilot the question before using it for a grade.

▶ Be sensitive to equity issues when writing the question or designing the product.

Open response questions can assess information that other forms of assessment do not reach. With the suggestions we offer, we hope you will find open response questions as valuable in your assessment process as we have in ours.

Start Slowly and Keep It Simple

With any form of assessment, some teachers have the tendency to jump in only to find out that the water is a little deeper than expected. We suggest that you start slowly, perhaps by using a single dimension question with one of your classes. Open response questions can be time-consuming to evaluate, and there is no feeling worse than knowing that you have 175-plus bad questions to evaluate! With practice, your questions improve and your rubrics become easier to use. Also recognize that open response questions are probably a new form of assessment for students. A brief explanation about the purpose of the assessment, along with a strategy for completing it, saves both the teacher and student a lot of time in the long run. A single dimension question that would require 10 to 12 minutes for students to complete is a nice way to begin.

Use for Measuring Understanding of Major Concepts

Open response questions are an excellent option when a teacher wants to determine how well students really know the major concepts and if students can apply it to other settings. When the teacher is merely interested in knowing whether a student has acquired a certain body of knowledge, other assessment options are better choices. When a teacher wishes to assess more complex levels of thinking, open response questions are a wonderful vehicle for doing so. Open response questions require more time to write, administer, and score than other more traditional forms of assessment. However, when the teacher is interested in whether a student can take the information presented in class to the next level, open response questions are excellent options. Measuring cognitive ability in physical education, especially at higher levels of thinking

is not easy. However, with the emphasis that many schools have placed on critical thinking today, open response questions provide an opportunity to utilize such thinking. Open response questions are excellent choices for culminating assessments that look at the big picture of what the class has covered.

Consider Teacher Time

Open response questions require time to write and time to score. With the number of students a physical education teacher has enrolled in classes, requiring open response questions from all students simultaneously puts a huge burden on teacher time. Assessment should not punish a teacher; it should enhance instruction, benefiting both teacher and student. When an open response question is the best way to assess student learning, teachers might stagger when they are given to the classes, making the evaluation less of a burden. If a teacher were to grade 200 open response questions, limited time is available for each one. When teachers space the administration of questions, they have more time to devote to scoring each response, which improves the quality of the feedback given to students.

For example, teachers might use an open response question for two classes while staying with traditional assessments for the other classes (assuming all classes taught during the day are similar). Or, when teachers have some elective classes in their schedules (e.g., team sports, dance, advanced physical education) the open response questions might be done in one of the sections (e.g., dance class) and in another type of class in a couple of weeks (e.g., advanced physical education).

Consider Student Time

Teachers must also consider student time when having students write open response questions. Some open response assessments require time to do well, and given the limited amount of time available in physical education, teachers should make every minute count. Some single dimension questions could be completed when students are waiting for their team to play or to present their dance composition. Another possibility is for physical education teachers to work with other content areas. When teachers work together when giving open response questions, each grading it for the quality of response relative to that subject, both areas benefit. Many subject-area teachers are willing to give class time for administering the question. For example, English teachers might grade the question as a writing assignment, and the physical education teacher could then take this same question and evaluate it for content and understanding in physical education. Science and social studies also have content in common with physical education. Additionally, when a question is used for multiple areas, students sense an increase in its importance, which can also improve the quality of the response. Writing open response questions in several classes can become tedious for students. When students are required to do fewer open response questions, a more insightful response is likely to result, as students give quality rather than quantity.

Give Students a Rubric

Writing the rubric is one of the most difficult parts of creating an open response question. As a result, some teachers try to bypass this step, giving students the question without an explanation of how it will be evaluated. The first time a question is used you might have a checklist or point system rubric because the various levels of performance haven't been developed. At a minimum, however, the rubric should contain enough criteria to inform students of what is expected for a high-quality, thorough answer. This is not to say that the rubric accompanying the open response question should provide all the answers or explain the thinking process students should use to determine the answer. Informing students of the criteria used to assess an open response question is very different from telling them how to complete the question.

Avoid Indistinct Questions

It is important to remember that with open response questions, some fuzziness is to be expected. However, if the teacher has a lot of problems writing the question or the rubric, then it could be that either the question has been poorly defined or that the body of knowledge that the teacher wishes to access has not been clearly delineated. With open response questions, knowing the body of knowledge to be accessed is critical to having a quality

response. If the responses are not clearly focused, then chances are high that the question must be rewritten or redesigned.

Avoid Transparency With the Rubric

The rubric created for students must contain guidelines for helping them respond to the question appropriately; however, they should not be so thorough that students don't have to develop their own thinking or approach to solve it. Care must be taken that the scoring guide is not so transparent that students simply have to follow the procedure outlined to produce a quality answer. When writing a scoring guide for students, the criteria used should let them know teacher expectations without providing the answer or process that students should use to complete the response.

Consider Time to Complete

Open response questions must be broad enough to allow students to pull information from various sources; however, they should not be so large that students spend hours completing them. The actual amount of time required to complete an open-response question depends on the purpose of the assessment, the content of the question, and the age of the student. Obviously, with younger students the question should not be overwhelming or impossible to do. With older students the question should have sufficient breadth so that students are challenged. For older students, a question should require between 45 and 90 minutes to complete, although this should not be considered an absolute time frame. The purpose of the assessment along with other contextual factors and considerations dictates the amount of time required to complete it. A reliable way to estimate the time required to complete the question is to give it to a colleague and calculate that students would need about twice as much time to complete it.

Pilot the Question Before Using It for a Grade

When teachers create open response questions, they often make assumptions about what students will do when answering them. As a result of the teacher "assuming" that the student will know what to do, the desired product is not clear to students. With an unclear product, students might interpret the question differently than how the teacher intended. The desired product or outcome should be clearly stated for students. Before using it for evaluation, a pilot administration of the open response question is a good way to work the "bugs" out.

Be Sensitive to Equity Issues

Please read and consider the following open response prompt:

Fitness is a key component of many physical education programs. Twenty years ago, teachers led exercises, and students followed without giving much thought about explaining the value of different exercises or sports to students. Today many of these adults want to increase levels of fitness, but they may not have the necessary information to choose or develop an exercise program that meets their needs. Describe your current fitness levels and what would be necessary to become fit at the present time. Develop an exercise program for keeping fit while at college that addresses all five components of fitness.

Although this looks like an excellent question for getting students to think about applying principles of fitness after graduation, this question raises an issue of equity. An assumption is made in the question that the student will attend college; however, this is not the case for every student graduating. This assumption might be a sensitive issue for students, causing them not to do their best. Going to college is really not an important part of this question. The focus should be on assessing student knowledge of fitness components and the ability to develop an exercise program as an adult.

When creating open response questions, teachers must be aware of language that may cause students to not do their best when generating the response. Teachers should avoid using language that is sensitive. Gender, ethnicity, race, and levels of fitness are obvious areas to consider when desensitizing open response questions.

Additional equity issues might arise if teachers required students to complete the open response on a computer. Socioeconomic status might also enter into equity issues if teachers assumed students had a computer or access to the Internet at home. No student should do poorly on an open response question because of external factors.

Allowing student choice in deciding how to respond to a question helps avoid having equity factors influence the student response. Student choice open response questions can be an excellent option when dealing with potentially sensitive or biased topics. Because teachers are trying to assess a concept, several prompts can address the desired information or content. When students are allowed to select their topic, it gives students some control over the topic, and equity issues tend to be less of a problem.

Conclusion

Open response questions provide teachers with another alternative for measuring cognitive or affective domains. Students must apply facts and knowledge learned in class, using higher-level thinking skills to formulate a response to a real-world prompt. Because open response questions can be answered in a variety of ways, with one approach as valid as another, students are encouraged to think out of the box. Open response questions can be challenging for students, while at the same time, reveal to teachers areas of student understanding and misunderstanding.

As with most performance-based assessments, open response questions require more time to develop, administer, and score. For this reason, teachers should carefully examine what they wish to assess to determine if this is the best form of assessment for the content knowledge they wish to evaluate. Careful attention must also be paid to the language used in the question to ensure that equity factors don't negatively influence a student response. Although questions should be broad, they should not be so grand that they become unmanageable in terms of student and teacher time and with respect to the rubric or scoring guide that accompanies the question.

When the various issues and factors discussed in this chapter are attended to, the result is a viable form of assessment that actually can be enjoyable to both students and teachers alike. Physical education teachers are encouraged to begin using open response questions to assess not only student understanding and application of knowledge but also the ability to use them in realistic, lifelike situations.

CHAPTER SIX

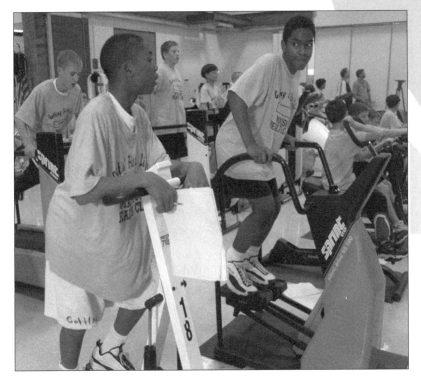

Portfolios

Because artifacts are collected over time, portfolios offer a dynamic, visual presentation of a student's abilities, strengths, growth and achievement of standards, and areas of needed improvement. (Melograno 2000, p. 99)

With the current widespread emphasis on the use of performance-based, continuous, and authentic assessment of student work to determine their level of achievement of targeted goals and standards, the portfolio has emerged as a new, exciting, and broadly used form of alternative assessment in the middle and secondary schools. You simply need to look at the latest professional literature to see that portfolio assessment is used in physical education (Wilson and Roof 1999; Kulinna et al. 1999; Melograno 1994, 1998; Kirk 1997).

The **portfolio** is "a purposeful, integrated, collection of actual exhibits and work samples showing effort, progress or achievement in one or more areas. It presents a broad, genuine picture of student learning" (Melograno

1999). The portfolio is actually not a new form of assessment and evaluation. Artists, architects, journalists, photographers, and models have gathered and presented their best work in portfolios as evidence of their talent and abilities for years. Only recently, educators have realized the tremendous potential that the portfolio process holds as a learning and assessment tool for K-12 students, as well as for preservice teachers (Melograno 1999).

The portfolio can provide not only a body of work for evaluation, but also a process for learning and assessment (Herman, Aschbacher, and Winters 1992). Students can actually choose from a variety of assessment tools to include in their portfolios for evaluation. The portfolio becomes the "receptacle" for "the collection of student work that documents students effort, progress and achievement toward a goal or goals (Siedentop and Tannehill 2000, 191). It is this process of completing the variety of learning and assessment tasks across time, self-selecting those that are the most representative of the student's effort and achievement, and reflecting on how the collection of artifacts provide evidence of the student's achievement of targeted goals, in which additional student learning occurs. Therefore, the portfolio is not only a collection of work for assessment, but also a learning process in which the students gain insight about themselves as performers and learners (Siedentop and Tannehill 2000).

The portfolio is a tremendously exciting and flexible learning and assessment tool in physical education. It can be used in a variety of ways that meet the needs of the teacher, the program, and the students. Introducing students to portfolio assessment and implementing the process is demanding, requiring considerable planning, organization, and usually a change in teaching styles for the teacher. The results are well worth the effort . . . though occasionally frustrating. The teacher can observe students as they become more actively involved in the learning and self-assessment process. Integrated learning and assessment tasks become more authentic and realistic to students' lives, which often results in higher levels of student interest and motivation (Mitchell 1992). Portfolios include displays of students' progress, improvement, and learning that provide them the opportunity to demonstrate their achievement. The portfolio, in a sense then, is a celebration of student achievement in which the student, the teacher, the parents, and the school can all take pride in student performance (Siedentop and Tannehill 2000).

To help the physical education teacher better understand this process and to design and implement the portfolio process in their own programs, we will discuss the following topics that pertain to the use of portfolios as an assessment tool:

▶ Characteristics of portfolios

▶ Types of portfolios

▶ Portfolio guidelines in performance-based assessment

▶ Evaluation of the portfolios

The following sections explain these concepts and how to implement them.

Characteristics of Portfolios

The portfolio has many characteristics that make it an excellent learning and assessment tool for physical education. Those characteristics allow teachers and students to use portfolios to enhance and support student learning. The characteristics discussed in the following sections encourage

▶ the use of flexible and multidimensional forms of assessments;

▶ the documentation of student progress, improvement, and achievement of goals;

▶ student choice, self-evaluation, and reflection of the learning process;

▶ the provision of feedback and continuous evaluation of student progress toward goals;

▶ the increased motivation of students and teachers; and

▶ the use of portfolios to spotlight student achievement with the promotion of the physical education program displayed throughout the student work.

Flexible and Multidimensional

The portfolio is a very flexible form of alternative assessment (see figure 6.1). It is an alternative because it is so different from traditional forms of assessment, yet it may include both traditional *and* authentic pieces. The teacher must, however, have a clear vision of the purpose and scope of the assessment and must communicate this to the student at the beginning of the process (Mitchell 1992). Evaluation portfolios can be **representative** or **accumulative** (Siedentop and Tannehill 2000). Student work included in the portfolio may represent achievement for only one unit of instruction, or it can be an accumulative assessment in which the portfolio includes an accumulation of student work across a semester, an academic year, or school years (i.e., K-5, 6-8, or 9-12 grades). The portfolio can serve as a **single- dimensional** or **multidimensional assessment** as well. It may include many documents that focus on the attainment of one goal or standard, such as the achievement of a healthy level of physical fitness, or it may include artifacts as evidence for the achievement of

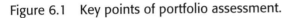

Portfolio Assessments

- Representative: Covers learning for one unit
- Accumulative: Represents learning across multiple units
- Single-dimensional: Represents the attainment of one goal or standard
- Multidimensional: Represents the attainment of two or more goals or standards

Figure 6.1 Key points of portfolio assessment.

multiple standards. Students may be required to provide work that represents the level of achievement of goals or standards that reflects not only the psychomotor domain, but also the cognitive and affective dimensions of educational development.

Documents Student Progress, Improvement, Learning, and Achievement of Goals

In the portfolio assessment process, students collect work and then choose their best pieces that most accurately document their targeted goals or standards for the identified scope of the physical education program (i.e., unit, semester, year, program). Students self-select and showcase a collection of their best work in the portfolio, which they submit for evaluation. The pieces included may compare earlier performances or products with later ones to demonstrate improvement, progress, or growth over time, as well as demonstrate achievement of the targeted goals (Westfall 1998). The documentation presented in the evaluation portfolio can provide a comprehensive view of student learning and achievement that is authentic and performance-based. Teachers and schools may ask students to present **artifacts** that provide evidence that they have progressed toward or have achieved state and local learner goals. Because several states have adopted the NASPE standards, students can be required to provide work that demonstrates that they are a "physically educated person" who has demonstrated a desirable level of achievement of the seven National Standards for Physical Education (NASPE 1995). A detailed log, in which the student dates and describes daily physical activity outside of class over a semester and which is signed by a witness, may be selected

by the student to include in the portfolio as evidence that the student is moving toward the achievement of National Standard for Physical Education #3: "Exhibits a physically active lifestyle" (NASPE 1995). Another student may include as evidence for the same standard newspaper reports or awards that focus on his or her training and participation in community and statewide mini-marathons.

Individualized Learning and Assessment

When using the portfolio as a form of performance-based assessment, students are encouraged to complete and choose the pieces of work that they will include as evidence for achievement of various goals and teacher guidelines. This process results in and encourages developmentally appropriate and individualized learning activities for students. Students work at their level of skill, knowledge, and ability, and on projects or tasks that are of interest to them (Kirk 1997). Because students come to class with a wide variety and depth of previous experiences and abilities, the portfolio process of assessment opens the door for teachers to individualize student goals, expectations, learning, and assessment tasks.

Within particular activity units and with the guidance of the teacher, students can identify individual goals that they will work to accomplish that address the broader class goals. For example, consider National Standard for Physical Education #1: "Demonstrates competency in many movement forms and proficiency in a few movement forms" (NASPE 1995). Juan may choose to submit documents that provide evidence that he has achieved proficiency in playing the game of tennis, while Emily may submit a portfolio that contains artifacts providing evidence of her proficiency in canoeing. Juan and Emily are both students in the same physical education class, but each is able to select a very different movement activity and provide a variety of choices of artifacts. Both students participated in each activity unit and made a decision regarding which of the activities, tennis or canoeing, he or she had developed at the proficiency level versus the competency level. In this instance, the portfolio assessment process encourages students to make individual choices about the activities in which they choose to develop proficiency, based on individual interest, skill ability, and achievement.

Even within the same activity unit, students may identify and work toward different individual goals. During a track and field unit in a ninth grade physical education class, Keeshana is very interested in sprinting and jumping events. She sets the following individual goals for herself: one, to high jump five feet using the flop technique; two, to long jump over 15 feet in the class track meet; and three, to run a personal best of 14 seconds in the 100-meter dash. Li, on the other hand, is more interested in throwing events and middle distance running, and he sets the following personal goals for himself: one, to shot put at least 40 feet; two, to throw the discus at least 100 feet; and three, to run a personal best of under 2 minutes and 50 seconds in the 800-meter run in the class meet. After identifying these goals, Keeshana and Li spend time in class working on the events in which they have some ability and interest. With the objectives clearly established, they are able to experience what it means to train and practice for these events and also to set and achieve personal goals (see figure 6.2).

Figure 6.2 Portfolio assessment permits students to work toward different goals.

They are able to decide how they will show progress, record work, and show achievement. Using the portfolio in this way, students are able to make choices about what they want to learn, how they will practice, and how they will demonstrate learning.

For adolescents, independence and choice are very important considerations for motivation and achievement. While each of the students chose different activities, their individual personal goals, projects, and performances could each satisfy National Standard #1, to develop competency in many movement forms and proficiency in a few (NASPE 1995).

Student Self-Responsibility and Active Learning

When students choose activities and skills and set individual goals for achievement to address broad class or program goals, the roles of the students and teacher change. "In order to complete products and assemble their best work as evidence of achievement of those goals, the students must work independently and take responsibility and ownership for their own learning" (Kirk 1997). The teacher then takes the role of facilitator or guide. Students must make choices and decisions about learning and assessment tasks (or products) that they will complete or select. In this new role, the student must be actively involved in the learning process, rather than an unengaged participant.

In our track and field unit example, the teacher may present the skill of high jumping to a group of interested students, take them through the initial steps of performing and practicing the skill, and make recommendations of tasks for continued practice. Initially the teacher introduces all skill events in the track and field unit to the entire class. Students then have an opportunity to try and practice all events. Teachers then organize the class by implementing the learning station approach for instruction and practice: Students identify track and field events in which they would like to develop proficiency; they set personal goals; then they rotate to those event stations to practice during classes. Keeshana may decide to seek more information about how to train and practice for the high jump. She might decide to interview the high school track coach or a varsity high jumper, attend a varsity track practice and observe the high jumpers practicing, search the Internet to find coaching tips from experts, or check out a videotape on high jumping from the library. Using the information that she found, Keeshana then may choose to design her own practice and training schedule for class. During class she may ask the teacher or a peer to videotape her performance so that she can complete a self-analysis of her performance. Keeping a log of practice performances may assist her in showing progress (or the lack of improvement); therefore, it helps her review her personal goals for performance and training strategies. If documented, any or all of these individual projects could provide evidence that she might choose to include in her portfolio. The opportunities for students to direct and engage in their own learning are limitless and much more authentic in nature.

Encourages Student Self-Evaluation and Reflection

The portfolio process encourages students to evaluate and reflect on themselves as learners. They must reflect on the quality of their work or performances to make decisions about which pieces present the best evidence of their effort, progress, and level of achievement. They should not only select artifacts to include in the portfolio, but also write convincing rationale explaining why each item was selected and how it provides evidence of progress or level of achievement toward targeted standards or goals. When reflecting, students must make personal judgments about the quality of their work and performances. The student might decide not to include an artifact that he or she originally thought provided evidence of achievement of a certain standard. While reflecting, the student determines that another artifact provides much stronger evidence for a higher level of performance of the standard.

By selecting documentation for evidence of improvement, the student must actually look at and compare performance artifacts that are accumulated throughout the unit. With this method, the student, as well as the teacher, clearly sees how much the student has learned and improved. Through participation in the portfolio process and building the evaluation portfolio, the student must look at his or her work with a critical eye and make decisions about his or her best work and to relate the artifacts to the targeted standards or goals. This process forces students to review their performances and gives them a clear picture of the level of performance and how much improvement was made. It is through this reflective process that the student is able to look at the big picture of his or her learning, rather than just separate pieces.

In my 1997 article (Kirk 1997), I demonstrated this concept in the example of providing students in a badminton unit with opportunities for daily practice of the long and short serve in a serve-receive game. I changed this daily assessment activity from having students simply record the number of accurate short and long serves made out of 10 when I realized that students who were completing 100% of their serves in practice were achieving a significantly lower percentage during game play. The practice had to be in a gamelike situation with an opponent returning the serve. This refinement added a new dimension to the goal of the practice in which the students not only had to serve the shuttles over the net and into the service court, but they also had to do it in such a way that the servers were not able to return them. Practicing in the modified game activity creates a realistic or authentic practice situation for the students. Data regarding the percentage of accuracy of shuttle trajectory, placement, criteria, and success are recorded daily by the student. This assessment activity provides data that students can use to chart progress, analyze performance across time, and make interventions for improvement when needed. The systematic recording, graphing, and analysis of this data then can be used as an artifact of evidence in the portfolio.

Feedback and Continuous Evaluation

The portfolio process encourages teachers to provide students with many opportunities to complete a variety of assessment tools continually throughout the unit, semester, or year. Because most assessments are formative or completed throughout the unit and integrated with learning activities throughout the portfolio process period, the teacher and student are provided with ongoing feedback about learning and progress of performance through systematic documentation. This process allows students and teachers to modify learning and practice activities to better meet the needs of the students. As students receive feedback regarding their progress, they may seek assistance from a peer or their teacher. To make changes in curriculum or instructional strategies, the teacher can also use the continuous feedback and evaluation information.

Motivates Students and Teachers

Students are more motivated by completing assessment tasks that are integrated with learning activities, reflective of real-life situations, and have personal meaning. Personal and realistic tasks for students include setting personal goals for daily participation in physical activity outside of class and keeping a daily log of the activities, which includes the amount of activity time, the type of activity, whether participation was completed alone or with someone,

and identifying a reason why participation was missed. This task allows the students to analyze and reflect on activity patterns and reasons for participation and nonparticipation so that they can make appropriate changes to encourage regular participation. This process is one that a student can use to motivate, analyze, and make interventions in physical activity patterns throughout a lifetime.

Allowing students the freedom to be creative and inventive in developing and participating in their own learning and assessment tasks can also be very motivating. Seeing students who are excited about and who take responsibility for their own learning can also motivate and inspire teachers. In the absence of this accountability, some students would not even attempt the task.

Students are also motivated by the knowledge that not every assessment completed inside or outside of class is evaluated or graded. This fact helps students try harder and attempt tasks that they might not normally attempt because of fear of failure. What is also very motivating to students is to allow them the time and opportunity to complete multiple practice and assessment tasks until they have met the criteria or until they are satisfied with their performance.

Giving adolescent students the opportunity (and ultimately the responsibility) to choose the artifacts for evaluation is highly motivating. By giving them choice, the teacher is saying to the students, "You are a responsible individual, and I trust you to make good decisions about your learning."

While teaching a badminton unit to a 10th grade class, I asked my students to create and complete a group assessment task. The task was one that they could use in their portfolios as evidence of their knowledge and skill of badminton and their ability to work cooperatively in a group to accomplish a goal. One group of five students chose to complete an instructional videotape on badminton. They opened the video with a shared presentation on the history and current status of the sport. Then each student introduced a different shot by presenting a rationale for its use in a game, identified performance cues, and gave several demonstrations of the shot, all the while other members of the group took turns directing and videotaping. To demonstrate their knowledge of the rules, four members served as players on the court while one student was the commentator explaining the rules as they were demonstrated. Students took turns serving as the commentator. It was very obvious to me as I observed this group that they were very animated, engaged, and motivated to complete a quality project.

The teacher derives tremendous motivation and renewed enthusiasm for teaching through observing his or her students as they develop the self-responsibility and initiative that are necessary to complete the portfolio task and the portfolio process. It is especially gratifying for the teacher when students take ownership and pride in their portfolios—when they genuinely take time to personalize their portfolios and are honestly anxious to share their work. In the badminton video mentioned previously, students provided other pieces of artifacts to illustrate their work on the video project, including written scripts, photos of the scripts in large print (used as monitors for the actors), and pictures that they took of the entire process. When students were asked to present their badminton portfolios to the class, this group was so excited to show their video and explain their process. These students were not always the best or most responsible students in the class, but because this was *their* project for *their* portfolios, they all enthusiastically engaged in the project. It was obvious to me that they were having fun both learning and developing evidence for their learning. It had become the centerpiece of their portfolio. As a teacher, this was one of those lightbulb moments!

Display of Student Work

"A portfolio is like a trophy case for a student's accomplishments" (Wilson and Roof 1999). Just as athletic trophy cases display the accomplishments of teams and individual athletes, portfolios can be used to showcase student work and accomplishments in the physical education program. Showcasing student portfolios is also an effective way to demonstrate teacher and program accountability. Student portfolios can also be displayed to provide evidence of student learning and achievement for goals and standards at the district, state, and national levels. During school open houses, instead of physical education teachers standing in front of groups of parents to explain the physical education program, parents could walk around the gym looking at student portfolios that are on display. Imagine the impressive scenario with students standing at tables with their portfolios displayed, surrounded by groups of parents, teachers, administrators, and other students, showing and explaining the arti-

facts included in the portfolio and articulating how each artifact provided evidence of his or her achievement of goals and standards. This method is a powerful way to demonstrate and measure the physical education program accountability.

Types of Portfolios

Portfolios can be designed for a variety of purposes. It is the selected purpose of the portfolio assessment that determines the type of portfolio that the teacher selects for the students to complete. Melograno (1998, 81) suggests that "once the purposes for implementing a portfolio system are clear, the type of portfolio should be determined that can best achieve these purposes." A variety of types of portfolios, which can be used alone or in combination, are the following (Burke, Fogarty, and Belgrad 1994; Kimeldorf 1994; Melograno 2000):

▶ Working portfolio

▶ Evaluation or showcase portfolio

▶ Thematic portfolio

▶ Multiyear portfolio

▶ Group portfolio

▶ Electronic portfolio

Working Portfolio

The **working portfolio** is the individual student's collection of daily or weekly work, projects, assessments, and assignments. The student collects these materials from class by placing them into a file folder, box, or envelope, which is either stored by the teacher or kept with the student. Each item is logged in or out on the portfolio register form, which is stored with the working portfolio. Periodically the student makes decisions regarding which items will be eliminated and which will be maintained as artifacts for evidence of the student's achievement of class goals in the evaluation or showcase portfolio.

Evaluation Portfolio

The finished product that is submitted by the student for evaluation is considered the **evaluation portfolio**. The evaluation (or showcase) portfolio contains a limited number of artifacts that are chosen by the student from the working portfolio to represent his or her best work. The pieces selected and included in this portfolio demonstrate level of achievement of personal, class, and program goals and standards, as well as student growth across time. This portfolio is developed in such a way that it can be showcased or exhibited to audiences beyond the teacher (peers, other teachers in the school, administrators, parents) to demonstrate individual student growth and achievement, as well as program promotion and accountability.

Thematic Portfolio

The **thematic portfolio** is used for a specific unit of study. The unit could extend from 2 to 12 weeks, depending upon the theme or activity. A variety of themes could be emphasized in a middle or high school physical education class that use the portfolio process for assessment. Some common thematic portfolios used in physical education include a focus on personal fitness, cooperation, teamwork, and self-expression through movement (Melograno 2000).

Multiyear Portfolio

The focus of the **multiyear portfolio** is to show student growth or achievement of goals and standards across years. For instance, middle school students could demonstrate improvement of skill performance in various physical activity units from sixth through eighth grade. They could also demonstrate the breadth of knowledge and skill development in a wide variety of physical activities: volleyball, basketball, soccer, badminton, in-line skating, dance, golf, tennis, ultimate Frisbee, gymnastics, track and field, canoeing, hiking, and orienteering. During the eighth grade, students could include in the portfolio a reflective writing assignment in which they identify the two to four activities in which they experienced the most joy, success, and interest. These activities could be pursued in a high school elective program. A multiyear portfolio approach could also be used effectively to help students and teachers follow growth in student knowledge, attitudes, improvements in personal physical fitness, and levels and types of participation in regular physical activities.

Group Portfolio

Melograno (2000) suggests that the use of **group portfolios** is an effective way for students to experience their initial exposure to the portfolio process because they go through it with their group instead of alone. Students might be asked to contribute individual or group work to the portfolio, which contributes to the achievement of group goals. Cooperation and teamwork can be effectively evaluated through the group portfolio process. The group portfolio is an excellent assessment form for teachers to use to evaluate group achievement in a sports education model unit approach.

Electronic Portfolio

The recent development of multimedia software, scanners, digital cameras, digital video cameras, CD-ROM drives, CD-writers, computers with videotape editing capabilities, and technology tools emerging today have made the development of the **electronic portfolio** possible.

The use of electronic portfolios in physical education creates endless possibilities (Mohnsen 2000). The electronic portfolio is created on the computer and saved on a floppy diskette or, more recently, a CD-ROM. The CD-ROM takes up less space and is easy to transport and store so that the student can work on the portfolio at school, in a computer lab, at the library, or at home. These technology tools make it possible for students in physical education to provide video sequences in which they demonstrate and display skill performance achievement, game play sequences, and dance and gymnastics performances. If the technological tools are available to students, using electronic portfolios as an assessment is an excellent way to implement technology into student learning in physical education.

Portfolio Guidelines in Performance-Based Assessment

To make portfolio assessment a positive and enjoyable process for all, it is extremely important that the teacher clearly explain and guide students through the process, especially the first time that students develop their portfolios. Teachers must remind themselves that using portfolios as a form of continuous performance-based assessment is a learning process for students. To be successful, the teacher must plan ahead and make the necessary preparations and attend to each of the following tasks:

1. Identify the learner outcomes that are to be demonstrated through the portfolio assessment.

2. Develop and communicate portfolio guidelines to students.

3. Build flexibility into the class schedule.

4. Provide a variety of performance-based learning and assessment opportunities for students.

5. Guide students in the creation of portfolio ideas.

6. Provide class time for students to work on their portfolios.

7. Provide opportunities for students to share or showcase their portfolios.

Guideline One

The teacher must begin the portfolio process with the identification of what students should know and be able to do by the conclusion of the unit, semester, year, or program. The objectives, goals, and standards that the students are expected to demonstrate must be clearly identified and shared with the students at the onset of the process. The goals and standards that must be achieved guide the student in the development of the portfolio. The student outcomes that are initially identified may include the following: very specific activity goals; sport unit goals; targeted, broad school district or state goals; or selected National Standards for Physical Education (NASPE 1995). The targeted, broad goals or standards can serve as the organizational format for the student portfolio. For example, if all seven National Standards for Physical Education are identified as desired outcomes of the semester or year, then the student may choose to organize the portfolio into seven sections, one for each standard, and provide at least one artifact to demonstrate level of achievement per standard. By sharing with the students the

expected destination at the onset, teachers can provide them with a better understanding of where they must go and what they must do to get there.

Guideline Two

Once the teacher has identified standards and decided that the portfolio will be the type of culminating product by which students will be evaluated, then a plan or guidelines must be established and shared with students. When students have had experience with portfolio development, the process is familiar to them, but they still need specific guidelines. When students do not have experience with portfolio assessment, it is crucial that the teacher guide them carefully throughout the process. The portfolio process must be designed for the setting in which it will be implemented. We have found that "if class time and space are limited, then the number and scope of tasks must be geared to the contextual limitations of the program (Kirk 1997, 30). Once dimensions and criteria of the portfolio have been identified, students should be given copies for future reference (see table 6.1). The teacher should carefully review the guidelines with students, making sure that all questions are answered and that all students have a clear understanding of what is expected.

We have found that it is best to provide organized storage of student working portfolios at the physical education facility. Providing a milk crate for each class with hanging file folders or colored folders for each student works well. A different color plastic crate can be provided and labeled for each of the teacher's classes. The crates can be stacked and stored in the teacher's office or a secure storage room adjacent to the gym. The class portfolio crate can be placed in a designated gym area so students have easy access to their portfolio materials during each class. A supply of pencils or pens should be provided near the file so students can record new documents.

Daily Storage of New Materials

Each assessment task or item should be dated or numbered and recorded in the artifact registry taped to the front of the working portfolio container (see figure 6.3). Melograno (1999) suggests that this provides a chronicle of when and why items are included, removed, and

Table 6.1 Guidelines for Portfolios

Recommendations or requirements for how the portfolio should be contained and submitted

Some suggestions include file folders, three-ring binders, photo albums, hanging files, large envelopes, computer diskette, or CD-ROM.

How the portfolio should be organized

In standards-based educational programs, the students may be required to provide a section with a specified number of artifacts for each targeted state or program standard or for each of the National Standards for Physical Education (NASPE 1995). The teacher might recommend or require that the students provide dividers with labeled tabs to separate sections by goal or national standard, or to color code each section, which corresponds to the table of contents. In the final evaluation portfolio, a table of contents of all items should be required to help students better organize their work and to assist the evaluator in locating materials.

Where and how the students' working portfolios are stored and how they gain access to them

The working portfolio is where all student work is collected until selections are made and the evaluation portfolio is compiled and submitted. Teachers must address the following questions regarding the storage of working portfolios: Are students to be responsible for keeping their own working portfolio, or does the teacher provide accessible space in the gym area to store them? Do students have access to stored working portfolios outside of class time?

Name: _____	Class: _____	Semester: Fall Spring	
Date	Document title/description	Added	Deleted

Figure 6.3 The working portfolio record form helps students keep track of all documents entered into or deleted from their working portfolio.

replaced with ongoing student reflection. This process makes it much easier for students when it is time to make decisions and to assemble the final evaluation portfolio. Without a written record of when and why artifacts were originally included, it may be difficult for the student to remember the information from weeks ago.

Sample Assessment Tasks

Teachers should provide suggestions, but they should also remember to allow students some choices if they expect students to take ownership of their portfolios. A list of some possible task ideas are presented later in this chapter. When giving students ideas about sample tasks, the teacher must focus on the targeted student outcomes and ask "What tasks can students complete that demonstrate a level of achievement of at least one of the outcomes?"

Student Written Reflections

Students should provide written reflections regarding why each artifact is included and how it shows growth, progress, and achievement (see figure 6.4). The reflection statement should provide a connection between the targeted student outcomes and the artifact.

Time Lines and Progress Checkpoint Dates

This strategy helps to ensure that it is a continual assessment process and that it also allows the teacher to give students feedback along the way. The teacher should encourage students to make early decisions regarding possible assessment tasks or projects that they would like to complete to submit in their final portfolio. The most effective way to encourage this organization is to provide a time table with checkpoints in which students compile

Name: _____	Class: _____	Semester: Fall Spring
Artifact/document	Goal/standard/objective	Reflection (Why is it included?)

Figure 6.4 This form assists students in the selection, organization, and justification of artifacts for inclusion in the evaluation portfolio.

specific parts of the portfolio and schedule conferences with the teacher. An efficient way to periodically check student portfolio progress is to set up a portfolio check station in the corner of the gym, away from the action. While the class is engaged in practice or game activities, the teacher calls students individually or in small groups to the station to check progress and answer questions.

Provide a Rubric

A rubric helps to guide them as they construct the final portfolio. As indicated in chapter 3, the rubric is a scoring guide that is used by the teacher to evaluate the portfolio, and it is also used by students to help guide the construction of their portfolio. The rubric identifies for the student the criteria that must be met to achieve each level identified in the rubric. Sample rubrics are found in chapter 3, and they can be found in this chapter in figure 6.7 and table 6.3.

Provide Models of Student Portfolios

Often students are unable to visualize what the completed portfolio should look like or the types of items that could be included. By viewing model portfolios, students develop a better understanding of the finished product. Model student port-

folios (with the student's permission) could be placed on reserve in the school library, kept on a table in the teacher's office, or in a table in the gym for students to view and ask questions. It is important, however, to remind students that they should create and personalize their own portfolios, not just copy another.

Encourage Personalization

Suggest the inclusion of their own artwork, computer graphics, colors, photos, stickers, or memorabilia. Adolescence is a time when the need for independence strongly emerges. By personalizing their portfolio in this way, students can be creative and individualize their work. When students are encouraged to personalize their work, they are more enthusiastic and take more pride in the portfolio.

Guideline Three

The teacher must build flexibility into the class schedule, organization, and instructional format to accommodate a successful and positive portfolio process for students (Kirk 1997). Students must be provided with time, space, equipment, materials, and learning or assessment opportunities (see figure 6.5).

Figure 6.5   The gym should be organized into a variety of learning stations to encourage students to work in small groups or independently on different types and levels of portfolio projects or assessments.

Instead of a large open space, the gym can be organized into separate work, practice, and play areas, as well as learning stations or centers for students to

▶ practice and analyze skills, and skill combinations,

▶ apply skills and strategies in small group, gamelike situations (e.g., two-on-two, three-on-three),

▶ exercise in a strength training or aerobic workout area,

▶ create a dance,

▶ complete projects,

▶ videotape self-analysis,

▶ search the Internet for desired information,

▶ complete a fitness component self-test and record performance data in the computer using the FITNESSGRAM software (Cooper Institute for Aerobics Research 1999),

▶ plan group projects, and

▶ view pertinent educational videotapes or use resource materials provided by the teacher.

The gym then becomes a multipurpose learning center for physical education.

Teachers may choose to arrange time in a variety of ways. For example, if the physical education class is scheduled as a 90-minute block, the teacher may designate the last 20-30 minutes of each class (or every other class) as student project, assessment, or portfolio work time. During this time, students could work on individual or group projects or required assessment tasks for their portfolio. Some teachers may find that reserving one entire class during the week designated to work on portfolio tasks is more efficient. The key to a successful portfolio process for students is that units of instruction must be extended for longer lengths of time so that students have time to develop in-depth knowledge, skills, and complete portfolio projects. This is especially true for high school classes where students should be provided the opportunity to develop proficiency in at least two physical activities (NASPE 1995). How to provide flexibility in class time is discussed later in this chapter.

Guideline Four

In this chapter, we have provided suggestions for how teachers can integrate continual performance-based learning and assessment tasks into a unit of study through the planning process. Providing students with continuing opportunities to complete a variety of assessment tasks through the portfolio process is very important. This provides students with a steady supply of performance artifacts that they can catalog into their working portfolio. Later, when assembling their final portfolio (their evaluation portfolio), students will have many artifacts from which to choose to demonstrate the level of achievement of the targeted goals and standards. Teachers might require that students include some specific items, but they should also allow students to personalize the portfolio by granting them choices about other documents to include.

In my badminton units I require students to provide skill and game performance data. This data is collected during daily practice activity and class tournament game play. The assessment may take the form of counting the number of accurate shots made out of 10 in a specific partner practice drill each day and graphing the progress for the overhead clear, the dropshot, and the long and short serve. Game play data can be easily gathered: Have students design personal statistics sheets so that they can exchange them with other students to collect and calculate stats for each other. The student may create or choose a project that demonstrates in some way his or her knowledge of the rules and strategies of the game.

Possible assessments that may be completed in class or that can be completed as a project for the portfolio include (as explained in chapter 2):

▶ peer or self-assessment skill checklists,
▶ rating scales,
▶ student writings,
▶ group or individual event tasks,
▶ criterion-referenced skill tests,
▶ student logs,
▶ written tests and quizzes,
▶ exit slips,
▶ individual or group projects,
▶ contracts,
▶ task sheets,
▶ reflections,
▶ workbook or homework,
▶ teacher's analysis or anecdotal record,
▶ attitude surveys,
▶ artwork or drawings,
▶ skill self-analysis, and
▶ videotaped performances.

When students complete these assessments or the teacher completes the evaluation, they are entered into the student working portfolio collection file for later consideration.

Guideline Five

Teachers may require specific projects or tasks that are designed to be included in the portfolio, or they may give students choices of tasks to complete or prompts to help them create their own tasks. "The possibilities for student portfolio tasks are infinite, bounded only by the imagination and the creativity of the teacher and the student" (Kirk 1997, 33). The teachers must take care to make sure that the tasks are aligned with the targeted unit or program goals and standards. To modify instruction and thereby address individual student abilities and interests, teachers should allow students to choose, with guidance, the specific type of portfolio assessment tasks they wish to complete. Although the students should have the option to choose tasks, the teacher must check to ensure that each student is challenged at his or her ability level and encouraged to give his or her best effort. Teachers must help students to determine how many artifacts should be included. The number of artifacts, however,

depends on the quality and depth of the artifacts. One student may include one project that provides excellent evidence that the student achieved three of the five targeted standards, while another student may need to provide one project or artifact as evidence for each standard. Some suggested portfolio tasks that encourage student learning and self-responsibility for learning, interest, and motivation are listed in table 6.2.

Guideline Six

Build time within lessons for students to work on portfolio tasks, especially when students are attempting to complete a group project. Teachers can, however, also require students to complete some work on projects outside of class, especially if class time is limited. If the school has implemented block scheduling and the students are in class for 90 minutes, then the teacher could designate the final 30 minutes of class as "portfolio project work time." During this time, students could work individually or in groups on projects, or they could work on organizing and selecting items to include in the submission portfolio. Also, during this time, the teacher is available to help students with projects, complete portfolio progress checks, answer questions, give feedback, and encourage students in the process. Another way the teacher can build in time to work on portfolios during class is through providing learning stations in the gym. Some stations are specifically designed for students to work on skills and strategies for the unit activity, while others are designed for students to complete portfolio assessment tasks or to work on the portfolio. Students are rotated to each of the various learning stations so that every student gets the opportunity to work on the portfolio. During this time, the teacher observes and is available to assist students and to prompt ones that are slow starters.

Guideline Seven

When evaluation portfolios are due at the end of a grading period, semester, or year, provide class time when students can present their portfolios to each other in small groups. During parent open houses, set up tables in the gym and hallways for students to display. When students know from the start that they are expected to display or present their portfolio to

Table 6.2   Suggested Portfolio Tasks

Self-Analysis and Peer Assessment

Refer to figure 6.6, an example of a student log of practice scores, graph, and self-analysis.

A student log in which the student records the product of performance for practice activities across the unit (i.e., the number of accurate serves out of 10 in badminton) and a graph or chart of progress across time. The student can also analyze the learning and performance curve to indicate where in the curve an intervention was necessary and what that intervention strategy was.

After a specified number of practice or game sessions, the student completes a written self-analysis of skill performance with individual goals for improvement and possible intervention strategies.

The student keeps a daily journal to set goals, record successes, setbacks, and progress and then analyzes the situation to make recommendations for present and future work.

A series of continuous self-analyses and peer assessments of skill and playing performance across time to show student progress in a sport or activity (process and product assessments: skill checklists and rating scales, criterion-referenced tasks, task sheets, game statistics sheets, won-loss record with scores in a round-robin tournament).

With a partner, the students videotape each other playing a sport or performing a skill or an activity. They complete a written analysis of a videotape, evaluating their partner's performance and giving feedback for improvement.

Self-analysis of student's playing performance (application of skills and strategies) through the collection of game statistics (e.g., shooting percentage, assists, successful passes, steals, service aces, saves) and how the student used the data to improve performance.

Using self-analysis, peer observation and assessments, and teacher feedback, the students identify strengths and areas that need improvement. They select or design appropriate practice or training programs and complete practice schedules; then they record results.

After being videotaped performing in a game or practice situation, view the videotape and complete a self-evaluation or analysis of the performance with suggestions for improvement.

(continued)

Table 6.2 *(continued)*

Participate and Learn

Students provide documentation of participation in practice, informal game play, and organized competition outside of class. This could include a student descriptive log with witness signatures, score or statistics sheet (or statistics from intramural play or community recreational league participation) and reported statistics and articles in the local newspaper.

In small groups, students set up, conduct, and participate in a class tournament. They must keep a record of the collaborative process that the groups had to follow to accomplish the task. Evaluate after completion.

The student attends a youth sport, high school, college, or professional sports event and writes a report regarding some aspect of the event (e.g., displays of good and bad sporting behaviors by players, coaches, and fans; the role of the officials in maintaining a fair contest; the skills and offensive and defensive strategies that each player or team used; an account of the traditions that surround the contest).

The student records a play-by-play or color commentary of a class tournament game as a radio sports announcer (audiotape) or a television announcer (videotape), as if they are preparing a demo to apply for a job.

Create

The student creates and performs an aerobic dance, step aerobic, jump rope, gymnastic, ice skating or swing dance routine according to the criteria provided by the teacher. The evidence provided for the portfolio might include a routine script or videotape, or video clip on a CD-ROM of the performance.

The student creates a sculpture, or paints or draws a picture that represents some aspect of emotion or feelings of participation or observation of a sport or physical activity.

The student creates and maintains a physical education Web site for students and parents. It is updated with class schedule, current fitness information and research findings, class tournament standings and results, photographs and videotape segments of class games, activities, field trips, performances, and so on. It also includes links to other Web sites of interest.

The student writes an essay or poem about the feelings experienced while participating in a favorite and least favorite physical activity.

(continued)

Table 6.2 *(continued)*

Write a newspaper article reporting on the class tournament, or a game of the tournament, as if a sports reporter (must demonstrate knowledge of the game). In groups, put the articles together and design and publish the "PE Sports page" for students. Have one or two students serve as photographers during games, to provide photos in the sports page.

Write an essay titled "My biggest accomplishment: overcoming my fear of water in swimming class" (or any activity unit) and what I learned about myself and life in the process.

Research

Students research the community resources available for various physical activities and develop a community physical activity resource guide for students and teachers in the school. In a group, they write, design, and edit a class sport or fitness magazine, which addresses topics studied in class and provides the most current graphics or photographs to make the magazine interesting.

The student researches the latest training strategies for a skill or a sport on the Internet, in the library, or through interviewing high school, youth sport, and college coaches or athletes in the area. The student shows how the new strategies are applied in a personal training program to improve performance.

The student completes a written scouting report of the next opponent in a class tournament before playing them. The student identifies strengths and weaknesses and develops a game plan of offensive and defensive strategies that are used during the game. After playing them, the effectiveness of the game plan is evaluated.

In shall groups, students research the Internet, the library, or interview an exercise physiologist or fitness specialist for the latest information regarding physical activity and health. They design a fitness, wellness, or physical activity and health newsletter that includes helpful and accurate information for students, teachers, parents and administrators. Integrate the use of technology skills with this project by having students use publishing software and graphics.

The student interviews an athlete about an experience with a disability and overcoming adversity to compete. The student then applies the lessons learned to personal situation in audio, video, or written form.

Skill practice scores		Dates									
		9/1	9/2	9/3	9/4	9/5	9/8	9/9	9/10	9/11	9/12
Short serve	10	3	4	5	4	2	4	5	6	6	7
Long serve	10										
Serve return	10										
Defensive overhand clear	10										
Offensive overhand clear	10										
Drop shot	10										
Forehand or backhand drive	10										

Graph of Short Serve Progress

Score

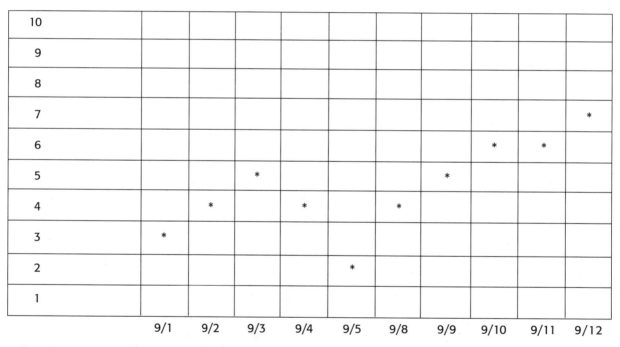

Student Self-Analysis and Actions Taken

From day one to day three, my short serve accuracy showed steady improvement. On day four and day five my performance declined. I kept hitting the shuttle into the net or short of the service area. On day five, I asked my partner to observe my short serve and to complete a Short Serve Performance Checklist. Following the observation we discovered that instead of dropping the shuttle from my hand and contacting it with my racket at knee level, that I was hitting the shuttle out of my hand. This meant that I was contacting the shutle at waist level or above, which is illegal, and making the shuttle travel high and short. This caused the shuttle to hit the net or land short of the service area because the shuttle was traveling in a short high trajectory.

Figure 6.6   Sample student log of practice scores, graph, and self-analysis.

an audience other than the physical education teacher, the stakes are higher for them. This is a motivation for students to provide their best work.

Evaluation of the Portfolio

When the teacher prepares a scoring guide or rubric at the beginning of the process, which is based on the set criteria and guidelines given to the students, the evaluation process is not that difficult. Preparing rubrics or scoring guides is addressed in chapter 3. In figure 6.7 and table 6.3, we have provided sample portfolio guidelines and a scoring rubric that are given to students at the onset of the unit.

Guidelines for a Badminton Unit Portfolio

At the end of the six-week unit on badminton, you must submit your badminton portfolio, which provides documents (pieces of your work) that demonstrate in authentic ways that you have achieved at an acceptable level the following unit goals. (Some suggested assessment project ideas are provided under each unit goal; you may, of course, come up with your own ideas.)

You will be able to do the following:

1. Demonstrate your knowledge of history, current status, equipment, court lines and areas, singles and doubles rules, and scoring procedures of the sport of badminton.

    Assessment ideas:

    - Create an informational pamphlet on the sport of badminton.
    - With a small group, create an instructional video on the sport of badminton.
    - Officiate or serve as a score keeper of games during the class tournament.

2. Demonstrate the ability to identify critical learning cues; observe and analyze your own and your peer's skill performance; make recommendations for practice to help improve performance of the following skills: short serve, long serve, offensive and defensive overhead clear, underhand clear, drop shot, smash, forehand and backhand drive.

    Assessment ideas:

    - Student journal
    - Videotape analysis
    - Use of skill observation checklist with written feedback
    - Create an instructional videotape

3. Demonstrate the ability to effectively perform the badminton skills (shots) listed in the second objective while playing badminton in the class tournament.

    Assessment ideas:

    - Peer- and self-observation skill checklists
    - Daily class practice scores and graphs and self-analysis
    - Game play observation statistics sheets
    - Videotape analysis of game play
    - Tournament record and results

4. Demonstrate respect and caring for your fellow classmates by helping them to improve their skill performance and game play through verbal feedback, practice suggestions, encouragement, and practicing with them.

    Assessment ideas:

    - Journal entries
    - Written feedback and practice suggestions
    - Practice log

(continued)

Figure 6.7   A sample of a guideline sheet that a teacher could provide to students that states unit goals with assessment ideas for each standard to include as an artifact in their badminton unit portfolios.

5. Demonstrate personal improvement in performance of skill performance and game play.

Assessment ideas:

- Journal
- Skill performance checklists
- Daily practice scores, graph of scores
- Tournament record
- Videotape analysis

6. Demonstrate the ability to explain and use (*a*) the basic offensive strategy of covering court space and returning to home and (*b*) the defensive strategies of hitting the ball to open spaces and moving the opponent out of position by using a variety of shots.

Assessment ideas:

- Instructional videotape
- Peer teaching
- Game play statistics
- Video sequences in which you demonstrated the strategies on CD-ROM
- Create an audio tape of you as a radio sports announcer calling a tournament game
- Create a videotape of you as a TV sports announcer covering a game

You must provide at least one artifact as evidence of achievement for each of the unit goals.

In some cases, you may need to provide more than one artifact as evidence for a particular goal. Remember, if you provide only one artifact, it must provide strong evidence for that goal.

Some of your artifacts may be actual assessments that you completed in class, while other evidence may be documents (group projects, journals, etc.) that you choose to complete during the six weeks.

You need to collect artifacts that are developed each day in class and place them in your working portfolio. Each student has a file with their name printed on it. The files are placed in alphabetical order (please keep them in order) in the milk crate provided for and marked for your class. You select your best work as evidence for your evaluation portfolio.

In the front of your portfolio, you must include the completed artifact registry form (see figure 6.4).

List all artifacts and the goal for which it provides evidence, and include your reflection statement. In the reflection statement, you explain why you have included the artifact and how it provides evidence that you have achieved the goal.

If you have chosen special personal or group projects, they should be identified by the beginning of the second week of the badminton unit so that you have sufficient time to complete them. Check with me before beginning such a project. *You must complete at least one small group cooperative project to be included in your portfolio.* The choice is yours, but you must keep and submit in your portfolio a record of your collaboration with the group.

You may personalize your portfolio. As long as it is organized with a table of contents and a tabbed section for each unit goal, which contains at least one rich artifact for each goal, the form in which you present your portfolio is up to you. Feel free to use color, computer graphics, pictures, drawings. Some of you techno-wizards may even want to submit your portfolio on a CD-ROM.

Figure 6.7 *(continued)*

Table 6.3   Rubric for a Badminton Unit Portfolio

Levels	Organization and presentation	Content
4 Proficiency level	–Neatly and effectively organized –Tabbed section provided for each goal –Artifacts clearly marked and placed according to the table of contents –Complete title page provided –Well-organized table of contents; each artifact listed in each goal section –All materials neatly and creatively displayed –Portfolio registry and reflection page provided after title page –Presentation creative and personalized	–Provides solid evidence of achievement of all unit goals –Clearly demonstrates student growth and improvement across the unit –Demonstrates a personal contribution to a cooperative effort –Represents a wide variety of assessment projects –Artifacts all listed in the registry –Provides a rich explanation of reflections of why and how artifacts were included –Includes appropriate graphics, pictures, or drawings to personalize
3 Competent level	–Neatly organized –Tabbed section provided for each goal –Title page provided –Table of contents provided –Displayed moderate creativity in presentation –Portfolio registry and reflection page provided after title page	–Demonstrates achievement for all but one of the unit goals –Provides evidence of growth and improvement across the unit –Provides evidence of cooperative group effort –Represents a variety of assessments –Provides reflections that show a clear connection between the artifact and the unit goals –Includes graphics, pictures, or drawings
2 Novice level	–Some organizational problems –Sloppy display of artifacts –Table of contents did not list artifacts under each goal section –Portfolio registry and reflection page does not follow the title page –Some creativity evident –Sections provided for each goal but are not tabbed	–Artifacts not provided for two or more of the unit goals –Clear evidence of achievement of goals not provided for some artifacts –Weak evidence provided for growth and improvement across the unit –Evidence of cooperative group effort provided –No variety of assessment tasks; many are similar –Reflections not clear or thoughtful –Some graphics, pictures, or drawings included
1 Needs improvement level	–Unorganized and messy presentation –Sections not clearly divided or tabbed –No table of contents provided –Missing the portfolio registry and reflection –Lack of creativity and general effort	–Lacks evidence for most of the unit goals –Weak evidence of achievement provided –No reflections provided –Lack of variety of assessment types; most are similar –No evidence of cooperative group project –Weak evidence for growth and improvement across the unit

This rubric was developed using the criteria that are identified in figure 6.7.

Conclusion

As more states move to standards-based educational programs and away from traditional forms of assessment, the further widespread use of the portfolio is observed. Using the portfolio process as an authentic, performance-based form of assessment in physical education is an exciting and promising alternative to traditional assessment. Students are able to complete projects and performances, gather and present artifacts in their portfolios, all of which provide evidence that they have met or achieved program and national standards. Although the implementation of the portfolio process of assessment involves much planning and organization, it is well worth the effort for both students and teachers. The process encourages students to become self-sufficient learners and provides an excellent way for teachers to individualize teaching and learning to meet the needs and interests of all students. Those teachers who have implemented the portfolio process successfully indicate that students are more actively engaged in the learning assessment process and are highly motivated. This process holds much promise for those teachers who are willing to challenge themselves and their students.

CHAPTER SEVEN

Developing Culminating and Progressive Assessments

Authentic assessment is an integral part of a never-ending hypothesis-verification-conclusion learning cycle . . . however, unless the students have a chance to reflect on their actions in light of the feedback they receive, and then make other trials in action, true learning may never occur. (Grehaigne, Godbout, and Bouthier 1997, p. 513)

In the previous chapters, we present reasons for integrating assessment into your teaching. We also present various types of performance-based and authentic assessments that teachers can use to design assessments. In this chapter, we begin the process of how to design the following: culminating (or summative) assessments for units of instruction, which are linked to identified broad standards and spe-

cific unit goals; and formative (or progressive) assessments, which are integrated with learning activities and help prepare students to successfully complete the culminating performance or product. You are provided with sample culminating and progressive assessments in three units: tumbling, golf, and archery. In chapters 8 and 9, we then take you through the entire process of designing standards-based instructional units with integrated formative and summative assessments, and we include a sample unit in tennis and soccer, each with sample assessments.

Culminating Assessments

The **culminating assessment** is generally a final performance or product that the student completes and should provide evidence that students have demonstrated achievement of broad standards and specific unit goals (Kentucky Department of Education 1993). The identification of the standards and unit goals is the first step in the five-step, standards-based planning process, which is described in detail in chapter 8. To guide you through the sample culminating assessments in this chapter, we also provide the national standards and specific unit goals that would normally be identified during this first step. The teacher can use the National Standards for Physical Education (NASPE 1995) and individual state or district goals as broad targeted goals, which serve as the student destination in the planning and teaching process. More specific unit goals, which lead to the broad standards and goals and pertain to the individual unit activity, are also identified by the teacher before the development of the culminating assessment. The targeted standards and goals are the destination—the culminating performance or product—indicating to the student and the teacher that the student has arrived at the destination.

Once the standards and goals have been identified and the teacher knows where the student is headed, the teacher then must design a culminating assessment to determine if the student arrived at the destination (see

figure 7.1). The teacher must address the question, How will the teacher and the students know if they have achieved the unit goals and targeted standards and at what level? The culminating unit experience, in which students participate at the end of the unit, can provide much information toward the final assessment of student learning. In standards-based instruction, this culminating assessment should be a demonstration of the student's learning and achievement of the goals and also the progress they have made toward the targeted standards. Students should provide a rich demonstration of the application of the knowledge and skills they have learned in an authentic or realistic engaging task or performance. The culminating performance or product then serves as the accountability measure for both the students and the teacher.

When designing the culminating assessment, the teacher must consider the unit goals and targeted standards, and they must think of how students can demonstrate the achievement of the unit goals and progress toward targeted standards in a real-to-life situation. This final assessment should be designed before the implementation of the unit, and it should take into consideration the length of the unit and available time. This final assessment should consist of a group or individual performance, a completed product in which the student assumes a real-life role with a specific audience identified, or a student portfolio. The culminating performance, product, or portfolio and the corresponding scoring guides or rubrics should be shared with students at the beginning of the unit so that they know from the outset what is expected of them. The culminating performance may take

---

Initial Steps in Standards-Based Physical Education Planning

1. Identify broad targeted National Standards for Physical Education (NASPE 1995) and state and local school district broad student goals.

2. Identify specific goals that are relevant to the unit activity and directly link to the achievment of the broad standards and goals.

3. Design a summative or culminating assessment performance or product that engages students and demonstrates their ability to apply knowledge and skills in a setting that is realistic to the activity and to the achievement of standards and goals.

4. Design a series of progressively more complex formative assessments that students participate in throughout the unit that are linked with learning activities. These progressive assessments should provide students with feedback about their progress toward the culminating assessment and goals.

Figure 7.1   These steps can help the teacher link standards, goals, and assessment to the demonstration of student learning.

the form of a project that students work on for several weeks, or it could be an event task that they complete during one or two class periods. This final assessment should be authentic or realistic, and it should be one that is engaging to the students. The culminating experience is the ultimate learning experience as well as the summative assessment. It is this final performance or product that ultimately demonstrates the students' level of achievement of unit goals and standards.

Once you have established the student goals for your unit, then you must think about ways that students could provide evidence of the achievement of those goals through the demonstration of the knowledge, skills, and abilities in a culminating performance or the creation and submission of a final product. Culminating experiences should provide the students with the opportunity to apply what they have learned in a way that is authentic to the activity or in a real-life application. To help guide you as you design a culminating assessment for an activity unit, ask yourself the questions featured in figure 7.2. Using these guiding questions, we have developed culminating performances and the progressive assessments examples for three activity units—tumbling, archery, and golf.

In the culminating performance or product, the student may take on the role of an athlete, a coach, a sport or fitness writer, director, sports announcer, or other roles that are appropriate to the task. The performance or product may take the form of the following items in figure 7.3.

Progressive Learning Activities and Assessments

Progressive learning activities and assessments should be designed to help the student achieve the broad targeted standards and specific unit goals. Therefore, the progressive learning activities should relate directly to the unit goals and provide students with experiences in which they are able to learn the essential, identified knowledge and skills that are needed to complete the culminating assessment successfully. Performance-based assessments should be interwoven with the learning activities throughout the unit so that students receive feedback on how they are progressing toward goals. The teacher also receives information about the appropriateness of instruction. These formative assessments are

---

Guidelines for Designing Culminating Assessments

1. What is the nature of the activity? In this activity, how are students expected to use the skills and knowledge?

2. How can my students demonstrate that they can apply knowledge and skills authentically in this activity?

3. How can I design the assessment so that it is meaningful and has real-life applications for my students?

4. How can I make this culminating assessment an interesting and fun learning experience that fully engages my students?

5. Should the culminating assessment be a performance or a product that students complete? What is my rationale? Should I have students complete both?

6. How can I design the culminating experience so that I am assessing all three educational domains: psychomotor, cognitive, and affective?

7. What is the culminating assessment?

8. Should it be a group or individual effort?

9. Is the culminating assessment designed so that students of all ability levels can complete the assessment successfully at their level of performance?

10. What criteria should students have to achieve when completing the culminating assessment? How can I encourage students to use higher-order thinking skills: synthesis, evaluation, analysis, and so on?

11. How do I evaluate student performance on the culminating assessment?

12. How much does the culminating experience contribute to the student's learning and grade?

13. Is the culminating assessment efficient?

Figure 7.2 These guidelines provide questions that the teacher can ask to design effective culminating assessments that authentically measure student learning and achievement goals.

Possible Culminating Performances and Products

- Perform a gymnastic routine.
- Develop a brochure on fitness and good sporting behavior.
- Develop a multimedia presentation.
- Choreograph and perform a creative dance routine.
- Create a folk or square dance.
- Develop a display of fitness centers in the community.
- Develop a class newspaper.
- Design and teach an aerobic dance routine.
- Make a videotape about a sport, dance, or fitness.
- Assume the role of a sports writer and write a collection of columns, articles, or editorials.
- Play in a sport tournament.
- Develop a slide show with script.
- Write and perform a skit.
- Develop a portfolio.
- Officiate or score a game.
- Write a journal about learning experiences dealing with sport or fitness.
- Develop a fitness or sport Web site.
- Plan and direct a tournament.
- Be a radio or TV announcer for a game.
- Keep a log of physical activity.
- Coach a youth sport team.
- Design a personal fitness program.
- Teach younger children skills, games, or dance.
- Analyze a video performance of an athlete or dancer.

Figure 7.3   Here is a list of various types of assessments that could be used in a wide variety of units as culminating assessments to measure achievement of standards or goals.

progressive because they require the students to learn, perform, and apply more difficult strategies, concepts, skills, and skill combinations as the unit progresses—all of which gradually move the student toward the accomplishment of the culminating performance or product. They provide feedback both to the teacher and to the students about their progression toward the achievement of the culminating assessment and, therefore, the broad and specific goals.

Because the assessments are integrated with the learning and practice activities throughout the unit, this assessment is referred to as a *continuous performance-based assessment.* The progression of instructional and assessment activities should include and extend from learning activities that begin with the initial practice of a skill in which the focus is to learn, practice, and ultimately demonstrate the critical performance elements (also referred to as learning cues). The progression of learning activities are the **extension, refinement,** and **application**

tasks (Rink 1998) in which the skills are then performed in controlled situations that model the ways the skill is performed in a game play situation (e.g., tennis) or a performance activity (e.g., gymnastics).

Tumbling Unit

Gymnastics and tumbling are popular activities with adolescents. A unit in tumbling can provide students with many challenging and fun learning activities. Participation in tumbling can help students develop upper-body strength and endurance, flexibility, coordination, and balance. Working together in partners and small groups gives students opportunities to develop social skills: As they learn and practice their routines, they also assist and encourage one another. Because students come with varied levels of interest and abilities, it is important to build individual choice into learning and assessment tasks. Each of the assessment samples (figures 7.4 and 7.5) presented provide general guidelines under which students are free to make choices about the skills in each category that they will master and perform in their routines.

Culminating Assessment and Rubric

A sample culminating performance for a tumbling unit and a sequence of continuous, "checkpoint" (Lambert 1999) progressive assessments, which are integrated with learn-ing activities, are presented in figure 7.7. Table 7.1 summarizes the culminating performance guidelines for the unit.

It is important to note that in this per-formance-based assessment, the students are permitted to choose the skills they wish to perform and how they plan to transition from one skill to another. The routines are optional: The students create them according to criteria that are authentic to the sport of tumbling. This strategy also allows for individual stu-dent differences, abilities, and preferences. Students of all levels of ability can be very successful and enjoy the experience.

Relevant National Standards for a Tumbling Unit

1. Demonstrates competency in many movement forms and proficiency in a few forms.
2. Applies movement concepts and principles to the learning and development of motor skills.
5. Demonstrates responsible personal and social behavior in physical settings.
7. Understands that physical activity provides opportunities for enjoyment, challenge, self-expression, and social interaction.

Figure 7.4   Four National Standards for Physical Education (NASPE 1995) are identified for student achievement through participation in this unit of instruction.

Reprinted from *Moving Into the Future: National Standards for Physical Education* (1995) with permission from the National Associa-tion for Sport and Physical Education (NASPE), 1900 Association Drive, Reston, VA 20191-1599.

Goals for a Tumbling Unit

1. Students master four or more tumbling skills at their assigned level in each of the following categories: upright balance, inverted balance, upright agility, inverted agility, forward and backward rolls (United States Gymnastics Federation 1992). Lists are provided to students with tumbling skills at the beginning, intermediate, and advanced level for all of the skill categories.
2. Students demonstrate the ability to analyze skills in each of the six tumbling skill categories at their performance level, and they apply the biomechanical principles learned to give feedback to peers.
3. Students are able to put skills together according to event guidelines to perform sequences of 3 to 10 skills.
4. Students demonstrate the ability to work positively and collaboratively in a small group to accomplish group goals.
5. Students demonstrate the ability to accurately judge peer tumbling sequence performances.
6. Students demonstrate the ability to work independently within a small group to improve skills and to develop and refine skill sequences.
7. Students identify feelings that they experienced while learning, refining, and performing skills and skill sequences and while helping members of their team improve during the unit.
8. Students demonstrate the ability to be creative by composing skill sequences or routines according to class guidelines.
9. Students demonstrate knowledge of principles of training to design a personal conditioning routine to help improve strength and flexibility for tumbling.

Figure 7.5   The goals, which are identified here for this tumbling unit, were developed by the teacher to lead students toward the achievement of specific unit goals and the broader-based national standards identified in figure 7.4.

Reprinted from *Moving Into the Future: National Standards for Physical Education* (1995) with permission from the National Associa-tion for Sport and Physical Education (NASPE), 1900 Association Drive, Reston, VA 20191-1599.

Figure 7.6   Gymnastics can be enjoyable for all levels of ability.

Culminating Performance for a Tumbling Unit

Perform a routine in at least two events in the class gymnastics meet. Select two events, then create the routine in each event according to the guidelines for the event. You may choose from the following events: vaulting, balance beam, pommel horse, uneven bars, parallel bars, rings, and horizontal bar. You must also serve as a judge for two events in which you are not performing. This means you need to attend a judges' training session held during class for each event you choose to judge. There will be three meets held during the unit. Your best performance on each event serves as your individual evaluation. If you would prefer not to perform in front of a live audience, you may perform your routine at another time while being videotaped. The judges then evaluate your videotaped performance as you meet performance. Everyone is encouraged to perform in person, as it is more authentic to the sport of gymnastics. The class is divided into four teams of seven students. Team scores are the sum of the top four scores for each team on each event.

Figure 7.7   This culminating assessment requires students to create and perform routines in class meets and to evaluate other performances. This is an example of a culminating performance that is authentic to the activity.

Table 7.1   Guidelines for the Culminating Performance of a Tumbling Unit

At the completion of the tumbling unit, each student creates and performs a sequence of tumbling movements in a routine for a class meet according to the following criteria:

The sequence must contain 10 movements.

The sequence must include a variety of movements, with at least one skill from each of the following categories: forward and backward rolls, upward agility movements, inverted agility skills, upright balances, and inverted balances.

The sequence must contain movement in forward, backward, and sideward directions.

The sequence must have a definite beginning and ending.

The sequence should be continuous, with no stops (with the exception of balance skills, which must be held for at least three seconds), and it should have smooth transitions from one movement to the next.

The movements should be performed with amplitude and good form.

You may choose to perform the sequence for the class or for only the instructor and judges.

You may choose to perform the routine with or without music.

Before performing the tumbling routine, you must submit the routine form, which includes the names of the skills and the order and direction in which they will be performed. Also on the routine form, you must include a diagram of the floor pattern for the routine.

A scoring guide or rubric should be developed and shared with students before the culminating performance. Students may then use the rubric to score each other during practice performances for feedback. A sample of a scoring rubric is provided in table 7.2.

Continuous Performance-Based Assessments

To give students continuous feedback in a progressive manner as they participate in learning activities to prepare for the culminating

Table 7.2 Culminating Performance Scoring Rubric for a Tumbling Unit

	Level
Gold Medal Performance	A

Contained a variety of at least 10 different movements.
All skills were performed correctly.
Contained at least one skill from each of the six categories.
Contained movements in forward, backward, and sideward directions.
Contained an observable beginning and end.
Demonstrated smooth transitions from one move to the next.
All movements and transitions were performed with good form and high amplitude.

Silver Medal Performance   B

Contained a variety of at least 10 different movements.
Most skills were performed wthout error.
Contained at least one skill from each of the six categories.
Contained movements in forward, backward, and sideward directions.
Routine had a definite beginning and end.
Sequence was continuous with smooth transitions.
Performed with good form and good amplitude.

Bronze Medal Performance   C

Contained at least 10 movements but repeated one skill.
Errors occurred in at least two skills.
Contained skills from at least five of the six skill categories.
Contained movements in two directions only.
Contained a definite beginning and ending.
Sequence was continuous, but transitions lacked fluidity.
Some form breaks and breaks in amplitude.

Novice Performance   D

Contained less than 10 movements and repeated more than one movement.
Errors occurred in more than two skills.
Did not include skills from five or more categories.
Contained movements in two directions only.
Contained a definite beginning but did not hold the ending.
Sequence had frequent stops and breaks and was not continuous.
Had many skill-form breaks and a total lack of amplitude.

This rubric is designed to incorporate the performance criteria that appeared in the guidelines that students received at the beginning of the unit.

performance, the teacher should include a series of shorter and similar—yet progressive—performance assessments throughout the course of the unit. After students have been introduced to a group of skills and have had an opportunity to learn, practice, and master them, it is a good time for this type of performance assessment. Following Lambert (1999), we refer to these progressive authentic assessments of students' performances, which are spaced strategically throughout the unit, as *checkpoints*. A checkpoint is a designated point in the unit (e.g., one day each week or every two weeks) that is set aside for a performance-based assessment to check student progress toward the accomplishment of the culminating experience.

A checkpoint in this example would mean that students would put together a few chosen skills that they have learned at this point in the unit into a short performance sequence. The culminating experience is a performance of a sequence of skills learned in the unit that meet the criteria of the assessment. Therefore, performing short sequences of skills learned along the way prepares the students for the culminating performance, and it gives them feedback on their progression. The idea of using checkpoints to ensure continuous, progressive assessment in a unit of instruction is discussed in chapter 2. Figure 7.8 illustrates examples of progressive formative assessments, which can be used as checkpoints that the teacher could design and implement throughout the unit to enhance student learning.

The continuous performance-based assessments that are provided in figure 7.8 are progressive. That is, each assessment is more difficult: They each require the analysis and refinement of new skills, and they each finish with the performance of such skills in gradually longer and more complex sequences. This series of progressive, performance-based, formative assessments prepare the student for the culminating performance. As the students move from one formative assessment to the next, they gain confidence and build their skill repertoire. They develop the ability to perform skills from the six categories and move from one to the next with a smooth transition, all of which are requirements for the culminating performance. When it comes time for students to design and perform the culminating tumbling sequence, they are experienced and prepared as a result of their participation in continuous, progressive assessments during the unit.

Target Archery Unit

In this section, we provide examples of both culminating assessments and continuous progressive assessments that can be used by you and your students in a target archery unit as checkpoints to determine and monitor student progress (see figure 7.9). Target archery is a recreational activity that students may choose to participate in for a lifetime of enjoyment, challenge, and social interaction. The following goals, standards, and authentic assessments help students develop the skills, knowledge, and competence that are necessary for participation. *Archery: Steps to Success* (Haywood and Lewis 1997) was used as a resource in the development of the learning and assessment tasks provided in this sample. The culminating product in this unit is a student-developed evaluation portfolio. Please note that many of the suggested artifacts from which students may select are performance assessments that students will participate in throughout the unit that are integrated with learning activities. Some of these assessments can be designated as checkpoints so that students and the teacher can check how the student is progressing toward the achievement of the culminating experience and the unit goals.

As in the gymnastics and tumbling unit, the development of the culminating assessment must begin with the identification of broad goals and standards, in addition to specific unit goals and objectives. Before you design assessments to determine how the students will demonstrate and apply the knowledge and skills learned, you must identify what students should know, feel, and be able to do during and at the completion of the unit. In figure 7.10, we have identified four broad National Standards for Physical Education (NASPE 1995) that students could accomplish through participation in the archery unit and through the achievement of the unit goals, and in figure 7.11, we list the specific goals for the unit. We used the unit goals to design both the culminating and progressive assessments for the target archery unit.

Continuous Performance-Based Assessment for a Tumbling Unit

As each skill category and skills are introduced and during student practice of the skills, students complete the following assessments.

1. Use skill check sheets for each skill, which include critical performance elements of the skills for students to use as self-assessments, peer observations, or teacher observations. A sample is included in figure 7.8a.

2. Use a teacher observation, class skill performance checklist, or rating scale. The teacher may include all skills in the category checklist or rating scale. These may be skills that students learned and practiced during a one- or two-week period. As students are ready to perform the skill for evaluation, they inform the instructor. This demonstration gives both the student and teacher information regarding the number of skills the student is mastering and where assistance and more practice is needed. A sample is provided in figure 7.8b.

3. The teacher or a partner videotapes students while they perform target skills. Students then view their own performance of a skill and compare it with a correct videotape performance. Students then analyze and write a paragraph comparing their personal performance with the model performance. In the analysis, the student identifies areas for improvement and strategies for improvement.

4. Following the introduction and demonstration of a new skill or category, students practice the skill in partners or small groups. During practice, students work on analyzing the critical performance elements of the skill. Students write the answers to the following analytical questions:

   • Describe the preparatory position.
   • How is the momentum developed, transferred, and controlled during the skill performance?
   • Describe how the momentum is controlled and absorbed as the skill ends.
   • Describe the ending position.
   • How can the performer move smoothly from the completion of this skill into or out of another skill movement?

   Following the analysis phase of this learning and assessment activity, students can be asked to share their analysis with other groups or the entire class for evaluation and comparison.

   Students develop and perform short sequences of skills as skill categories are introduced and practiced. Through participation in these assessments, students develop competency and confidence in creating and performing skills together in increasingly longer and more challenging sequences. Through this assessment strategy, students progrssively develop their tumbling abilities and get feedback along the way about how they are doing. The teacher may also include specific skill combinations in which students practice beginning and ending differently so that they develop a variety of transitions from which they can later choose as they create and perform the shorter sequences. Students are confident and well prepared when the time arrives for the culminating performance because they have been progressing toward the performance by taking small steps each day throughout the unit. A progression of a sample checkpoint assessment is presented in the following sequence.

5. Design and perform a sequence that includes a forward roll variation. The sequence must begin and end with two different balance skills. the sequence should be smooth and continuous with a graceful transition between skills. The balance skills must be held for at least three seconds. Challenge yourself to include skills that you really had to work at to learn. You perform the sequence in front of the teacher when you are ready for evaluation.

6. Design and perform a sequence that includes a balance skill at the beginning and end of the sequence, a backward roll variation, and an upright agility skill. make sure that you move smoothly from one skill to the next. Be sure to hold the balance skills for at least three seconds to show control, then move into the next skill with a smooth transition.

7. Design and perform a sequence that begins and ends with a balance skill (either upright or inverted), contains a forward roll variation, a backward roll variation, and an upright agility skill. Make sure one skill flows smoothly into the next skill and that you show balance skills for at least three seconds.

8. Design and perform a sequence that contains six skills. The sequence should include at least one skill from each of the tumbling skill categories: rolls, upright and inverted balances, and upright and inverted agility skills. Your sequence should include at least two changes of direction and smooth transitions between skills. Perform your sequence for your partner and use the feedback to go back and polish your performance. When you are ready, you will perform the routine for me for evaluation.

Figure 7.8   In this figure, a series of progressive assessments are included that students complete during the unit to help prepare them for the culminating performance and to give them continuous feedback on the progress of their performance.

Handstand Forward Roll Observation Checklist

Performer: _____ Evaluator: _____ Date: _____

Instructions

1. Stand to the side of your partner as he or she performs the handstand forward roll.
2. Observe your partner perform the skill five times.
3. After each observation, check each of the performance cues that you observed.
4. Focus on only one part of the skill during each observation.

Preparation

__ Arms/shoulders stretched overhead

__ Step into a lunge position

__ Body stretched

Handstand Execution

__ "Teeter-totter" action (as hands go down, back leg goes up)

__ Hands placed on floor shoulder-width apart

__ Shoulder angle remains extended

__ Strong push-off and lift-up with support foot

__ Legs come together

__ Head between arms

__ Body tight and aligned over hands

__ Maintain balance for 2 counts

Forward Roll Execution

__ Hips and legs shift forward beyond the hands to initiate an off-balance position

__ Head tucks

__ Arms bend for soft landing

__ Shoulders and back are rounded

__ Hips and knees tuck

__ Smooth roll out to feet

__ Body stretched with arms extended overhead

Write feedback statements to help your partner improve his or her performance.

_____

_____

_____

_____

Figure 7.8a   A sample tumbling observation skills checklist. A teacher could design this type of checklist for the observation and assessment of tumbling skills.

Performer: _____ Class: _____ Date: _____

Forward Rolling Skills

__ Rocker

__ Tip up

__ Look back

__ Tip over

__ Rock up to feet

__ Squat forward roll

Perform at Least Six of the Following Skills

__ Forward roll to a knee scale

__ Forward roll to a V-seat

__ Forward roll walk-out

__ Forward roll to a lunge

__ Forward straddle roll

__ Forward pike roll

__ Forward roll to a scale

__ Forward roll from a scale

__ Forward roll jump

__ Jump, forward roll

__ Two continuous forward rolls

Figure 7.8b   Forward rolling skills checklist.

Balance skill: _____

Transition: _____

Forward roll variation: _____

Transition: _____

Backward roll variation: _____

Transition: _____

Upright balance: _____

Draw a diagram of your floor pattern in the square below. Mark the beginning and the end of your sequence with an X.

(continued)

Figure 7.8c   Tumbling sequence performance.

Peer Evaluator Feedback

Things you did really well:

_____
_____
_____
_____
_____
_____

Things you can improve:

_____
_____
_____
_____
_____
_____

Figure 7.8c   (*continued*)

Figure 7.9   Archery is an excellent sport for adolescents because it is challenging and fun, and it can develop into a lifetime activity.

Culminating Assessment and Rubric

Once you have identified the broad standards and specific goals that students should strive to achieve, the next step is to design the culminating performance or product that students must complete at the conclusion of the archery unit. Our sample culminating experience for a target archery unit is a culminating product, which the students must submit for evaluation at the end of the unit. We chose to provide an example of a portfolio for the culminating product. We call this final assessment an *archery sportfolio*. The portfolio as an assessment tool in physical education is discussed in more detail in chapter 6. The portfolio, or archery sportfolio, that we describe provides for not only a summative student product but requires students to participate in and collect artifacts of continuous formative assessments throughout the unit.

Through the use of this form of culminating assessment, students attach meaning to and see the value of participation in continuous performance-based assessments throughout

---

Relevant National Standards for a Target Archery Unit

1. Demonstrates competency in many movement forms and proficiency in a few movement forms.

2. Applies movement concepts and principles to the learning and development of motor skills.

3. Exhibits a physically active lifestyle.

7. Understands that physical activity provides opportunities for enjoyment, challenge, self-expression, and social interaction.

Figure 7.10　Four National Standards for Physical Education (NASPE 1995) are identified for student achievement through participation in this unit of instruction.

Goals for a Target Archery Unit

1. Students demonstrate knowledge of names and functions of parts of bow, arrows, and use of safety equipment; information necessary to purchase appropriate equipment; and how to repair and properly store equipment.

2. Students identify, rationalize, and apply safety rules that must be followed before, during, and after shooting a round of target archery.

3. The students are able to identify and demonstrate the critical performance cues for each part of the process of shooting: stance, grip, nocking the arrow, drawing, anchoring, aiming, release, and follow-through.

4. Students are able to identify and demonstrate the cues for how to aim at a target using the point-of-aim method or using a bow sight.

5. The students are able to identify possible errors in the shooting process through the identifcation of arrow groupings in the target and make adjustments to their own shooting technique in addition to their peers' technique to improve shooting accuracy and scores.

6. The students demonstrate improvement across the unit in shooting performance scores while participating in individual and team class shooting rounds of various distances.

7. The students articulate their feelings about their skill development and participation in the sport of target archery, and they develop a plan for how they can continue to participate in the sport, if desired.

Figure 7.11　The goals, which are identified here for this target archery unit, were developed by the teacher to lead students toward the achievement of specific unit goals and the broader-based national standards identified in figure 7.10.

the unit, and as a result, they take them more seriously. Compiling a working portfolio and putting together the final product or evaluation portfolio is not only an *assessment* process but also a *learning* process for the students. In the following section, we provide a sample portfolio guideline and sample rubric (see figures 7.12 and 7.13), which provide students with specific criteria that they must achieve based on the unit goals. You would provide the students with a copy of the guidelines and rubric or scoring guide and explain them at the beginning of the unit.

Listed in the portfolio guidelines as possible artifacts, which the student may include as evidence of achievement of broad and specific unit goals, are possible progressive performance-based assessments that you may include as formative assessments across the length of the unit. These sample progressive assessments provide the students with feedback about their progress and assist them in the completion of the

archery sportfolio, the culminating product assessment.

Continuous Performance-Based Assessments

In this section, we provide you with sample continuous, progressive performance-based assessments that are linked with learning and practice activities in which students participate across the archery unit to develop knowledge and skill and to receive feedback (see figure 7.14). Students are encouraged to select from these formative assessments artifacts to include in their portfolio, those that provide the best evidence of their achievement of the unit goals and the portfolio criteria.

Through participation in the sequence of continuous, progressive performance-based assessments throughout the unit, which were designed to link to the broad standards and specific unit goals, students are provided with

Guidelines for a Target Archery Unit Portfolio

You complete and submit an archery sportfolio for this unit, in which you provide evidence of your knowledge, skill improvement, and skill performance level in the sport of target archery. In order to collect documents for evidence during the unit, you must participate in assessments that are integrated with learning and practice activities, must complete individual projects throughout the unit, and then must file them in your working portfolio folder. Be sure to record your artifacts in your record log. Later you make judgments about which artifacts show improvement and what your best work is to determine inclusion in your evaluation archery sportfolio. You should organize your portfolio via your artifacts, all of which provide evidence of the following:

- Your knowledge of target archery equipment, purchasing information, repair, and storage
- Safety rules that must be followed when shooting in a group (in class or outside of class), alone, or with a friend
- How to aim at a target with or without a bow sight
- Knowledge of critical elements of the shooting stance and process: stance, grip, nocking the arrow, drawing, anchoring, aiming, release, and follow-through
- Identification of errors and corrections that you can make in the critical elements of the shooting process
- Evidence of your competence of the shooting process

Your evaluation archery sportfolio will be submitted on the final day of the archery unit. Your portfolio will be evaluated based on the portfolio scoring guide or rubric, which is found on the second page of this handout.

Figure 7.12 These guidelines include specific performance criteria that students must follow when developing their portfolio for the target archery unit. Students should receive the guidelines at the beginning of the unit.

Levels of Organization, Presentation, and Content

	Level
Outstanding	A
• Portfolio is very well organized and neatly presented.	
• Sections are divided by unit goals and clearly marked.	
• A table of contents is provided with each artifact listed in order, under the correct unit goal.	
• All materials are neatly and creatively displayed.	
• Complete title page is provided.	
• Portfolio registry and reflection page is provided after the title page.	
• Artifacts provide solid evidence of achievement of unit goals.	
• Artifacts clearly demonstrate student improvement across the unit.	
• Reflections provide a rich and clear explanation of each artifact and why it is included as evidence.	
Very good	B
• Organized and neat.	
• Divided into sections by unit goals, marked but not clearly.	
• Table of contents included.	
• Complete title page provided.	
• Portfolio registry provided with reflection.	
• Documents provide evidence of achievement of most goals.	
• Documentation provides evidence of improvement in some areas.	
• Reflections lack depth and explanation.	
Needs improvement	C
• Unorganized and sloppy.	
• Artifacts are not divided into sections by unit goals.	
• Table of contents not included or unorganized.	
• Title page missing.	
• Portfolio registry missing or incomplete.	
• Documents provide little or weak evidence of some unit goals.	
• Reflections lack depth of explanation.	
• Little or no evidence of improvement provided.	

Figure 7.13 This rubric for a target archery unit incorporates the criteria from the portfolio guideines and is used to evaluate student portfolios.

Continuous Performance-Based Assessment for a Target Archery Unit

1. Shooting process checklist and rating scales completed and signed by a partner or the teacher while student shoots an end of arrows. This assessment should be completed every other day during the first week of shooting practice.

2. Complete a videotape segment of each student shooting an end of arrows. Students view personal shooting segments and complete the shooting process checklist, then view a model performance. Each student then writes a self-performance analysis, in which he or she identifies strengths and weaknesses and proposes recommendations for how to improve the weaknesses in the shooting process.

3. Evidence of student participation, practice, and progress in target shooting from the beginning to the end of the archery unit. Some possible choices for assessments that students could use as artifacts for their portfolio may include any of the following:

   • Dated score cards for various shooting distances
   • Graph of shooting progress at various distances across time
   • Arrow grouping charts that show improvement in accuracy
   • Arrow grouping charts across consecutive shooting events for each shooting distance with a written analysis of shooting errors that may have been causing each grouping of the arrows in the target and a plan for improvement. These should be followed with further grouping charts that show improvement.

   Refer to the sample in figure 7.14a

4. Scorecards from rounds shot at various distances during class practice, which demonstrate improvement in shooting ability across time. Students may show improvement by developing a graph in which they chart scores across dates for each distance.

   Refer to the sample in figure 7.14b

5. Scorecards from formal student participation in competitive contests inside or outside of the class, or scorecards from practice outside of school.

6. In groups, students plan and implement a class tournament. Duties for groups would include tournament planning committee, officials, awards committee, media committee, and special events committee.

7. Students participate in the repair of class archery equipment during and at the end of the unit.

8. Students develop a resource guide on target archery by gathering information from the Internet, books, or experts in the community. The resource guide could be used for the next class in target archery.

9. Students develop a plan for how they will continue to participate in target archery outside of school.

10. Students develop a plan for how to secure their personal equipment: what it will cost and how they will raise the money.

11. Students identify facilities or space where they can participate in target archery.

12. Students develop a proposal to start a target archery club at school or in the community so that they can participate in target archery activities with friends or family members.

13. Students write an essay in which they describe why or why they would not pursue involvement in target archery beyond this class.

Figure 7.14   In this figure, a series of progressive assessments are included that students complete during the unit to help prepare them for their culminating product, the archery sportfolio.

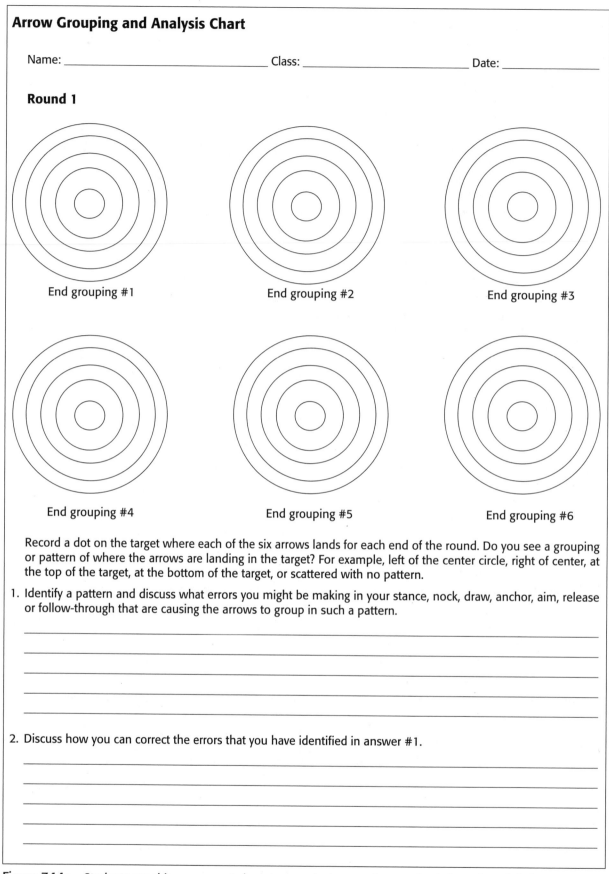

Arrow Grouping and Analysis Chart

Name: _____ Class: _____ Date: _____

Round 1

End grouping #1

End grouping #2

End grouping #3

End grouping #4

End grouping #5

End grouping #6

Record a dot on the target where each of the six arrows lands for each end of the round. Do you see a grouping or pattern of where the arrows are landing in the target? For example, left of the center circle, right of center, at the top of the target, at the bottom of the target, or scattered with no pattern.

1. Identify a pattern and discuss what errors you might be making in your stance, nock, draw, anchor, aim, release or follow-through that are causing the arrows to group in such a pattern.

_____
_____
_____
_____
_____
_____

2. Discuss how you can correct the errors that you have identified in answer #1.

_____
_____
_____
_____
_____
_____

Figure 7.14a Students use this assessment chart to record where each arrow lands in each end during a round of shooting to determine if there is a grouping or pattern that can be linked to a particular shooting error.

Name: _____ Class: _____ Date: _____

Round #1 20 feet

1	2	3	4	5	6
T					

Round #2 20 feet

1	2	3	4	5	6
T					

Round #3 20 feet

1	2	3	4	5	6
T					

Round #4 20 feet

1	2	3	4	5	6
T					

Figure 7.14b   Archery scoring forms and performance graph.

many assessment documents for inclusion in their working portfolio. Students can consider these documents to make decisions about how to provide documentation of their achievement of broad and unit goals and how to complete the evaluation portfolio as a culminating assessment.

Golf Unit

We have included sample assessments for a unit of golf because it is a very popular lifetime sport and a healthy form of physical activity (figure 7.15). Through an in-depth instructional unit in which assessments are continuous, progressive, authentic, and linked with learning activities, students gain knowledge, skill, competence, and experience, which may ultimately encourage them to participate in golf for a lifetime. It is important to remember at this point that the more progressive and authentic the learning and assessment activities, the more students develop competence, confidence, experiences, knowledge, and skills that are realistic to the sport of golf. A student could stand on a mat and hit golf balls into the curtains for weeks, but that practice alone does not prepare them to play a round of golf. Practice and assessment of performance in a variety of realistic golf situa-

Figure 7.15   Golf is a very popular lifetime sport.

tions are needed. For example, they can hit from uphill and downhill sites, from different distances and at different targets, or with different clubs. Through this type of experience and feedback, along with the development of competence and confidence in their abilities and decisions, students are more likely to participate in golf throughout a lifetime. *Golf: Steps to Success* (Owens and Bunker 1995) was consulted as a resource in the development of these learning and assessment tasks.

Similar the tumbling and target archery units, here we identify broadly what we want students to accomplish in physical education and those national standards that we think students can achieve through participation in an in-depth golf instructional unit. We also identify specific goals for the golf unit to give the teacher direction for planning and to give the students goals to work toward. To accomplish these standards and goals, the unit must be of sufficient length and depth. Just introducing students to skills, rules, and knowledge does not guarantee that they will develop to the point at which they are able and willing to apply them in a realistic setting, which in this case is playing a game of golf. To help them develop confidence and competence in their ability as players, we must provide students with enough appropriate learning and assessment experiences in which they test these skills and knowledge. They can do so when they learn a progression of simple-to-complex skills and when they practice in a variety of environmental settings, which is really the essence of golf. The standards, as identified from the National Standards for Physical Education (NASPE 1995) and the specific goals for a unit on golf are provided in figures 7.16 and 7.17. We used these standards and goals as the guides in the development of the culminating and progressive performance-based formative assessments presented here for golf.

Culminating Assessment and Rubric

After we identified the standards and unit goals, we were then able to develop the unit culminating assessment. As we read through the goals, it was obvious that the culminating assessment would need to be a performance-based assessment in which students were

---

Relevant National Standards for a Golf Unit

1. Demonstrates competency in many movement forms and proficiency in a few forms.
2. Applies movement concepts and principles to the learning and development of motor skills.
3. Exhibits a physically active lifestyle.
5. Demonstrates responsible personal and social behavior in physical activity settings.
7. Understands that physical activity provides opportunities for enjoyment, challenge, self-expression, and social interaction.

Figure 7.16   Five National Standards for Physical Education (NASPE 1995) are identified as possible targets for student achievement through participation in this instructional unit.

Reprinted from *Moving Into the Future: National Standards for Physical Education* (1995) with permission from the National Association for Sport and Physical Education (NASPE), 1900 Association Drive, VA 20191-1599.

Goals for a Golf Unit

1. Student is able to demonstrate how to grip the golf club, using either the interlocking or overlapping grip.
2. Student is able to demonstrate the ability to correctly address the ball and assume the correct stance for a full swing.
3. Student is able to identify and demonstrate the process and performance cues for the full swing with a wood while hitting balls from a tee.
4. The student is able to analyze his or her full swing performance as well as that of a peer through observation and offer corrective feedback for improvement.
5. Student defines and appropriately uses identified golf terms.
6. Student is able to name and identify the areas of a golf hole and course.
7. Student is able to identify errors in ball flight: hook, slide, topping the ball, a mulligan, and they are able to identify how to correct the swing to avoid these errors.
8. Student is able to identify and demonstrate the performance cues when hitting a chip and pitch shot from a mat or the grass.
9. Student is able to identify and make necessary adjustments to the lie of the ball, the stance, the distance to the target, and the selection of the club when hitting a shot from the fairway, the rough, a sand trap, or an approach stroke.
10. Student is able to demonstrate a correct grip and stance, preparation, swing, and follow-through for putting.
11. Student is able to demonstrate the ability to play three rounds of nine holes on a par-three golf course.
12. Student is able to identify and apply the correct procedures, rules of play, and rules of course etiquette when playing on a golf course.
13. Student can keep track of their shot progress, golf skill, and knowledge development, both during practice and play.
14. Student can keep track of practice that they participate in outside of class during the unit.
15. Student is able to articulate their feelings about playing golf as a leisure activity.

Figure 7.17   The goals, which are identified here for this golf unit, were developed by the teacher to lead students toward the achievement of specific unit goals and the broader-based national standards identified in figure 7.16.

asked to apply skills and knowledge in an authentic situation. If the unit is taught as an in-depth, multiple-week unit in a high school with block scheduling, then the culminating assessment described in figure 7.18 would be appropriate for the students.

Continuous Performance-Based Assessments

To prepare for the culminating experience and assessment of playing three rounds of golf, the students must participate in a series of progressive learning, practice, and assessment activities throughout the course of the unit. Some suggested learning and assessment activities that can serve as continuous or formative assessments and checkpoints are provided in figure 7.19. These assessments and learning activities were designed to gradually prepare students to be able to complete the culminating assessment and achieve unit goals.

Culminating Assessment for a Golf Unit

You play three rounds of nine holes of golf at the par-three golf course near the school with the class while on a field trip the last two weeks of the unit. Each round has a shotgun start to save time. For each round, you submit a scorecard with scores for each hole and the total score. One member of your foursome signs the card for formal verification. In addition, you need to complete the log sheet for each hole, which will be provided to you. On the log sheet, you record and describe each shot, that you take for each hole, give the approximate distance from the hole, the club used for each shot, and a description of the results. On the log sheet, there is a diagram of each hole on which you diagram each shot. Completing the log sheet for each hole helps you recall, reflect, analyze, and make future corrections in your game play.

Following each round of golf, which is spaced three to five days apart, you use the log reflection and analysis to seek assistance or to modify your practice activities to help improve your play in the next round. You must submit a comparison of the three rounds. If improvement does not occur in your score, you should write a narrative describing any improvements that you observed in your play, despite the score.

During the final round, students participate in a team, "scramble" tournament. Everyone hits their next stroke from the spot where the best of the foursome's ball landed.

During each of the three rounds of golf, the teacher observes you playing at least one hole. During the observation, the teacher evaluates how well you know and demonstrate playing etiquette and the rules of the game.

Figure 7.18   This authentic, or real-to-life, culminating performance and product can be used to assess student learning and achievement of goals and standards.

Continuous Performance-Based Assessments for a Golf Unit

Use the checklist provided by the teacher to have partners observe and assess each other's full swing while hitting balls in an outdoor environment. Students use feedback for further practice to improve stroke. This assessment should be used frequently for further practice to improve stroke. The assessment should be used frequently throughout the unit for the full swing, with woods and long swings (like drives), to irons with shorter swings (like chipping and pitching).

Students are videotaped while hitting golf balls outside. They then observe their own swing and compare it with a videotape of a model swing. They assess their swing using a checklist or rating scale provided for them.

Students hit plastic practice balls with various clubs into designated target areas marked in the gym or on the field. This activity helps students learn how to adjust their stance and line up to the ball, and it helps them select the appropriate club for the specific lay, distance, and situation. To assess the performance, students could record the number of balls that land within 10 yards of the designated target.

Students hit real balls in a school field or at a community driving range near the school. This activity and assessment are very similar to the previous one that was completed at school with plastic practice balls. Students attempt to hit a specific number of balls (15-25) while trying to hit the ball to designated targets of various distances. Students record the number of balls that land within 10-20 yards of the flag. This exercise is completed a number of times so that the student can determine the percentage of balls landing within range of the flag. Students may graph their progress or lack of progress. As they hit balls, a partner uses a target form and charts on the form where the balls are landing in relation to the flag. Students and teacher can then analyze the chart to see if students are developing consistency in their swings or are having directional problems, such as topping the ball, slicing, and hooking, so at that point, they can develop a plan to eliminate the error.

Each group of five students designs a golf hole in the field adjacent to the gym. Each hole must have a tee area, fairway (straight or dog-legged), rough, a water hazard or a sand trap, and a green. Materials to create hole areas are available (i.e., rope to mark off the rough and hazards). Each hole must be at least 100 yards in length. Each group designs a diagram of their hole with designated par and score card. All students have the opportunity to play each group's hole and evaluate the design. Each group evaluates another group and gives them feedback on how well they followed the rules of etiquette and of the game.

Students view a videotaped golf tournament. The videotape includes no audio. Their job is to analyze and write (on audiotape) the commentary that they would hear from the sports announcer on three consecutive holes. Through their analysis and commentary, the students demonstrate knowledge of the rules of golf and an understanding of their strategies that players use while playing different holes (e.g., choices of clubs, how they play the lay of the ball, the wind, the situation such as bunkers, water, trees).

On a field trip, students play three holes of golf and write reflections on how well they played and on how well they know and applied the rules. Students repeat this assessment three times before the culminating assessment.

Figure 7.19   A series of progressive learning and assessment activities are presented here to prepare students for successful completion of the culminating assessment.

Conclusion

In this chapter, we addressed how you can link assessments in physical education to targeted standards and goals in physical education. These initial steps of integrating meaningful, standards-based assessment into the planning process for units of instruction in middle and secondary physical education help you ensure that students learn and achieve important goals in physical education. The first step in this assessment planning process in the standards-based education approach is the identification of targeted broad standards and also the student goals that are specific to the unit activity. We recommend that you first select the broad standards and goals from the National Standards for Physical Education (NASPE 1995) and from your state and local school district goals. Second, you should develop specific unit goals that create a direct link to the broader goals. Once you have identified what students should know, value, and be able to do, you are then able to design the final or culminating assessment performance or product in which students demonstrate the application and achievement of those targeted standards and goals.

We have provided sample standards, goals, and assessments for units in three individual sports. We have taken you through the process by identifying broad standards and specific unit goals and by linking them to a culminating assessment. We then provided samples of a sequence of continuous performance-based assessments, which students complete throughout the unit to prepare for the completion of the culminating assessment. The assessment tasks that we provided in this chapter are samples, which teachers can use as models from which to develop their own assessment tasks for other individual, dual, and group sports and activities. In chapters 8 and 9, we take you through the entire unit planning process for a standards-based physical education program.

The important message that we hope you take away from this chapter is one of accountability! When you expect students to learn and achieve broad standards and specific goals in your classes, you must plan for that to occur. Give them goals to reach, then plan how they can achieve them and how they and you will know when they have accomplished them. Hold yourself *and* your students accountable for learning.

CHAPTER EIGHT

Planning for Continuous Performance-Based Assessment

Rather than merely assessing an isolated skill such as the forehand or backhand drive in tennis, teachers need to focus also on holistic assessment in which the overall quality of the game, tennis in this case, is judged. (Hensley 1997, 22)

This textbook is about the improvement of student learning and achievement in physical education through standards-based instruction and continuous performance-based assessment of student progress toward the exit standards or expectations for student learning. To successfully implement performance-based assessments continuously throughout a unit of instruction, the teacher must begin with the standards-based planning process. When continuous assessment is not planned before the implementation of the unit, it usually does not occur or the attempt at assess-

ment is piecemeal at best. In this chapter, we take you through the planning of a high school tennis unit using the standards-based planning process. This process is first explained in the following section.

The focus of this chapter is to take the reader through the process of standards-based instructional planning in which assessment is a continuous and an integral part of the planning process. It is through this process that teachers begin to see that the progression of learning and assessment tasks and activities can be integrated in the learning process. In this chapter, we take you through the planning process step-by-step, from the identification of unit objectives and national and program standards to the design of scoring guides and learning and assessment tasks for a beginner's tennis unit in high school.

The "design-down, deliver-up" (Hopple 1995) or "backward or reverse curriculum mapping planning process" (Lambert 1999; Kentucky Department of Education 1993) will serve as the foundation of the planning model adapted by us to guide the teacher in the unit of instruction planning process. We have used the analogy of a staircase to graphically represent the standards-based, backward mapping planning model (figure 8.1). In this model, the targeted standards are identified and placed at the top of the staircase. The teacher designs

the unit down the staircase from the standards, then delivers instruction up from the bottom of the staircase. Each step provides what students need to help get them to the next step and ultimately to reach the top, where they demonstrate the achievement of the targeted standards.

In the **five-step, standards-based planning process**, the teacher first determines (1) the major focus of the unit through the identification of three parts: (*a*) the central organizer and (*b*) the targeted national and program standards and unit goals that relate to the standards or program goals. The teacher then develops (*c*) essential questions, which students should be able to answer during and at the completion of the unit. Once the major unit focus and essential questions are stated, then

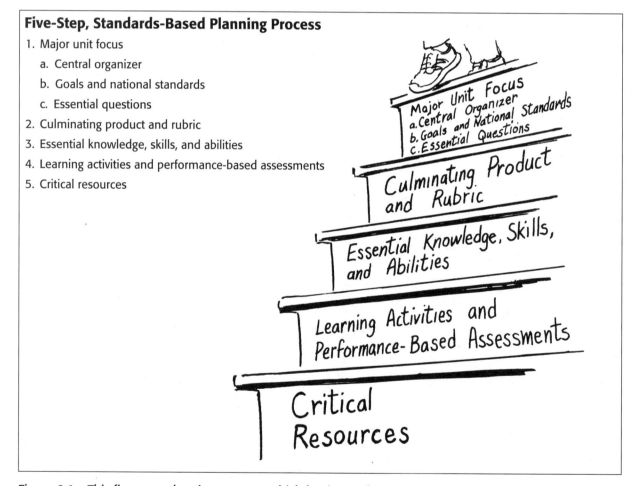

Five-Step, Standards-Based Planning Process

1. Major unit focus
   a. Central organizer
   b. Goals and national standards
   c. Essential questions
2. Culminating product and rubric
3. Essential knowledge, skills, and abilities
4. Learning activities and performance-based assessments
5. Critical resources

Figure 8.1   This five-step planning process, which begins at the top of the stairs and proceeds downward, includes the steps shown in this figure (Kentucky Department of Education 1993). Instruction is then "delivered up", leading students from the bottom step to the top.

Adapted, by permission, 1993, *Transformations: Kentucky's curriculum framework* volume 1 (Frankfort, KY: Kentucky Department of Education), 53-60.

the teacher develops (2) the culminating performance or product assessment and rubric. This is the final (or summative) assessment. In the culminating assessment, students should be expected to apply and demonstrate knowledge and skills that they have learned in an authentic assessment task. The final performance should relate closely to the unit goals and objectives as well as to the overall program standards or goals. Once the items of the major focus, the culminating performance or product, and the rubric are completed, the teacher has officially identified the destination to which the students aspire. The next step is to ask the question, "What do students need to know and be able to do to get to the destination?" The teacher answers this question through the identification of (3) essential knowledge, skills, and abilities or demonstrators that students must learn and apply to successfully complete the culminating performance or product to demonstrate the achievement of the targeted goals and standards. The next step that the teacher must complete in the planning process is to identify the route that students must travel to reach the destination through the careful creation of (4) the progressive instructional activities and assessments that students engage in to learn the necessary knowledge, skills, abilities and demonstrators to be able to reach the destination. In the final step, teachers must identify (5) the critical resources that are needed for the learning and assessment activities. It is at this point that students take the first step in the deliver-up instructional process through engagement in the initial learning and assessment activities and move one step at a time to reach the destination.

This process is referred to as the **curriculum backward planning map** (Kentucky Department of Education, 1993) because the teacher first establishes the destination (where the students should be and what they should know and be able to do), then how the students will get to the destination (learning activities), and finally how the students and teacher will assess their progress as they move toward the destination (progressive assessments and culminating performance).

Unit Major Focus

The major focus of the unit is the starting and the ending point of the planning process. It includes three interrelated sections: the central organizer, targeted broad standards and specific unit goals, and the essential questions. The major focus and its three interrelated sections identify for the teacher and the student what the student should know and be able to do within this unit to accomplish the broader targeted standards. The central organizer statement focuses the unit content around a particular theme, concept, problem, skill, issue, or content, which relates back to the targeted standards and goals. The central organizer should both captivate and motivate the students. To explore and understand the central organizer, the students must be able to ask and eventually answer the essential questions that the teacher generates for the unit. The major focus (and answer) derives from the question, "What should students know and be able to do as a result of participating in this unit of instruction?" In the following section, the three parts of the major focus are discussed in more detail, and examples are provided for the beginning tennis unit.

Central Organizer

Identifying the major focus of the unit is a critical first step for the teacher. The establishment of the major unit focus involves first the identification of the **central organizer**. The organizer can be a theme, a concept, content, a skill, an issue, a problem, or a question that is relevant to students. The central organizer can focus on any one of these or may include more than one. For instance, the teacher may select the skill theme of *striking with an implement* as the central organizer for a sixth grade middle school unit. The focus of this unit may center on how the skill patterns of striking with various rackets, sticks, and clubs are used in a variety of games and sports. A high school physical educator might identify the following problem as the central organizer for a backpacking class: How can we enjoy the wilderness while at the same time make the least impact? The central organizer for our sample instructional unit is illustrated in figure 8.2.

Targeted Standards and Goals

The next step in the planning process is to identify targeted standards, specific unit goals, and objectives that relate to the organizer. There are many sources that can be used to

Concept and theme

Tennis is a sport that you can enjoy playing with others for a lifetime. If you learn the skills, strategies, and knowledge that allow you to play tennis successfully and confidently early in life, then you are more likely to enjoy playing tennis for physical activity and socialization throughout your life, and well into your senior years.

Content and skills

The performance and application of the basic strokes, rules, scoring procedures, rules of etiquette, and singles and doubles strategies of tennis during game play are essential to success in recreational tennis.

Figure 8.2   The unit central organizer for a tennis unit provides a theme, problem, question, content, or skills around which the unit can be developed.

help identify the appropriate objective, such as the following:

► National Standards for Physical Education (NASPE 1995)

► State outcomes or goals

► Local school district or school goals

► Individual student needs, abilities, and interests

The National Association for Sport and Physical Education developed and published *Moving Into the Future: National Standards For Physical Education* (NASPE 1995) to assist school districts, administrators, and teachers in the identification of outcomes that students should achieve as a result of participating in a quality physical education program from grades K-12. All of the seven National Standards for Physical Education are listed in chapter 1, page 4. To provide further assistance to the teacher in curriculum planning, the standards document provides sections for grades K, 2, 4, 6, 8, 10, and 12, in which areas for emphasis, sample bench- marks, and samples of assessments are provided for each of the seven standards for that particular grade level.

For the sample 10th grade beginning tennis unit of instruction presented in this chapter, the teacher began by consulting the chapter for 10th grade in *Moving Into the Future: National Standards for Physical Education* (NASPE 1995, 73-88) to identify appropriate targeted goals and unit content goals for the unit of instruction that relates to the organizer. The targeted standards that were identified by the teacher for the high school tennis unit are defined in figure 8.3.

The number of unit goals is determined by a number of factors including

► the developmental level and ability of the students,

► the length of the unit,

► the amount of time that students are in physical education, and

► the equipment and facilities available.

The teacher determines what is reasonable to expect students to accomplish. Remember: There is no set number! With these targeted national and program standards in mind, specific tennis unit goals are identified that students should achieve throughout or by the end of the unit (see figure 8.4).

The standards, goals, and outcomes that are identified in figure 8.4 now serve as a destination to which students will travel during the unit. They identify what each student should know, understand, and be able to do throughout and at the conclusion of the tennis unit of instruction. They serve as a guide for the teacher as he or she identifies learning activities and assessments in which students will participate to help them reach their destination.

Essential Questions

The third component of the major focus of the unit plan is the **essential questions**, which organize the several targeted standards and focus the unit of study. In the essential questions, the teacher identifies questions that students should be able to answer throughout and by the end of the unit to achieve the unit goals and move toward the accomplishment of the targeted standards. These questions help both the teacher and the students narrow the focus of the learning: They divide

Relevant National Standards for a Tennis Unit

1. Demonstrate competency in many movement forms and proficiency in a few.

   The emphasis is on the demonstration of competence (basic skills, strategies and rules) in an increasing number of more complex versions of at least 3 of the following different types of movement forms: individual and dual sports, team sports, dance, and aquatic. (NASPE 1995, p. 76)

2. Applies movement concepts and principles to the learning and development of skills.

   The emphasis is on the identification and application of critical elements to enable the development of movement competence/proficiency, and to identify and apply characteristics of highly skilled performance to enable the development of movement competence/proficiency.

3. Exhibits a physicaly active lifestyle.

5. Demonstrates responsible personal and social behavior in physical activity settings.

7. Understands that physical activity provides opportunities for enjoyment, challenge, self-expression, and social interaction.

Figure 8.3   Five National Standards of Physical Education (NASPE 1995) were identified as broad goals for students to achieve through participation in the tennis unit.

Reprinted from *Moving Into the Future: National Standards for Physical Education* (1995) with permission from the National Association for Sport and Physical Education (NASPE), 1900 Association Drive, Reston, VA 20191-1599.

Goals for a Tennis Unit

1. The student demonstrates knowledge of and ability to perform the critical performance elements using the following forehand and backhand skills: ground strokes, volleys, and lobs. The student also serves properly. Students work to improve skills through analyzing and giving feedback to partners and through self-evaluation.

2. The student is able to apply and demonstrate the rules of tennis and the rules of etiquette and fair play while participating in class activities and the class tennis tournament.

3. The student applies and demonstrates the offensive strategies of covering court space and the defensive strategy of hitting to open space while playing in the class tennis tournament.

4. The student demonstrates improvement in the performance of the skills of the forehand and backhand drive, volley, lob, the overhand serve, and smash over the course of the unit through participation in progressive practice activities.

5. The student is able to successfully apply appropriate strategies and demonstrate the following skills: the forehand and backhand drive, volley, and lob, and also the overhand serve while participating in the class tennis tournament.

6. The student demonstrates the ability to participate in the game of tennis outside the school setting to demonstrate participation in a physically active lifestyle.

7. The student experiences personal satisfaction and enjoyment while pursuing personal goals while participating in tennis in a competitive and recreational setting.

8. The student recognizes that playing tennis can provide a positive social environment for activities with others.

Figure 8.4   Specific unit goals that are directly linked to the broad national standards are identified for student achievement.

the central organizer into logical, sequential parts for instruction. The questions should require students to think, analyze, and apply knowledge acquired during the unit, and they should be acutely relevant to the students. Only five to seven questions should be identified. The number of questions should be kept to a reasonable number so that they can be answered by students during the course of a unit. The questions should address all of the goals, but they do not necessarily need to be parallel. Because the essential questions help guide learning and assessment, they should be shared with students and posted in the gym. In fact, the questions could be developed with student input. Essential questions that have been identified for our tennis unit appear in figure 8.5.

Essential Questions for a Tennis Unit

1. What are the benefits of playing tennis throughout a lifetime?

2. What are the necessary skills to play tennis successfully? What are the critical performance elements and cues for each of the tennis skills?

3. What major movement concepts and mechanical principles apply to the performance of tennis skills? How do they apply?

4. What are the rules that are necessary to successfully participate in a tennis match?

5. What social skills, rules of etiquette, and sportsmanship are necessary to develop to successfully play and enjoy tennis?

6. What offensive and defensive strategies should you use while playing tenis to outplay your opponent?

7. How can you continue to expand and improve your tennis skills and playing ability beyond this one class? Can you identify effective practice and learning strategies?

Figure 8.5   These are questions identified by the teacher (and sometimes the students) that students should be able to answer to help accomplish goals and standards.

Culminating Assessment and Rubric

Once the elements of the major focus have been identified and the teacher knows where the student is headed (the destination), then the teacher must design a culminating or summative assessment to determine if the student arrived there. Therefore, the following question must be addressed: How will the teacher and the students know if they have achieved the unit goals and targeted standards and at what level? The culminating unit experience in which students participate at the end of the unit can provide much information toward the final assessment of student learning. This final experience (the culminating performance or product) is the final and summative assessment for the unit. In standards-based instruction, the summative assessment should be a demonstration of the student's learning and achievement of the goals and the progress they have made toward the targeted standards. Students should provide a rich demonstration of the application of the knowledge and skills they have learned in an authentic or realistic engaging task or performance. The culminating performance or product then serves as the accountability measure for both the students and the teacher.

When teachers design the culminating experience, they must consider the unit goals and targeted standards. They also must think of how students can demonstrate the achievement of the unit goals and thus progress toward the achievement of the targeted standards in a real-to-life situation. This final assessment should be designed before the implementation of the unit, and it should take into consideration the length of the unit and available time. The culminating assessment should consist of a group or individual student performance, a completed product or project in which the student assumes a real-life role with a specific audience identified, or a student portfolio. The culminating performance, product, or portfolio and the corresponding scoring guides (or rubrics) should be shared with students at the beginning of the unit, so they know from the outset what is expected of them. The culminating performance may take the form of a project that students work on for several weeks, or it could be an event task that they complete during one or two class periods. This final assessment should be authentic or realistic, and it should be one that engages the students. The culminating experience is the ultimate learning experience as well as the summative assessment. It is this final performance or product that ultimately demonstrates the students' level of achievement of unit goals and standards. It is through the completion of this culminating experience that students take the final step to the top of the curriculum planning staircase.

In the culminating performance or product, the student may take the role of an athlete, a coach, a sports or fitness writer, director, sports announcer, or other roles that are appropriate to the task. The culminating performance or product should richly engage the students, and it will probably be multidimensional. The task should be designed to allow children to show their learning in different ways so that all students can succeed at their level of ability. For our beginning tennis unit, the multifaceted culminating performance or product is identified in table 8.1.

Table 8.1 Culminating Performance and Product for a Tennis Unit

Performance

You will demonstrate and apply the basic strokes of tennis, knowledge of the rules and etiquette of the game, and the offensive and defensive strategies appropriately while playing in the class singles and doubles tournament. In addition, you will also serve in some capacity as a tournament official to help the tournament run smoothly.

Choose From Either A or B

A. Portfolio

Your portfolio should include evidence that you have achieved unit goals. The following artifacts must be included in your portfolio:

1. Answers to the unit essential questions, including performance cues for each of the tennis strokes.

2. A reflective journal of your daily class goals, practice activities, and practice performance and assessment results.

3. Graphs that represent your practice progress over the unit for each stroke.

4. A summary of your playing performance statistics for each tournament match and a summary of totals and averages for the entire tournament. Write a reflection of your performance during the tournament.

5. A log of practice and playing episodes outside of class.

6. Documents of your choice. Please check with me before developing your own documentation.

B. Project

In a group of five, prepare for and produce a videotape that promotes tennis as a valuable, accessible, and enjoyable lifetime physical activity. The videotape presentation should also be instructional and address the essential questions of the unit. The videotape should be edited and be of high quality so that it could be used for classes and community recreation programs, for placement in the community library, or for the school's physical education Web site to promote the sport of tennis as a lifetime physical activity.

The culminating performance and products offer opportunities for the students to take a real-life role in three authentic tasks that demonstrate and apply what they have learned during the tennis unit. Allowing the students to choose the assessments they would like to complete gives them an opportunity to work at a level compatible with their ability and learning style. It is important to remember that the teacher must be prepared to allow students class time to complete the culminating performance and products, and serve as a facilitator to assist students when necessary.

Once the design of the culminating performance or product is completed, then the teacher must design a rubric or a scoring guide that is used by the students to help guide their performance and is used by the teacher to evaluate the performance or the product. More information about developing rubrics can be found in chapter 3. The rubric for the unit culminating performance game play is provided in table 8.2.

Essential Knowledge, Skills, and Abilities

Once the teacher has written the culminating performance or product, the next step in the standards-based, five-step planning model is to clearly identify the knowledge, skills, abilities, and demonstrators that students must learn to be able to successfully complete the culminating performance or product. At this point the teacher must ask the following question: "What do my students need to know, understand, and be able to do to successfully complete the final assessment, demonstrate that they have reached the unit goals, and establish their progress toward the targeted standards?" In this tennis unit example, the teacher performed a task analysis to clearly identify what the students must know, understand, and apply about tennis to successfully play in the class tournament and to continue to play tennis beyond their physical education class. It is at

Table 8.2   Culminating Performance Rubric for a Tennis Unit

Proficient Level

Consistently demonstrates the ability to select and successfully use the appropriate strokes

Consistently anticipates ball placement and moves to the ball

Consistently demonstrates appropriate stroke form

Consistently applies and follows the appropriate rule for play and scoring

Consistently applies an appropriate offensive strategy with success

Consistently moves to cover appropriate space on the court, which results in successful play

Consistently follows rules of game etiquette and fair play

Consistently demonstrates the rules of the game and scoring

Competent Level

Demonstrates the ability to select the appropriate stroke and attempts to use it the majority of the time

Demonstrates appropriate stroke form a majority of attempts

Demonstrates the ability to anticipate ball placement and move to the ball a majority of the time

Consistently applies and follows the appropriate rules for play and scoring

Consistently selects the appropriate strategy, but play does not always end with success

Attempts to move to cover appropriate space on the court but is not consistently successful

Demonstrates good sporting behavior consistently and follows game etiquette most of the time

Novice Level

Inconsistent attempts to select and use appropriate strokes

Frequently demonstrates incorrect stroke form

Often is unable to anticipate ball flight and move to ball

Applies and follows appropriate rules for play and scoring

Little evidence of attempts to apply appropriate strategies to the situation

Does not move to appropriate space on the court, often caught out of position on a play

Does not consistently demonstrate appropriate game etiquette or good sporting behavior

this point in the planning process that the teacher again asks the question, "What should students know and be able to do to accomplish the unit goals?" In figure 8.6, the essential knowledge is identified for the tennis unit.

The teacher, through analysis of the game of tennis and possibly through the consultation of tennis resources, identifies skills and abilities that students must learn and apply to successfully participate in the class tournament and in out-of-class recreation. It is not likely that physical education teachers are able to complete this task without the use of helpful resources. *Tennis: Steps to Success* (Brown 1995) was a very useful resource in the preparation of this tennis unit plan. We strongly recommend that teachers consult experts and other resources to complete this step and also

the next step of the planning process. The identified essential skills, abilities, and demonstrators are indicated in figure 8.7.

The identification of essential skills, abilities, and demonstrators and the development of the instructional, learning, and assessment tasks are the "heart of the unit planning process". These items represent the steps that students climb to reach the targeted standards and goals and a higher level of performance in the standards-based, five-step planning model (i.e., the staircase planning model).

Once the teacher has identified the essential knowledge, skills, abilities, and demonstrators for students, the teacher then uses this information to identify and develop a progression or sequence of **integrated instructional and assessment activities.** It is these

Essential Knowledge for a Tennis Unit

- Names, functions, and locations of lines and areas for the singles and doubles tennis courts
- Rules and procedures of playing singles and doubles tennis
- Scoring systems used in tennis: traditional, no-add scoring, and tiebreakers
- Rules of etiquette
- Singles strategies for ground stroke, serve, volley, and lob
- Doubles play strategies: up and back, side-by-side
- Critical performance elements and learning cues for: forehand drive, backhand drive, forehand volley, backhand volley, serve, and lob
- Benefits that can be derived from playing tennis regularly

Figure 8.6 When designing the unit, the teacher must identify essential knowledge that students must possess to answer essential questions, to complete the culminating assessments, and to achieve goals and standards.

Essential Skills and Abilities for a Tennis Unit

1. Begin in and always return to the ready position ("home position")
2. The eastern forehand and backhand grip and the continental grip for the serve
3. Court footwork (shuffle steps, crossover, split stop)
4. Forehand drive and backhand drive
   - Reverse pivot to create space between player and the ball
   - Moving forward, backward, to the side to return the ball
   - Placement of the ball by hitting deep to opponent's baseline, both crosscourt and down the line, or shallow to the forecourt
   - Receiving and returning an opponent's serve with a forehand or backhand
   - Placing the ball in open space on the court—moving the opponent out of position or balance
5. Forehand and backhand volley
   - Hitting an approach stroke to safely go to the net
   - Hitting a volley to the opponent's court
   - Moving to the right or left to return a shot with a volley
   - Placing the volley to the outside baseline corners and the outside service corners
6. Overhand serve
   - The punch serve
   - Consistent toss
   - Flat serve/Eastern forehand grip
   - Spin serve/Continental grip
   - Placement of serve within the service court of opponent on the first or second serve
   - Hitting a hard and fast second serve
   - Placing the service into the back corners of the opponent's service court
7. The lob: forehand and backhand
   - Offensive lob (low, deep trajectory)
   - Defensive lob (high, deep trajectory)
   - Moving to hit a forehand and backhand lob
   - Using the lob at the correct time
   - Accurate placement of the lob
8. Stroke combinations
   - Serve, receive, return
   - Approach stroke, net position, return, volley
   - Volley, lob
   - Forehand and backhand; crosscourt and down the line
   - Rally continuously with a partner
9. Court singles and doubles strategies
   - Return to home base and ready position
   - Make opponent move to get to the ball
   - Up and back
   - Side-by-side

Figure 8.7 The skills and abilities identified here are essential for students to learn and apply to complete the culminating assessment and reach unit goals and standards.

instructional and assessment activities in which the students will participate to learn, practice, improve, and apply the knowledge and skills that they will need to utilize to accomplish the culminating assessments. The learning and assessment activities help move the students up to the next step toward the achievement of the targeted goals and standards.

Progressive Learning Activities and Assessments

This section is the heart of the unit plan. In this section, the teacher identifies and designs activities that engage the student with the content in ways that encourage cognitive and psychomotor learning. The learning and practice activities should eventually lead the student to the achievement of the broad targeted standards and more specific unit goals. This achievement is demonstrated through each student's level of performance on the culminating assessment; therefore, the learning activities should relate directly to the unit goals. They should provide students with experiences that allow them to learn the identified essential knowledge and skills to perform the culminating performance or complete the culminating product successfully. In other words, they need the right experiences to demonstrate the achievement of targeted standards. A variety of performance-based assessments are integrated with learning and practice activities throughout the unit so that students receive feedback on their progress. The teacher also receives information about the appropriateness of instruction. Because the assessments are integrated with the learning and practice activities throughout the unit, this practice is referred to as *continuous assessment*. The progression of instructional and assessment activities should include and extend from learning activities that begin with the initial practice of a skill in which the focus is to learn, practice, and ultimately demonstrate the critical performance elements (also referred to as *learning cues*). The progression of learning activities are the extension, refinement, and application tasks (Rink 1998) in which the skills are then performed in controlled situations that model the ways the skill is performed in a game play situation (e.g., tennis) or a performance activity (e.g., gymnastics). The extension tasks may include such tasks as

▶ moving forward to hit a forehand drive across the net to the opponent,

▶ returning an opponent's hit with a backhand drive to a strategically desired area of the court (crosscourt or down the sideline), and

▶ putting skills together in combinations that are required in a game play situation (hitting a good approach stroke to move the opponent out of position so that the player can move to the net to volley the next return and put the opponent at a disadvantage).

Each activity should assist students in the ability to select and perform the strategically correct skills and skill combinations in a variety of situations that they are likely to encounter in game play or an activity performance. Both learning and assessment activities are designed to systematically move students toward mastery of the unit goal—playing the game of tennis. The assessments, which are integrated with the learning tasks, should provide continuous information to students about their progress. The assessments should also allow the teacher to make informed decisions about subsequent instruction and learning tasks. A progression of learning activities and **integrated assessment tasks** for the beginning high school tennis unit of instruction is illustrated in table 8.4.

Developing a Schedule

After the identification and development of learning and assessment activities, the teacher must develop a time frame for the delivery of the learning and assessment tasks. We recommend that this time table be accomplished through the use of a block plan (see figure 8.8). The teacher identifies the order and duration for which students participate in these activities. Each day, the instructional unit is assigned specific learning and assessment activities. This time line later assists teachers as they develop lesson plans for each class. Through the completion of the block plan, the teacher actually places the learning and assessment activities on the calendar. When developing the block plan, the teacher should keep in mind that the time line should be flexible because students may need more time to learn skills, practice strategies, and complete activities.

Table 8.4 Learning Activities and Continuous Performance-Based Assessment for a Tennis Unit

Tennis Instructional/Learning Activities and Assessments Tasks Forehand Drive (FHD)

Instructional/Learning Activities

1. Observe the teacher perform the FHD on the court, by returning a ball to a hitter across the net. 5x (Following instruction in which critical performance cues are identified and students perform cues w/o a ball while mirroring the teacher.)

2. The student, standing 15 feet from the fence, drops and hits the ball with the FHD to the fence, 15x.

3. Partner Toss/FHD/on court. From baseline area, student hits partner tossed ball with FHD, so that the ball lands in the singles court 8 out of 10x. Repeat for 4 days as a warm-up.

4. Partner Hit/FHD/on court. Same as #3 but partner increases the speed of hits so that hitter must react to the ball more quickly. Criteria: 8 out of 10x, complete 4x.

5. Partner Toss/FHD/Move to Ball. Performer at center baseline, tosser tosses ball to right and left of center, so that performer must shuffle or crossover to hit ball. Criteria: 8 out of 10x, complete 4x. Then increase speed of hits. Use same critiera.

6. Performer Toss/Hits/FHD/Move Forward/Backward. Performer at center baseline, tosser tosses/hits ball so that performer must shuffle back behind baseline to hit the ball and run forward to hit the ball. Criteria: 8 out of 10x, complete 4x.

7. Reverse Pivot to hit a FHD. Hitter at center baseline, tosser tosses/hits ball close to hitter, must use reverse pivot to hit FHD so that ball lands in opponent's singles court. Criteria: 8 out of 10x, complete 4x.

8. Placing the Ball–Hitting the FHD Cross-court. From center baseline, hit a tossed/hit ball so that it lands along the opponent's opposite sideline near the baseline. Criteria: 7 out of 10x, complete 5x.

9. Placing the Ball–Hitting the FHD Down the Sideline. From center baseline, hit the tossed/hit ball so that it travels and lands along the opponent's sideline near the baseline. Criteria: 7 out of 10x, complete 5x.

Assessment Tasks

1. Use the FHD Checklist to identify cues performed by the teacher. (This is to help students become familiar with the observation of the cues and checklist)

2. Peer Observation Assessment #1. Partner observes performance while focusing on the performance of the CPE and uses the FHD Checklist/shares the checklist with student.

3. a. Repeat Peer Observation use FHD Checklist.

   b. Use Practice Record Form to record the number of accurate hits each time–chart progress.

4. a. Use Practice Record Form to record the number of accurate hits each time–chart progress.

   b. Use Peer Observation to check performance cues during at least one trial.

   c. Self Evaluation of FHD progress. Based on data available from previous assessments: Write a paragraph describing progress of FHD & strategies for improvement.

5. Practice Record Form–record successful hits, chart progress.

6. Practice Record Form–record successful hits, chart progress.

7. Practice Record Form–record successful hits, chart progress.

8. a. Practice Record Form–record successful hits, chart progress.

   b. Complete Hit Chart. Mark a dot on the court chart in the area where each hit landed.

   c. Self-Observation/Videotape. Use the FHD Skill Checklist.

9. a. Practice Record Form–record successful hits.

   b. Complete hit chart. Mark a dot on the area of the court on which each ball landed.

   c. Self-Assessment/Videotape. Use FHD Skill Checklist.

(continued)

Table 8.4 *(continued)*

Tennis Instructional/Learning Activities and Assessments Tasks Forehand Drive (FHD) *(continued)*

Instructional/Learning Activities	Assessment Tasks
10. Placing the Ball–Hitting deep to the Baseline. From center baseline, hit tossed/hit ball so that it travels low and lands near opponent's baseline, by applying topspin. Criteria: 7 out of 10x, complete 5x.	10. a. Practice Record Form–record successful hits. b. Complete hit/trajectory chart.
11. Placing the Ball–Hitting the ball into the Forecourt. From center baseline, hit tossed/hit ball so that it travels low and lands in forecourt. Criteria: 7 out of 10x, complete 5x.	11. a. Practice record Form–record successful hits, chart progress. b. Complete hit/trajectory chart.
12. FHD Rally with a partner. Hit the ball back and forth with a FHD with a partner. Move to hit the ball back. Hit ball cross-court to right handed hitter, and down-the-line to a left-handed hitter.	12. a. Count the number of times that you and your partner hit back and forth four or more times. Record longest rally. b. Teacher/Peer Observation. Use Rally Rubric/FHD Checklist.

Backhand Drive (BHD)

Instructional/Learning Activities	Assessment Tasks
1. Observe the teacher perform the BHD on the court, by returning a ball to a hitter across the net. (Following instruction in which critical performance cues were identified and students performed cues w/o a ball while mirroring the teacher.)	1. Use the BHD Checklist to identify 5x cues performed by the teacher. (This is to help students become familiar with the observation of the cues and checklist.)
2. The student, standing 15 feet from the fence, drops and hits the ball with the BHD to the fence 15x, while focusing on the performance of the CPE.	2. Peer Observation Assessment #1. Partner observes performance and uses the BHD Checklist/shares the checklist with student.
3. Partner Toss/BHD/on court. From baseline area student hits partner tossed ball, with BHD, so that the ball lands in the singles court 8 out of 10x. Repeat for 4 days as a warm-up.	3. a. Repeat Peer Observation using BHD checklist. b. Use Practice Record Form to record the number of accurate hits each time, chart progress.
4. Partner Hit/BHD/on court. Same as #3 but partner increases the speed of hits so that hitter must react to the ball more quickly. Criteria: 8 out of 10x, complete 4x.	4. a. Use Practice Record Form to record the number of accurate hits each time, chart progress. b. Use Peer Observation to check performance cues during at least one trial. c. Self Evaluation of BHD progress. Based on data available from previous assessments: Write a paragraph describing progress of BHD.
5. Partner Toss/BHD/Move to Ball. Performer at center baseline, tosser tosses ball to right and left of center, so that performer must shuffle or crossover to hit ball. Criteria: 8 out of 10x, complete 4x. Then increase speed of hits. Use same criteria.	5. Practice Record Form–record successful hits, chart progress.
6. Performer Toss/Hit/BHD/Move Forward/Backward. Performer at center baseline, tosser tosses/hits ball so that performer must shuffle back behind baseline to hit the ball and run forward to hit the ball. Criteria: 8 out of 10x, complete 4x.	6. Practice Record Form–record successful hits.

(continued)

Table 8.4 *(continued)*

Backhand Drive (BHD) *(continued)*

Instructional/Learning Activities	**Assessment Tasks**
7. Reverse Pivot to hit a BHD. Hitter at center baseline, tosser tosses/hits ball close to hitter, must use reverse pivot to hit BHD so that ball lands in opponent's singles court. Criteria: 8 out of 10x, complete 4x.	7. Practice Record Form–record successful hits, chart progress.
8. Placing the Ball–Hitting the BHD Cross-court. From center baseline, hit a tossed/hit ball so that it lands near the opponent's opposite sideline near the baseline. Criteria: 7 out of 10x, complete 5x. A dot on the court chart in the area where each hit landed.	8. a. Practice Record Form–record successful hits, chart progress. b. Complete Hit/Trajectory Chart. c. Self-Observation/Videotape. Use the BHD Skill Checklist.
9. Placing the Ball–Hitting the BHD Down the Sideline. From center baseline, hit the tossed/hit ball so that it travels and lands along the opponent's sideline near the base-line. Criteria: 7 out of 10x, complete 5x.	9. a. Practice Record Form–record successful hits. b. Complete Hit/Trajectory Chart. Mark a dot on the area of the court on which ball landed. c. Self-Assessment/Videotape–Use FHD Skill Checklist.
10. Placing the Ball–Hitting Deep to the Baseline. From center baseline, hit tossed/hit ball so that it travels low and lands near opponent's baseline, by applying topspin. Criteria: 7 out of 10x, complete 5x.	10. a. Practice Record Form–record successful hits. b. Complete Hit/Trajectory Chart.
11. Placing the Ball–Hitting the ball into the fore-court. From center baseline, hit tossed/hit ball so that it travels low and lands in fore-court. Criteria: 7 out of 10x, complete 5x.	11. a. Practice Record Form–record successful hits. b. Complete Hit/Trajectory Chart.
12. FHD/BHD Rally with a partner. Hit the ball back and forth with a partner using both the FHD & BHD. Move to hit the ball back.	12. a. Count the number of times that you rally 4x or more. b. Teacher/Peer Observation. Use Rally Rubric/FHD checklist.

Serving and Receiving

Instructional/Learning Activities	**Assessment Tasks**
1. Observe the etacher perform the Punch Serve on the court 5x. Attempt the Serve without/ball–mirror 8x.	1. a. Teacher Observation & instructor feedback. b. Question students for understanding of the cues.
2. Practice the toss, behind baseline, allow the ball to drop on the court, inside baseline in direction of service court. 20x. Criterion: 10 out of 20x lands in target area.	2. Partner observe toss & give feedback.
3. Overhand throw into the service court. Standing behind service line, use an over-hand throwing action, throw the ball to opposite service court, 5x to each court. Criterion: 8 out of 10x. Move back to baseline and repeat. Criterion: 8 out of 10x.	3. Record # of throws that land in correct service court. 4. a. Use Skill Practice/Progress Record (SPPR), record the # of accurate serves out of 15. b. Partner observes and uses Serve Checklist Form to assess serve form–shares feedback with student. *(continued)*

Table 8.4 *(continued)*

Serving and Receiving *(continued)*

Instructional/Learning Activities

4. Serve to the Fence. Using the punch serve, face the fence, stand inside baseline, serve ball to fence. Land between 3' and 4' from ground. (15x).

5. Serving on the Court. Standing behind service line, serve five good serves, diagonally across to opponents service court (5 to each service court).

6. From a spot 1/2 way between service line and baseline, serve 5x diagonally across to each service court. If 70% of serves are good, move back to baseline and complete #7, if not repeat #6 until reach criterion.

7. Serving from the Baseline. From behind base-line, stand in appropriate area & stance, serve 5x diagonally across to Punch Serve each of opponent's service courts. Repeat 5x. If not at 70% continue to practice each day.

8. Placing the Serve. Divide each service court into quarters (w/chalk, tape, cones). Serve the ball so that it lands deep in the back R & L corners, 3 out of 10x. Then serve to the front outside corners 3 out of 10x. Repeat 4x.

9. Present tips for receiving the serve to FHD & BHD. Provide demonstration.

10. Serve and Return Practice. Groups of 3, server serves from the baseline, alternating between the R & L serving, service courts. One receiver in each service area returns the serve. 10x to each court. Rotate positions.

11. Serve and Return Only Modified Game. W/partner, only use serve and reception in the game. Scoring: successful serve/return = 1 pt. Play to 15 pts.

Assessment Tasks

5. Student uses SPPR, record the number of accurate serves for each trial of 10.

6. Student uses SPPR, record number of successful serves for each trial of 10.

7. a. Peer Observation using the checklist to evaluate serve form. Provide feedback to performer, focus on missing or weak cues.

   b. Partner videotapes performer serving. Student views videotape performance w/instructor for feedback. Completes written self-evaluation.

   c. Student uses the SPPR, to record the # of successful serves for each trial.

8. Student uses the SPPR to record performances.

9. Question students for understanding of things to do to receive the serve.

10. Student uses SPPR, then records # of successful serves and aces. When receiving, records the # of successful returns to server's singles court.

Tennis

Rules, Unwritten Rules of Etiquette, Scoring, History, Current Status, Equipment

Instructional/Learning Activities

1. Present areas/lines of the singles & doubles tennis court. Students receive court handout. Self-test for homework.

Assessment Tasks

1. a. Complete Tennis Court.

   b. Written Quiz/Oral Quiz.

2. a. Complete Scoring Self-Test.

   b. Written Quiz.

(continued)

Table 8.4 *(continued)*

Tennis

Rules, Unwritten Rules of Etiquette, Scoring, History, Current Status, Equipment *(continued)*

Instructional/Learning Activities

2. Game, set, match–scoring:

   a. Traditional

   b. No-add

   c. Tie breakers

   Students receive handout.
   Demonstration games using each of the scoring systems.

3. Students play games: w/traditional scoring, no-add scoring, and tie breaker scoring.

4. Introduce singles and doubles rules. Demonstrate game in which rules are applied. Students are given handout.

5. Introduce Unwritten Rules (Etiquette), honor system, rules of fair play. Students are given handout.

6. Students use the Internet to find information regarding history, current status, how to select proper equipment, conditioning, and common tennis injuries and treatment.

Assessment Tasks

3. Instructor observes to give feedback of scoring.

4. Complete Rules Self-Test.

5. a. Demonstrate application of knowledge during modified games/teacher observation.

   b. Play "You Be the Judge". View tennis game videotapes–stop after a play and students identify the next call and next procedure.

6. Each student is assigned a topic–writes a report and shares with other students through a presentation or handout.

Forehand & Backhand Volley/Playing the Net

Instructional/Learning Activities

1. Identify critical performance cues of the FH Volley–teacher demonstrates on court. Students receive copy of FH Volley Checklist to follow.

2. Students perform FH Volley without/ball–mirroring teacher. Attempt 10 times while focusing on the critical performance cues.

3. Repeat #1 & #2 for the Backhand Volley. Students receive copy of BHV Checklist.

4. Reacting to the ball. Standing at the center net, 3 ft away, partner tosses ball to FH side. Reach out and catch (using a blocking action of the volley to catch) 10x. Repeat for the BHV 10x.

5. Volley with Back to the Fence. Standing with heel of back foot against the fence, partner tosses to FH. Volley ball back to partner. Emphasis on a short backswing and moving forward to hit the ball 10x. Repeat for Backhand Volley, 10x.

Assessment Tasks

1. Question students on cues to check for understanding.

2. Teacher observation gives individual and group verbal/visual feedback.

3. Check for understanding through questions/teacher observation & feedback.

4. Peer feedback.

5. Peer observation and verbal feedback

6. a. Peer Observation–students use FH Volley Checklist. Give feedback to performer.

   b. Student uses SPPR to record # of successful FHV.

7. a. Peer Observation–student use BH Volley Checklist. Give feedback to performer.

   b. Student uses SPPR to record # of successful BHV.

(continued)

Table 8.4 *(continued)*

Forehand & Backhand Volley/Playing the Net *(continued)*

Instructional/Learning Activities	**Assessment Tasks**
6. Partner Toss to FH Volley. Hitter at center net (3 ft away), tosser near service line across net, tosses balls to FH side, hitter returns w/FH volley–lands anywhere in opponent's singles court. 10x. Complete 4x. Gradually increase speed with which ball is tossed. Criterion: 8 of 10x.	8. Peer Feedback–student use SPPR to record # of successful FHV & BHV.
	9. Students use SPPR to record # of successful FHV & BHV.
7. Partner Toss to FH Volley. Hitter at center net (3 ft away), tosser near service line across net, tosses balls to FH side, hitter returns w/FH volley–lands anywhere in opponent's singles court. 10x. Complete 4x. Gradually increase speed with which ball is tossed. Criterion 8 of 10x.	10. a. Check students for understanding through questioning.
	b. Students complete exit slips.
	11. Students use SPPR to record the results.
8. Partner Toss to FH & BH Volley. Hitter at center net, 3 ft from net. Tosser at service court line, tosses unpredictably to the FH or BH volley. 10x to each FH & BH.	12. Students use SPPR to mark the areas of the court where the ball landed for each hit.
9. Partner Hit to FH & BH Volley. Partner at baseline, hits balls to performer's FH & BH side unpredictably. Performer returns the ball with a FH or BH volley to opponent's singles court. Feeder mixes hits up so that the performer must move to contact the ball. 10x to each side.	13. Students use SPPR to record the # of successful passing shots.
10. Getting to the Net. Introduce the approach stroke, run to net, split stop, ready position. Emphasize importance of only going to net after hitting a strong approach stroke, which takes opponent out of position or off balance. Demonstrate on court a number of times.	
11. Hitting an Approach Stroke. Students rally from baseline, when opponent is moved out of position or caught off balance, run to net, split stop, ready. Return ball with FH or BH Volley to opponent's court. 10x each.	
12. Hitting Volleys at Target Areas. Hitter at net position, partner hits ground stroke to FH 10x then BH 10x. Hitter attempts to volley ball first to service court outside corner then baseline outside corner, using the down-the-line or cross court shot. 10x FH & 10x BH. Criterion: hit target 3 out of 10x.	
13. Defending Against the Volley. Hitting Passing Shots. W/a partner at the net position, hit FH drive at him/her. Partner returns a volley to FH/BH baseline corner, return a passing shot down-the-line to opponent's back corner baseline 10x each.	

(continued)

Table 8.4 (*continued*)

Lobs: Offensive and Defensive

Instructional/Learning Activities

1. Introduce the FH Lob critical performance cues. Demonstrate on court, point out difference between the offensive and defensive Lob: cues and placement. Students are given FH & BH Lob Checklist. Go over.

2. Students perform the FH Lob without ball, mirroring the instructor, 10x. Repeat w/BH Lob, 10x.

3. Self-Drop Ball to hit FH/BH Lobs. Standing behind baseline, drop ball to FH side, hit a defensive Lob to opponents' baseline area, 10x. Repeat with BH Lob, 10x. Criterion: 7 out of 10x. Repeat 3 times.

4. Self-Drop Ball to hit FH & BH Lobs to target Areas. Standing behind baseline, drop ball to FH side, hit an offensive Lob to opponent's FH and BH baseline corners. Complete 10x. Repeat for BH Lob, 10x. Repeat 4x for each. Criterion: 6 out of 10x.

5. Volley and Lob with Partner. With partner at net, stand at baseline, hit FH or BH drive to partner, partner volleys to either FH or BH side. Return with an offensive Lob to opponent's FH or BH baseline area. Partner runs back to attempt to return with a defensive Lob. 10x to each side.

Assessment Tasks

1. Question students on the critical performance cues of both FH & BH Lob, and differences between offensive and defensive Lob.

2. Teacher observation and group and individual verbal/visual feedback.

3. a. Peer Observation, using FH & BH Lob Checklist. Provide feedback.

   b. Student records score on the SPPR.

4. a. Peer observation using Lob FH & BH Lob Checklists.

   b. Student records score on SPPR.

5. Student records score on SPPR.

Playing the Game of Tennis: Tournament/League Play

Instructional/Learning Activities

1. Students view a videotape of U.S. Open, Wimbledon, French Open, NCAA, tournament match, or attend a varsity high school or a community tennis tournament match.

2. Students are taken on a class field trip to Beechmont Racket Club, Lunken Airport Recreation Park Tennis Center, or the Four Seasons Indoor Tennis Facility. Students will have the opportunity to observe league play and to play on the indoor courts and receive a lesson from the club professional.

3. Participate in the P.E. class round-robin tournament as a player (singles or doubles) and as a tournament official: tournament committee member, tournament director, official scorer, statistician, line judge, umpire, ball person, awards committee, or athletic training staff.

Assessment Tasks

1. Using the Game Analysis Form Assignment, analyze or assume the role of a sports writer and write an article about the match. Include an interview of a player.

2. a. Write a reaction paper to the field trip experience.

   b. Take a tour of your neighborhood to locate tennis courts which you could use to play tennis with family or friends.

3. a. Each student keeps a record of his/her tournament matches, & individual play stats. From this information, student evaluates and analyzes his/her individual or doubles team performance and makes decisions about what and how to practice.

   b. As a member of the tournament committee, student researches and reports to the committee a list of duties for his/her assigned position. Write a self-reflection about participation as an official in tournament.

Block Plan for a Tennis Unit

Week 1

DAY 1

Learning Activity	Assessment
FHD #1	FHD #1
FHD #2	FHD #2
FHD #3	FHD #3
FHD #4	FHD #4, A,B,C
Introduce game of tennis	#1
Tennis court markings	#1 A

DAY 2

Learning Activity	Assessment
Review FHD	
FHD #4	#4 A,B
FHD #5	#5
Introduce BHD	
BHD #1	#1
BHD #2	#2
BHD #3	#3
Quiz on tennis court markings	BHD #4

DAY 3

Learning Activity	Assessment
Review	
FHD #4	#4 A,B,C
FHD #5	
FHD #6	#6
Review BHD	
BHD #2	#2
BHD #3	#3 A,B
#4 A,B,C	Exit slip on BHD cues
Exit slip on FHD cues	

DAY 4

Learning Activity	Assessment
Review FHD	
FHD #6	#6
FHD #7	#7
Review BHD	
BHD #3	#3
BHD #4	#4 A,B,C
BHD #5	#5
	BHD #5

DAY 5

Learning Activity	Assessment
Review & refine FHD	
FHD #5	#5
FHD #6	#6
FHD #7	#7
Review & refine FHD	
BHD #4	#4 A,B, C
#5	
BHD #6	#6
BHD #7	#7

Week 2

DAY 6

Learning Activity	Assessment
Introduce the serve	
S/R #1	#1 A,B
S/R #2	#2
S/R #3	#3
S/R #4	#4 A
S/R #5	#5
Review & refine FHD & BHD	
FHD #6	#6
FHD #7	#7
BHD #5	#5
BHD #6	#6

DAY 7

Learning Activity	Assessment
Review the serve	
S/R #1	#1 A
S/R #2	#2
S/R #4	#4 A,B
S/R #6	#6
S/R #7	#7 A
Review & refine FHD & BHD	
FHD #5	#5
FHD #6	#6
FHD #7	#7
BHD #6	#6
BHD #7	#7

DAY 8

Learning Activity	Assessment
Review and refine serve	
S/R #7	#7 A,B,C
S/R #9	#9
S/R #10	#10
Introduce placing the ball–FHD	
FHD #8	#8 A,B
FHD #9	#9 A,B
Review moving to hit the ball–BHD	
BHD #5	#5
BHD #6	#6
BHD #7	#7

DAY 9

Learning Activity	Assessment
Checkpoint Assessment	
Teacher evaluates student performance on FHD	
FHD #5 & #6	
Use FHD skill checklist	
Students submit records of performance and self-evaluation on the FHD	
Review serving & receiving	
S/R #7	#7 A,B,C
S/R #10	#10

DAY 10

Learning Activity	Assessment
Checkpoint Assessment	
Teacher evaluates student performance on BHD	
Use BHD skill checklist	
Students submit records of performance and self-evaluation on the BHD	
Review & refine serving & receiving	
S/R #7	#7
S/R #10	#10
BHD #6	#6
BHD #7	#7

(continued)

Figure 8.8   In a block plan, the teacher maps out the progression of the learning and assessment activities for each week and day.

Week 3

DAY 11

Learning Activity	Assessment
Introduce tennis rules—singles	
T #4	#4
Review placing the ball–FHD	
FHD #8	#8 A,B
FHD #9	#9 A,B
Introduce placing the ball–BHD	
BHD #8	#8 A,B
BHD #9	#9 A,B

DAY 12

Learning Activity	Assessment
Placing the serve	
S/R #8	#8
Modified game	
S/R #11	
Tennis rules—singles quiz	
Introduce tennis doubles rules/ rules of etiquette	
T #4 & 5	

DAY 13

Learning Activity	Assessment
Introduce FH & BH volleys	
FHV #1	#1
FHV #2	#2
BHV #3	#3
FHV & BHV #4	#4
FHV & BHV #5	#5
FHV #6	#6 A,B
BHV #7	#7 A,B
Review placing the ball	
FHD & BHD #8 A,B,C & 9 A,B,C	

DAY 14

Learning Activity	Assessment
Review placing the ball	
FHD & BHD #8	#8 A,B
FHD & BHD #9	#9 A,B
Review FH & BH volleys	
FHV & BHV #6	#6 A,B
FHV & BHV #7	#7 A,B
FHV & BHV #8	#8
Review and practice serve	
S/R #8	#8
Tennis rules	#5 A,B

DAY 15

Learning Activity	Assessment
Review and extend volley	
FHV & BHV #9	#9
Introduce the approach stroke	
FHV & BHV #10	#10 A, B
FHV & BHV #11	#11
Modified game	
S/R #11	
Quiz on tennis rules	

Week 4

DAY 16

Learning Activity	Assessment
Review and refine serving	
S/R #10	#10
Review & refine placing the ball	
FHD #8 & BHD #8	#8 A,B,C
FHD #9 & BHD #9	#9 A,B,C
FHD #10 & BHD #10	#10 A,B
FHD #11 & BHD #11	#11 A,B
Review and refine approach and volley	
FHV & BHV #9	#9
FHV & BHV #11	#11

DAY 17

Learning Activity	Assessment
FHD & BHD rally	
FHD & BHD #12	#12 A,B
Introduce scoring in tennis	
T #2	#2 A
Play games using various scoring systems	
Practice serving	
S/R #8	#8
S/R #10	#10
Assignment: T #6	

DAY 18

Learning Activity	Assessment
Review approach & volley	
FHV & BHV #12	#12
FHV & BHV #11	#11
Hitting passing shots	
FHV & BHV #13	#13
Play games with tiebreaker scoring	
Quiz on tennis scoring systems	

DAY 19

Checkpoint Assessment	
Teacher observes and evaluates student	
Performance on the serve and receiving	
Use skill observation checklist	
Practice approach, volley, & passing shots	
FHV & BHV #12	#12
FHV & BHV #11	#11
FHV & BHV #13	#13
Assignment T#6 due	
Assignment #6 due	

DAY 20

Learning Activity	Assessment
Introduce offensive & defensive lobs	
FHL #1	#1
BHL #1	#1
FHL & BHL #2	#2
FHL & BHL #3	#3 A,B
FHL & BHL #4	#4 A,B
Playing the game of tennis	
Assignment #1	

(continued)

Figure 8.8 *(continued)*

Week 5

Day	Learning Activity	Assessment
DAY 21	Practice FHV & BHV FHV & BHV #12 FHV & BHV #11 Review FHL & BHL FHL & BHL #3 A,B FHL & BHL #4 A,B FHL & BHL #5 Play a set of tennis doubles	#12 #11 #3 #4 #5
DAY 22	Practice skills as needed Playing the game of tennis Assignment #1 due	Checkpoint assessment Teacher evaluates FHV & BHV using skill observation check sheet Students submit practice performance record for FHV & BHV
DAY 23	Playing the game of tennis Field trip to indoor tennis club	#2A,B
DAY 24	Playing the game of tennis Doubles partners practice Skills as needed #3 Select tournament committees and give committees duties Committees work together to plan doubles/singles class tournament	
DAY 25	Playing the game of tennis Doubles partners practice skills as needed Play doubles set of tennis Committees work on planning class tournament Assessment #3 A,B	Assessment #2 A,B due

Week 6

Day	Learning Activity	Assessment
DAY 26	Committees organize and conduct class tennis tournament Class doubles and singles tournament begins	Assessment #3 A,B Students not playing take stats Teacher evaluates students during game play using the game play rubric Assessment #2 A,B playing the game of tennis due
DAY 27	Committee organizes and conducts tennis tournament Class doubles and singles tournament continues	Assessment #3 A,B Students not playing take stats Teacher evaluates students during game play using the game play rubric
DAY 28	Same as day 27	
DAY 29	Same as day 27	
DAY 30	Same as day 27 Class tournament completed Winners receive awards	Students submit assessment #3 A,B on Monday

Figure 8.8 *(continued)*

Depth Versus Breadth

It is important that teachers plan units of sufficient duration so that students have ample time to learn, practice, and apply skills and strategies that are necessary to successfully play or participate in the sport or activity. Traditionally, physical education programs have units that last two to three weeks in which students only have time to review skills that they have not previously mastered. Rarely are they introduced to more advanced skills and strategies, and they continue to play the game or participate in the activity for which they lack the skills and strategies to be successful. Units should extend over a sufficient period of time—6 to 12 weeks, relative to the activity—so that students are given the necessary opportunities to master the knowledge, skills, and strategies to become proficient or at least competent in the activity (Siedentop and Tannehill 2000). Students do not learn skills and strategies after one class period. For students to learn and be successful participants, they must practice skills and strategies many times and in a variety of situations, all of which ultimately lead to gamelike applications. If the teacher takes the time to plan developmentally appropriate, progressive, challenging, interesting, authentic, and fun learning and assessment activities, the students become enthusiastic and highly motivated to participate because they see that they are making progress toward the unit goals. When this is the case, the teacher no longer hears students whine the proverbial "Do we have to do more drills?" and "When are we going to play the game?"

Critical Resources

Finally, in the unit planning process, the teacher must identify, secure, and schedule the necessary resources needed to provide the planned activities and educational experiences for the students. Critical resources may include many items such as

- adequate facilities,
- sufficient equipment for all students,
- arrangements for off-campus community facility use or outsourcing,
- arrangements to invite guest experts to teach, lecture, or demonstrate,
- printed or media materials needed to support learning and assessment,
- technology to support the learning process, or
- reference materials needed by the teacher to assist in planning and teaching.

The critical resources should be secured and scheduled before the beginning of the unit for best results and to avoid the unavailability of any of the necessary resources. For the critical resources needed in the tennis unit, see figure 8.9.

Critical Resources for a Tennis Unit

1. Use the six high school tennis courts and one half of the gym for class on bad weather days.
2. Twenty-six tennis rackets and three balls per student.
3. Field trips planned to Riverfront Park Tennis Courts (12 courts) and to Beechmont Racket Club indoor courts. Tennis professionals work with students at each site for one class each.
4. Books: Brown, R. 1988. *Tennis: Steps to success.* Champaign, IL: Human Kinetics.
5. Tennis Internet Sites: **www.tennisone.com**
   www.successfuldoubles.com
   www.professionaltennisinstruction.com
   www.education.Ed.ac.uk/tennis
   www.tenniss_tips.com
   www.tennis4you.com
   www.sportsonwheels.com
   www.altosports.com/tennis.html

Figure 8.9   In this section of planning, the teacher identifies all materials, equipment, facilities, and community resources that are essential to help students accomplish identified goals.

Conclusion

Planning is absolutely essential for the teacher to provide for continuous performance-based assessment and integration of assessment tasks with learning activities. When planning does not occur, teachers often find that the unit comes to an end before they have addressed student assessment. These circumstances are the reason that we tend to see more summative assessment than formative assessment in middle and secondary physical education programs. To accomplish the planning necessary to include continuous performance-based assessment, it is recommended that teachers follow the standards-based, five-step planning model presented in this chapter. In this chapter, we have taken you through the planning process and provided you with a sample unit plan for a 10th grade beginning tennis unit. You could implement this unit plan in your classes or use it as a model by which to develop other activity unit plans in which continuous performance-based assessment is an integral part of student learning experiences.

Using this model for curriculum development, you design from the top of the steps, where targeted standards and goals are identified as the students' destination, down to the learning and assessment activities. The instruction is then delivered upward. You deliver instruction up the steps toward the targeted standards and goals from learning and assessment activities at the bottom of the steps. During the unit, you continue to move the students up the steps where they gain the necessary knowledge and skills to reach the culminating experience. At that point, they demonstrate the achievement of those targeted standards. When students begin at the bottom of the steps and participate in learning and assessment activities that provide them with feedback about their learning, they have an opportunity to gradually move up the steps to the achievement of targeted goals and standards at the top of the stairs.

PART

III

Implementing Continuous Performance-Based Assessment

This section is designed to provide additional examples of performance-based assessments. Grading is frequently one of the biggest problems for teachers, so we have provided our thoughts about implementing an effective grading system. The book concludes with a variety of hints and suggestions designed to help you as you begin to incorporate performance-based assessments into your physical education curriculum.

CHAPTER NINE

Continuous Performance-Based Assessment in Team Sports

Many instructional arrangements seem "contrived," but there is nothing wrong with that. It is the teacher's function to contrive conditions under which students learn. It has always been the task of formal education to set up behavior which would prove useful or enjoyable later in a student's life. (B.F. Skinner)

As we indicated in chapter 8, to effectively assess student performance continually throughout a unit of instruction so that students are made aware of their progress and to inform future instruction, the teacher must plan ahead. In this chapter, we provide you with a sample team sport unit plan: middle school soccer (for sixth graders). We prepared and wrote this unit using the five-step, stan-

dards-based planning model presented in chapter 7. It provides examples on how to integrate continuous performance-based assessments with appropriate learning activities throughout the unit. For the soccer unit plan, we provide the following:

▶ Unit Major Focus

▶ Central Organizer

▶ Targeted Standards and Goals

▶ Essential Questions

▶ Culminating Assessment and Rubric

▶ Essential Knowledge, Skills, and Abilities

▶ Learning Activities and Continuous Performance-Based Assessments

▶ Critical Resources

▶ How to Use the Student Soccer Portfolio

The presentation of the unit sample was done in this manner so that the reader can see the continuous nature of performance-based assessment and how assessment is integrated throughout the unit and integrated with the learning activities through systematic planning. This planning process is also undertaken to make sure that there is definite alignment between learning activities and assessments, and the goals of the unit of instruction and overall program goals. When instructional alignment exists, the learning activities, content, and assessments should prepare students for what they should know and be able to do to achieve unit and program goals. The program goals that are identified for this unit are taken from *Moving Into the Future: National Standards for Physical Education* (NASPE 1995) for the sixth grade level. Starting with the national standards helps the teacher to identify appropriate goals, content, and benchmarks for the grade level desired. For each standard the appropriate content and benchmarks are also identified for the teacher. *Soccer: Steps to Success* (Luxbacher 1996) was used as a resource in the development of this instructional unit.

Unit Major Focus

The major focus of the unit identifies a central organizer, targeted goals and standards, and essential questions that relate to the central organizer. These three items identify for the teacher and students what the unit is about, what students are to accomplish both broadly and specifically, why this unit is important to the students, and what questions they need to answer.

Central Organizer

The central organizer is stated to the students to catch their attention, to draw them into the content, and to get them excited about learning and participating in this unit activity. It may

Figure 9.1   Soccer can be an enjoyable group activity

be a problem, a theme, a skill or set of skills, a concept, an issue, content, or a question that is relevant to the students. The teacher should share the central organizer with the students and post it in a prominent place in the gym so that students are constantly reminded of it during the unit. Teachers may even ask students to identify and write the central organizer for the unit to really engage them. The central organizer of the soccer unit (figure 9.2) accomplishes three relevant goals: First, it is formally stated for the students; second, it is relative to them; and third, it is an issue, a problem, a theme, skills, or content.

Targeted Standards and Goals

For a sixth grade physical education class, we have identified the following broad goals, or National Physical Education Standards (NASPE 1995), that students should achieve through participation in this unit of study. We did this by turning to the sixth grade section of *Moving Into the Future: National Standards for Physical Education* (NASPE 1995). Under each standard, we looked at recommended content and benchmarks for sixth graders, then we selected those standards that we believed students could achieve through participation in the soccer unit. The materials that we found in *Moving Into the Future: National Standards for Physical Education* (NASPE 1995) that helped guide our planning are reproduced in figure 9.3.

These are more specific goals that are identified by the teacher for your specific unit and school context. There should be a direct

Central Organizer for a Soccer Unit

Soccer can be an enjoyable group activity in which to participate and make friends, whether it be in my school, my neighborhood, or my community. Being physically active by playing soccer regularly, I help to maintain and improve my heart strength and muscular endurance. To enjoy participating in soccer, I must be able to perform basic skills and strategies fairly well and know and follow the rules of the game. I do not necessarily have to be highly skilled to enjoy playing the game, but rather, I need to demonstrate reasonable competence in the skills and strategies. Therefore, I must practice them alone and with others to improve. Learning skills and strategies takes time, many trials, and effort, but it can also be a lot of fun. Practicing these skills regularly can help fulfill the recommended daily requirement for physical activity.

Figure 9.2   This central organizer is the theme around which the middle school soccer unit is designed.

Relevant National Standards for a Soccer Unit

National Standard for Physical Education #1: Demonstrates competency in many movement forms and proficiency in a few movement forms.

"The sixth grade student uses skills and combinations of skills appropriately in the context of actual performance situations. . . . Game skills are adapted to the requirements of increasingly complex strategies and are used in more complex, but still somewhat unstructured game environments (e.g., limited rules, modified equipment, small numbers of participants) . . . the student is beginning to acquire the basic skills of selected sport, dance and gymnastics activities.

The emphasis for the sixth grade student will be to:

- Demonstrate mature form for all basic manipulative, locomotor and nonlocomotor skills.
- Demonstrate increasing competence in more advanced specialized skills.
- Adapt and combine skills to the demands of increasingly complex situations of selected movement forms.
- Demonstrate beginning strategies for net and invasion games.

Sample Benchmarks:

2. Foot dribbles while preventing an opponent from stealing the ball.
4. Keeps an object going continuously with a partner.
5. Places the ball away from an opponent (NASPE 1995, 46).

National Standard for Physical Education #2: Applies movement concepts and principles to learning and development of motor skills.

"Students should be able to begin to identify principles of practice and conditioning that enhance movement performance. Students should be able to use information from a variety of sources (internal and external) to guide and improve performance. This student should be able to recognize and use basic offensive and defensive strategies."

The emphasis for the sixth grade student will be to:

- Identify and apply principles of practices and conditioning that enhance performance.
- Use basic offensive and defensive strategies in noncomplex settings.

Sample Benchmarks:

1. Detects, analyzes and corrects errors in personal movement patterns.
2. Identifies basic practice and conditioning principles that enhance performance (NASPE 1995, 48).

National Standard for Physical Education #3: Exhibits a physically active lifestyle.

"The intent of this standard for the sixth grade is the development of voluntary participation in out-of-class physical activities with the goal of developing interest and improving and maintaining an active lifestyle.

The emphasis for the sixth grade student will be to:

- Identify opportunities in school and community for regular participation in physical activity.
- Analyze personal interests and capabilities in regard to one's exercise behavior.

(continued)

Figure 9.3   The selected National Standards for Physical Education, demonstrators, and benchmarks identified for this soccer unit are taken directly from the National Association for Sport and Physical Education (1995). Using *Moving Into the Future: National Standards for Physical Education* (NASPE 1995) can help teachers identify relevant and appropriate goals, demonstrators, and bechmarks for instruction and assessment for unit planning.

Sample Benchmarks:

2. Participation in games, sports, dance, and outdoor pursuits both in and out of school based on individual interests and capabilities.

3. Identifies opportunities close to home for participation in different kinds of activities (NASPE 1995, 50).

National Standard for Physical Education #5: Demonstrates responsible personal and social behavior in physical activity settings.

"Sixth grade students identify the purposes for and participate in the establishment of safe practices, rules, procedures, and etiquette for specific activities. They develop cooperative skills to accomplish group or team goals in both cooperative and competitive activities. Students are expected to work independently to complete assigned tasks."

The emphasis for the sixth grade student is to:

• Participate in establishing rules, procedures, and etiquette that are safe and effective for specific activity situations.
• Work cooperatively and productively in a group to accomplish a set goal in both cooperative and competitive activities.
• Make conscious decisions about applying rules, procedures, and etiquette.
• Utilize time effectively to complete assigned tasks.

Sample Benchmarks:

1. Makes responsible decisions about using time, applying rules and following through with the decisions made.
2. Uses time wisely when given the opportunity to practice and improve performance.
3. Makes suggestions for modifications in a game or activity that can improve the game.
4. Remains on task in a group activity without close teacher monitoring.
5. Chooses a partner that he or she can work with productively.
7. Includes concerns for safety in self-designed activities (NASPE 1995, 50-51).

National Standard for Physical Education #7: Understands that physical activity provides the opportunity for enjoyment, challenge, self-expression, and social interaction.

"Sixth graders attach great importance to group membership; they will choose participation in physical activity to be with peers. . . . Physical activity can become an important avenue for self-expression for these students. Risk-taking, adventure, and competitive activities provide the opportunity for challenge, enjoyment, and positive social interaction."

The emphasis for the sixth grade student will be to:

• Recognize physical activity as a positive opportunity for social and group interaction.
• Demonstrate enjoyment from participation in physical activities.
• Recognize that success in physical activities leads to recognition from peers.
• Seek personally challenging experiences in physically active opportunities.

Sample Benchmarks:

1. Recognizes the role of games, sports, and dance in getting to know and understand self and others.
2. Seeks physical activity in informal settings that utilize skills and knowledge gained in physical education classes (NASPE 1995, 57-58).

Figure 9.3 *(continued)*
Reprinted from Moving Into the Future: National Standard for Physical Education (1995) with permission from the National Association for Sport and Physical Education (NASPE), 1900 Association Drive, Reston, VA 20191-1599.

relationship between the specific unit goals that you identify and the broad goals or standards and the central organizer. We have identified for each of the following specific unit goals the national standard to which it relates in figure 9.4.

Essential Questions

The essential questions help the students focus on and address the central organizer. They should be stated as if the students were asking the questions themselves. Like the central organizer, the essential questions should

Goals for a Soccer Unit

1. In a five-on-five, modified soccer game, students demonstrate competence in the performance of the following basic soccer skills: dribbling against an opponent, passing to a teammate against defenders, receiving and controlling the ball with the foot, thigh, and chest, shooting at the goal, and using the front and side tackle to take the ball away from an opponent. This goal relates to the first National Standard for Physical Education (NASPE 1995).

2. Students demonstrate the knowledge and ability of the basic, offensive off-the-ball strategy of creating space for a pass and on-the-ball strategies of passing into open spaces, leading the passer, and when in possession of the ball, putting one's body between the ball and the opponent, all of which in five-on-five, modified soccer games. This goal relates to the second National Standard for Physical Education (NASPE 1995).

3. Students demonstrate knowledge and ability to apply the basic defensive strategies of marking an opponent closely and moving to block the opponent's passing lanes in five-on-five, modified soccer games. This goal relates to the second National Standard for Physical Education (NASPE 1995).

4. Students demonstrate effective practice strategies and the ability to work independently or with a partner to complete assigned tasks. This goal relates to the second National Standard for Physical Education (NASPE 1995).

5. Students demonstrate the ability to work cooperatively in a group to accomplish the assigned tasks to organize and conduct a successful class, five-on-five, modified soccer tournament. This goal relates to the fifth National Standard for Physical Education (NASPE 1995).

6. Students demonstrate the ability to find the necessary information to solve problems that might arise while they carry out the duties assigned to their group when organizing and conducting the class soccer tournament. This goal relates to the fifth and seventh National Standards for Physical Education (NASPE 1995).

7. Students practice soccer skills and play games outside of school and keep a log to provide evidence of their participation. This goal relates to the second, third, and seventh National Standards for Physical Education (NASPE 1995).

8. Students are able to analyze the skill performance of themselves and other students and give feedback and suggestions for improvement. This goal relates to the first, second, and fifth National Standards for Physical Education (NASPE 1995).

9. Students will identify the benefits of participating in soccer and consider if this is an activity in which they would be likely to continue participation into adult years. This goal relates to the first and fifth National Standards for Physical Education (NASPE 1995).

10. Students should be able to identify facilities and programs in their communities where they can participate in soccer if they so desire. This goal relates to the third National Standard for Physical Education (NASPE 1995).

11. Students will demonstrate their knowledge of the rules of soccer when participating in a five-on-five, class soccer tournament, and they will demonstrate the ability to modify rules of the game to make the game more developmentally appropriate and fun. This goal relates to the first, second, third, fifth, and seventh National Standards for Physical Education (NASPE 1995).

12. Students will demonstrate knowledge of how to improve soccer skill performance by designing a personal practice plan for themselves and their team. This goal relates to the first and second National Standards for Physical Education (NASPE 1995).

Figure 9.4   The soccer goals are specific goals that students are expected to achieve during the soccer unit. In this figure, we have linked each of the unit goals to a National Standard for Physical Education (NASPE 1995).

Essential Questions for a Soccer Unit

1. Why and how can participating in soccer help me reach my daily recommended requirement for physical activity and stay active for life?
2. What offensive and defensive skills should I learn and become competent in performing to be successful and have fun playing soccer?
3. What offensive and defensive strategies do I need to learn and use to gain an advantage against my opponent in a soccer game?
4. What do I need to do to be a contributing member of a team to help reach team goals?
5. What rules of soccer are important to know and follow to make the game fun, safe, and fair for all?
6. What opportunities are available to me at school and in my community to continue to participate in soccer for fun, socialization, and exercise, and how can I work it into my schedule?

Figure 9.5   Students should be able to answer these questions at the end of the soccer unit. Developing essential questions during planning helps the teacher focus on instruction and assessment.

be shared with the students through posting them in the gym or giving them a handout with questions written on it. The questions help guide student learning and achievement of the unit goals and standards. In the box in figure 9.5, we provide essential questions for the middle school soccer unit.

Culminating Assessment and Rubric

In this section, we have provided a variety of different types of authentic performance-based assessments from which you can select one or possibly two as culminating assessments (see figure 9.6 and table 9.1). All of the sample culminating performances and products could be modified for use in other team sport units of instruction.

Essential Knowledge, Skills, and Abilities

In this section, we identify the skills that students must learn to complete the culminating performance and achieve the unit goals and standards. This forecasting is accomplished through a task analysis of the sport or activity in which we answer the question, "What do students need to know and be able to do to successfully complete the culminating experience and achieve the targeted standards and specific goals?"

Essential Knowledge

In this section, we answer the question, "What knowledge must my students know and apply to successfully complete the culminating performance?" In figure 9.7, we identify knowledge that students need to know and apply to successfully complete the culminating performance or product. The essential knowledge and skills that we identify then serve as the guide for developing learning and assessment activities. For this section, we analyze the sport or movement activity—in this case, soccer—and we identify the knowledge and skills that the student must know, apply, and perform to complete the culminating soccer performance or product.

Essential Skills and Abilities

In figure 9.8, we identify the skills that students must be able to perform in the culminating performance to achieve the targeted unit goals and standards. Most of the culminating performances in a team sport require the students to demonstrate the ability to successfully perform skills in a game or modified game situation as indicated in the essential skills identified in the figure.

Progressive Learning Activities and Assessments

The learning and assessment activities that are listed for this unit (table 9.2) represent a progression of learning and practice activities that are designed to help students learn, apply, and perform the skills, knowledge, and strategies in a progression of increasingly complex situations. The progression of complex situations should provide experiences that prepare the students to successfully play in a soccer game. These activities are designed to help students achieve the unit goals. Along with each learning or practice activity, a performance-based assessment is identified that gives the students and teacher information about their performance and progress. For this unit, we have prepared a student assessment portfolio booklet, "Keeping Track of My Soccer Performance" (see page 179 at the end of this chapter). In this soccer portfolio booklet, learning activities and the corresponding assessment record forms or directions are provided for the student.

Critical Resources

When planning your soccer unit critical resources, consider those elements that are absolutely necessary (equipment and facilities), and then those that are necessary to enhance student learning (good textbook resources, articles, appropriate Internet sites, community resources such as community facilities, where the class could be taught, speakers, and other sources of information to excite and invigorate learning). Figure 9.9 illustrates the critical resources that were used in our soccer unit. As you create your list of critical

Student Project

Collect, summarize, analyze, and graph individual game statistics to document improvement in skill performance and game playing ability. You need to demonstrate improvement in skill performance and game-playing ability throughout the class five-on-five, modified soccer tournament. The improvement is documented through the collection, summary, analysis, and graphing of individual game statistics for assists, scores, steals, blocked shots, and effective passes. You must also prepare a final written report in which you discuss your progress, areas of strength, and areas in which improvement is needed. Using the information in the report, you develop a practice plan for how to improve your soccer skills for game play.

Student Journal

Keep a personal journal about learning to play soccer. Each day of class write an entry that includes a summary of practice activities in which you participated, new skills that you learned, and your reaction to your performance in the practice activities and modified game. Was participating in class practice and games enjoyable to you? Why? Why not? Also include a daily log of any practice or soccer games in which you participated outside of class in the evenings or on the weekends.

Student Self-Assessment

At the end of the soccer unit, write a summary of your own assessment of your soccer skill and game play performance. Include a discussion of your strengths and areas in which you think you need to improve. Compare your soccer performance at the end of the unit with your performance as the unit began. In the report include a section in which you discuss why or why you would not choose to participate in soccer on a regular basis for physical activity outside of class. If you plan to continue to participate, discuss your plan for how to do this.

Group Event Task

In groups of four to six, design a modified soccer game that you could play in class or at home with siblings, friends, or neighbors. Give your game a name. List the equipment that is needed. Include a diagram of the playing area with dimensions. Write a sentence or two that states the main objective of the game. Provide a list and clear explanation of the rules and include the following: starting the game, number and position of players, restarts when the ball goes out of bounds, fouls and penalties, scoring, and length of game.

Make sure that your game is inclusive. Everyone on the team should have an opportunity to be actively involved in the game. Discuss modifications that you could make so that students of all abilities and any students with a disability could be contributing participants and enjoy the game. Once you have completed designing your game, try it out. Play the game with your group to see if it works as you planned. Evaluate the game and make any necessary modifications.

Complete the following:

- Write all the information requested on the form provided, to be handed in at the end of class.
- Teach the game to the class during the next class, and officiate the games to make sure students are playing correctly.
- Reevaluate the game after the other members of your class have played the game.

Portfolio Assessment—Soccer Sportfolio

See figure 9.10 at the end of this chapter.

Group Project

During the soccer unit, you each are assigned to a team, and each team participates in a five-on-five, round robin and championship round, double-elimination tournament. Everyone signs up for one of the four tournament committees:

- Tournament organization and rules committee
- Awards and souvenir committee
- Media, news, and sports information committee
- Officials committee: scorekeepers, statisticians, and officials

(continued)

Figure 9.6   Here are several culminating assessments that could be used in a soccer unit.

The tournament is organized and conducted by the members of the class through the cooperation of the tournament committees. The guidelines and recording sheets for each committee can be found in your "Keeping Track of My Soccer Performance" sportfolio booklet (pages 179-188). You will be given time in class to meet with and work with your committees. You may have to do some research to do your jobs well. Each committee is evaluated on how well they carry out the duties assigned to their committee and how well their part of the tournament is conducted.

Figure 9.6 *(continued)*

Table 9.1 Culminating Performance Rubric for a Soccer Unit

Level 3: Professional

Game Creativity

- Was simple and involved the use of soccer skills.
- Was fun and practical.
- Game name was related to the game.
- Play area diagram was clear and contained appropriate dimensions.
- Stated very clear game objectives.
- Rules were simple, clearly written, fair, and appropriate.
- Rules covered required items.
- Game provided appropriate and active inclusion strategies.
- Game form was complete and demonstrated considerable group effort.

Teamwork

- Group worked cooperatively to accomplish the task.
- All members participated, contributed equally, and were fully included in the project.
- Group members complimented and encouraged each other.

Game Presentation and Evaluation

- Group played the game and made necessary adjustments along the way.
- Group provided clear and concise directions to the class when teaching the game.
- Each group member officiated and helped clarify rules and procedures.
- Class members were able to quickly grasp the objectives and the rules of the game.
- Class members were able to play the game well and had fun while doing so.
- Group sought input from class members while evaluating the game and made appropriate modifications to make the game better.

Level 2: Varsity

Game Creativity

- Was a bit too complicated for the class.
- Incorporated some soccer skills.
- Was fun and practical.
- Game name was somewhat related to the game.
- Game objectives were stated.
- Rules were written at various levels: somewhat complicated, fair, and appropriate.
- Rules covered most of the required areas.
- Game provided inclusion strategies that were, for the most part, appropriate.
- Game form was completed and demonstrated group effort.

(continued)

Table 9.1 *(continued)*

Teamwork

- Group worked cooperatively to accomplish the task.
- Most members participated, contributed, and were included in the project.
- Group members encouraged each other.

Game Presentation and Evaluation

- Group played the game and made some adjustments along the way.
- Group provided directions to the class when teaching the game.
- Each group member officiated and helped clarify rules and procedures.
- Class members had some difficulty grasping the objectives and the rules of the game.
- Class members were eventually able to play the game well and had fun while doing so.
- Afterwards, the group evaluated the game and suggested modifications to make the game better.

Level 1: Junior Varsity

Game Creativity

- Was too complicated and restrictive for the class.
- Incorporated minimal soccer skills.
- Was not practical.
- Game name was not related to the game.
- Game objectives were not stated, or stated objectives were not clear.
- Rules were not fair or appropriate.
- More rules were required for a fair game to be played.
- Game's inclusion strategies were not provided or were inappropriate.
- Game form was incomplete and demonstrated little group effort.

Teamwork

- Group did not work cooperatively to accomlish the task.
- Most members did not participate, contribute, or were not included in the project.
- Group members did not encourage each other or were argumentative.

Game Presentation and Evaluation

- Group played the game, but did not make adjustments along the way.
- Group provided unclear directions to the class when teaching the game.
- Not all group members officiated or helped clarify rules and procedures.
- Class members had difficulty grasping the objectives and the rules of the game.
- Class members had difficulty playing the game well.
- Group did not evaluate the game or suggest modifications to make the game better.

Essential Content Knowledge for a Soccer Unit

1. Basic rules of soccer and modified soccer
   - Kick-offs
   - Fouls: direct and indirect free kicks
   - Restarts: throw-in, corner kick, goal kick, penalty kick
   - Positions: goalkeeper, fullbacks (sweepers), forwards (strikers, wings), midfielders (stoppers)
   - Field markings, lines, areas
   - Length of game
   - Substitution
   - Scoring

2. Critical performance elements
   - Dribbling with the inside, outside, and instep of the foot
   - Passing, kicking, and shooting with the inside, outside, and instep of the foot
   - Trapping a moving ball with the foot, the thigh, and the chest
   - Tackling the ball from an opponent: front tackle or side tackle (poke tackle)
   - Punting
   - Catching or deflecting the ball when playing goalkeeper: ground ball, line drive, ball kicked overhead
   - Throw-in

3. Basic offensive strategies
   - Off-the-ball movement to create open passing lanes
   - Off-the-ball movement to spread out the defense
   - Leading the receiver with the pass
   - Moving into open spaces

4. Basic defensive strategies
   - Marking the offensive player with and without the ball
   - Blocking passing lanes and moving into passing lanes to intercept passes

5. Elements of good sporting behavior

6. Working cooperatively as a member of a group to accomplish a goal.

Figure 9.7   This figure includes content knowledge about soccer that students must know to accomplish unit goals and standards.

Essential Skills and Abilities for a Soccer Unit

- Dribbling the ball and maintaining control with the inside and outside of the foot while moving at various speeds, distances, and pathways, alone and against an opponent.
- Placing the body between the ball and defender to shield the ball while dribbling or maintaining possession of the ball.
- Passing the ball to a stationary or moving teammate with a defender nearby (using the inside, outside, or instep of the foot).
- Shooting the ball with the foot from a dribble or pass at the goal from various angles and distances against a defender so that the ball has a chance to score.
- Trapping or stopping the ball on the ground or in the air to gain control of it with the foot, thigh, or chest.
- Closely marking an opponent who is in possession of the ball, using a front or side tackle to gain possession.
- Performing a legal throw-in to a teammate so that he or she gains possession of the ball.
- As a goalkeeper, catching or deflecting a ball kicked on the ground or into the air by an opponent and then either throwing or punting the ball to clear it away from the goal area.
- Performing a legal throw-in from the sideline to a team member on the field so that he or she can gain possession of the ball.
- Performing a stationary kick for distance and accuracy: free kick, goal kick, or corner kick.

Figure 9.8   These are skills and abilities that middle school students must develop and apply in a game situation to successfully achieve unit goals and standards.

Table 9.2 Continuous Performance-Based Assessments for a Soccer Unit

Soccer: Dribbling/Passing/Shooting/Defending	
Activity	**Assessment**
1. Each student, with a ball, dribbles in a straight line across the width of the gym/field varying the speed and keeping control of the ball (5x).	
2. Students repeat #1—Peer Observation Assessment—with a partner observing using an assessment checklist with performance elements listed, the partner checks those critical elements observed. Partners switch after one partner has completed the task.	Students use "Learning/Practice Activity #2 Partner Assessment Form found on page 180 in the student Soccer Sportfolio.
3. Each student dribbles a ball in space while changing direction quickly and using different pathways to avoid running into others, while maintaining possession of the ball. Assessment a: Peer and self-assessment. Students use a checklist/scoring guide. Peer gives feedback to performer then switch roles and repeat.	Students use L/P Activity #3 Peer and Self Assessment Rubric on page 180 of the Soccer Sportfolio.
4. Students dribble against an opponent in a small area, while trying to maintain possession of the ball, using dodging and feinting. Initially the opponent moves with the dribbler but does not attempt to get the ball. Partners switch roles and opponent attempts to get possession of the ball, while the dribbler tries to keep control	Peer Assessment using Performance Element Checklist/Self-assessment form completed by each student in which he or she answers questions about his or her performance. Use L/P Activity #4 Self Assessment Form on page 181 of the Student Soccer Sportfolio.
5. Student passes the ball with the inside of the foot to a large stationary target (the wall) and varies the distance of the pass to the wall.	Assessment: Self-assessment completed by student. Use Assessment Form #5 on page 182 of the Soccer Sportfolio.
6. Student passes the ball to a partner, who is stationary, partner must move to the ball and gain control of the ball. Students complete designated number, then switch roles.	Assessment: Self-assessment—Checklist for performance elements and criteria referenced record. Students use Assessment Form #6 on page 182 of the Soccer Sportfolio.
7. From a stationary position, student (passer) passes a ball to a partner (receiver), who is moving. The receiver gains control of the pass.	Assessment: Students use assessment form #7 on page 182 of the Soccer Sportfolio.
8. While dribbling with the ball, student (passer) makes passes to a partner (receiver) who is moving. The passer, gains control of the ball, and dribbles the ball to pass back to partner.	Use assessment form #8 on page 183 of the Soccer Sportfolio.
9. The student dribbles and passes in a restricted space, with a partner and an opponent (two-on-one). Students switch positions periodically.	Group assessment—Identify strategies that worked best when passing against an opponent. What strategies worked best in trying to intercept a pass. Students share and compare answers with other groups in class. Use assessment form #9 on page 183 of the Soccer Sportfolio.

(continued)

Table 9.2 *(continued)*

Soccer: Dribbling/Passing/Shooting/Defending	
Activity	**Assessment**
10. Students play two-on-two keep away in a restricted area.	Peer-Assessment—Students report the number of successful passes made over the total number of passes attempted, and the total number of intercepted passes over the attempted number of interceptions. They will be reporting performance statistics. Students will use assessment form #10 on page 183 of the Soccer Sportfolio.
11. Students will shoot the ball at a target (vary the distance and the angle), and record their results as the percentage of attempted shots made.	Students will use assessment form #11 on page 183 of the Soccer Sportfolio.
12. With a partner (passer), the student (shooter) will shoot a ball at a target (goal), from a pass, and then record his or her results as a percentage.	Students will use assessment form #12 on page 184 of the Soccer Sportfolio.
13. With a partner, students will pass and shoot at a defended target (two-on-one), and record the number of assists and goals over number of those attempted.	Students will use assessment form #13 on page 184 of Soccer Sportfolio.
14. Students will play in a three-on-three modified soccer game.	Group Assessment—Members of the teams will answer questions regarding strategies that they used and their effectiveness. Based on this information, students, in small groups, will plan and conduct a team practice to help improve their team's and player's performance. Students will use assessment form #14 on pages 184 in the Soccer Sportfolio.
15. Students will participate in a three-on-three soccer game and complete the assessment "Can I improve my fitness level by playing soccer." In this assessment, students will take their pulse and calculate their target HR.	Students will complete assessment form #15 on page 185 in the "soccer sportfolio."
16. Students will participate in a four-on-four modified soccer tournament. All students will serve on a tournament committee to help plan and implement the tournament: tournament committee, rules committee, officials committee, scorekeepers/statisticians committee, awards committee, news/media/sports information committee.	Members of committees produce a portfolio product by completing the appropriate assessment form #16 a on pages 185 to 187 in the "soccer sportfolio". During the course of a class tournament, every student will also keep a record of their performance progress, and will complete, assessment #16 b "My Tournament Evaluation" on pages 187-188 in the "soccer sportfolio".
17. Group Project: Students have been asked to help coach the third grade youth sports soccer team. Each member of the group (4 to 6) must prepare to teach a skill to the team of third graders. To do this you must identify performance cues for the skill, give a good	Students will use Assessment Form #17 on page 188 in the "Soccer Sportfolio".

(continued)

Table 9.2 *(continued)*

Soccer: Dribbling/Passing/Shooting/Defending	
Activity	**Assessment**
demonstration of the skill, and identify 3 learning/ practice activities in which the third graders will participate to practice the skill.	
18 Students will complete the following two assessments either at home as homework or at a portfolio work station in the gym station.	Students will complete individual Assessment #18 "Soccer: A Choice to Be Physically Active" on page 188 in the "Soccer Sportfolio".
19 Students will complete the following two assessments either at home as homework or at a portfolio work station in the gym station.	Assessment #19 "My Final Evaluation of My Soccer Performance and Progress" on page 188 in the "Soccer Sportfolio".

Critical Resources for a Soccer Unit

Equipment

- One soccer ball per student
- Cones and hot spots
- Four modified soccer goals

Facility

- Outdoor field divided into four small fields
- One gym court for bad weather days

Books

Luxbacher, J. 1999. *Soccer: Steps to success.* 2d ed. Champaign, IL: Human Kinetics.

Soccer Web Sites

www.soccerteam.com
www.hometown.aol.com/ayso
www.soccer-goalkeeping.com
www.fastfeet.com/fees.htm
www.coachingsoccer.net
www.eteamz.xom/soccer/instruction/tips/category.cfm/coaching
www.thesoccercoach.com

Community Resources

Speaker: Northern Kentucky University men's and women's soccer coaches and players

Field Trip

Town and Country Sports Center indoor/outdoor soccer facility in Wilder, Kentucky

---

Figure 9.9 The teacher must plan ahead for the materials, equipment, space, facilities, and community resources that are critical for student learning.

resources, be sure to keep in mind each of the earlier steps in the planning process, and how these resources fit into that plan. Depending on your major unit focus, the categories and types of resources that you focus on may differ from unit to unit.

How to Use the Student Soccer Portfolio

The students or their partners record performance results for each assessment so the students and the teacher can track progress during the unit. We recommend that the teacher provide an area where students may store their booklet after class. Using the prepared assessment booklet is an effective way to introduce students to the concept of the sportfolio (Marmo 1994) as a culminating project before requiring them to keep and submit a portfolio for assessment in a sport activity unit. Remember, a sportfolio is a portfolio that students complete as they participate in a sport unit of instruction. We designed this soccer sportfolio so that the assessments are integrated with the learning and practice activities and are arranged in a progression of simple to more complex. The students are then able to follow the class activities and complete the assessments as they go along. Students are receiving feedback or information about their progress as they complete the tasks in some cases. In other cases, the teacher may have to look at the student responses and give them written feedback about their performance.

The learning activities for the sixth-grade soccer unit are provided in figure 9.10. For each learning activity, we refer you to the corresponding performance-based assessment in the student soccer sportfolio booklet. We keep the student soccer sportfolios for each class in a separate box or crate. The box or crate is kept in the gym near the door with a box of clipboards and a box of pencils before the beginning of each class. Our students pick them up when they enter the gym. Time is provided at the beginning of class for students to go back and complete a task that they were unable to complete during the previous class, or they may choose to repeat a previous activity and assessment to see if they can achieve an improved score. When class begins, students move on to the next learning activity and assessment. Students complete the corresponding assessment in their soccer sportfolio booklet with the learning activity. When giving directions and demonstrations to the students for each learning activity, we refer them to the number and page number of the corresponding assessment directions and form. At the end of the class, students return their soccer sportfolios, clipboards, and pencils to the appropriate box as they exit the gym.

Conclusion

In this chapter, we have provided a middle school soccer unit plan. The plan was developed using the five-step, standards-based planning model in which the unit was designed down from the targeted goals and standards to appropriate content and learning and assessment activities. The learning and assessment activities are designed to enhance student learning and help them move up the steps to the top where their ultimate goal rests—the achievement of the targeted standards and goals. This unit provides an excellent example of how teachers can incorporate continuous performance-based assessment into the teaching of an activity or sport unit. The most valuable asset of this chapter is a unique assessment tool that is integrated with the learning activities in the student soccer sportfolio booklet. Each student is given a copy of the soccer sportfolio to use each day in class to complete assessments along with the learning and practice activities. Through this portfolio, the student and the teacher can track each student's progress and achievement throughout and at the end of the unit. The teachers can either choose to keep the student soccer sportfolios as evidence of student achievement, or they can allow students to keep their own work.

This approach has been used quite successfully by one of us. We encourage you to try this soccer learning and assessment approach or to design your own unit plan for another activity with this unit as a guide and model. You will find a variety of performance-based assessments that you can use as models. But most importantly, it demonstrates that you can incorporate continuous performance-based assessment into your program in a fun and interesting way.

"Keeping Track of My Soccer Performance"
6th Grade Physical Education
River Ridge Middle School

Name: _____

Date: _____

Teacher: _____

During our soccer unit learning/practice activities, you will be asked to keep track of your progress as you master the soccer skills of dribbling, passing, trapping, shooting, tackling, and defending and apply these skills and basic offensive and defensive strategies in modified game situations. You will accomlish this task by completing each assessment task found in this booklet either during or at the completion of the learning/practice tasks. By doing this you will be able to track your progress throughout the unit. This will help you identify skills that you need to work on both in class as well as outside of physical education class. This booklet will go with you to 7th grade physical education, so that you can continue to follow your progress in soccer skill and playing development.

At the beginning of class as you enter the gym, you will pick up your booklet and a pencil. Keep the booklet with you as you move around the gym, but make sure that it is in a safe place so that no one will step on it or trip over it. The best place to keep it is probably close to a wall. At the end of class, you will leave the booklet and pencil in the box on the table by the door as you exit the gym, unless you have a homework assignment and need to take the booklet home with you.

To get better at any skill or sport, you must practice, practice, practice!

We may not have enough time for you to practice skills as many times as you need to in order to get better. Therefore it is important for you to remember ways to practice skills that help you progress from one level of performance to the next. In the first section of your soccer portfolio, you will record the ways that you can practice the skills and when you practice at home, during lunch, on the weekends.

Learning/Practice Activity #1: My Practice Record

Skills	Practice Activity	Where	Date	Results

(continued)

Figure 9.10 The soccer sportfolio, which is given to each student at the beginning of the unit, contains guidelines and forms for the completion of individual, partner, and group continuous assessments throughout the unit. Students are able to keep track of their progress throughout the unit with this document.

Learning/Practice Activity #2: Partner Assessment

Directions: As your partner dribbles the ball across the floor and back, make sure that you are in a good position so that you can clearly see your partner dribble, and so that you can correctly evaluate his/her performance of the dribble.

Make sure that you record the results in your partner's booklet. Use the checklist provided below to complete this assessment. Place a checkmark in the space in front of each performance element that you observed your partner consistently demonstrate.

Remember this is not being used as a grade for your partner. It is used to help him/her improve his/her performance. You are the teacher or the coach.

Dribbling the Ball for Speed Checklist

Date Completed: _____ Name of Evaluator: _____

Comments: _____

_____ upright body position _____

_____ head up, looks down field _____

_____ looks at the ball _____

_____ taps the ball with the inside or top of the foot pushing it about three feet in front of dribbler

_____ head up, looks down the field _____

_____ runs quickly to the ball _____

_____ taps ball forward about three to four feet with the inside or the top of the foot

_____ maintains control of the ball _____

Learning/Practice Activity #3: Peer and Self Assessment Rubric

Directions: Observe your partner while he/she dribbles in space with other students dribbling at the same time. Rate your partner's performance using this rubric/scoring guide. Make sure you mark your partner's booklet. Circle the term that you think best represents your partner's level of performance. Write feedback comments which you think might be helpful to your partner to improve his/her performance as he/she continues to practice.

Changing Direction and Dribbling in Different Pathways

Date Completed: _____ Name of Evaluator: _____

Expert level

- was able to change direction quickly to avoid bumping into other students consistently
- maintained control of the ball during the entire time
- looked up frequently to watch for other students
- dribbled in curved, zigzag, and straight pathways
- changed speed when needed (slowed as approached another, changed direction and speeded up as moved away from another)

Intermediate level

- changed direction but not always quickly, bumped into other students a few times, but generally was able to avoid collisions
- maintained control of the ball most of the time, lost the ball only a fwe times and quickly ran to regain control
- looked up occasionally to watch for o ther students in path
- dribbled in at least two different pathways
- changed speed of dribble at appropriate times

(continued)

Figure 9.10 *(continued)*

Novice level

- was unable to consistently change direction when needed, frequently bumped into other students
- lost control of the ball frequently, was slow to regain control
- consistently looked down at the bal, rarely up at others
- dribbled in only one pathway
- speed of dribble was consistently slow, little changed in speed

Learning/Practice Activity #4: Dribbling Against an Opponent Peer Assessment

Directions: Observe your partner as he/she dribbles against a defender, use the checklist below to evaluate your students performance. You will be checking to determine if your partner is demonstrating the performance elements/cues that are necessary for successful dribble against an opponent. Place a check mark in the space provided on the checklist if your partner demonstrate the performance cue consistently.

Dribbling Against an Opponent Peer Assessment

Preparation

_____ knees bent

_____ low center of gravity

_____ body over the ball

Execution

_____ focus on ball

_____ use body fakes and deceptive foot movements

_____ control ball with appropriate surface of foot

_____ place body between ball and opponent

_____ change speed, direction or both

Follow-through

_____ maintain close ball control

_____ accelerate away from opponent

_____ look up and look down field

Evaluator's Comments: _____

_____

_____

Dribbling Against an Opponent Checklist—Self Assessment

(8-10 Awesome, 5-7 Good, 0-4 Needs Practice)

1. In 10 possessions of the ball, I maintained possession when confronted by an opponent _____ times.
2. The dodging tactic that seemed to work the best for me when dribbling and dodging an opponent was: _____

_____

3. The dribbling and dodging tactic which did not work well for me was _____

_____

(continued)

Figure 9.10   *(continued)*

Learning Activity #5: Passing the Ball to the Wall Self Assessment

(8-10 Awesome, 5-7 Good, 0-4 Needs more practice)

1. I was able to make quick passes from a stationary position so that the bal hit the target area on the wall from a variety of distances _____ out of 10 times.

2. I was able to make quick passes from a dribble from various distances so that the ball hit the target on the wall _____ out of 10 times.

Learning Activity #6: Passing a Ball to a Stationary Partner Self Assessment

(8-10 Awesome, 5-7 Good, 0-4 Needs improvement)

1. I was able to make quick, accurate passes to my stationary partner so that he/she was able to move forward and trap the ball _____ out of 10 times.

2. I was able to gain control of _____ passes that were kicked to me by my partner, out of 10 tries.

Peer Assessment of My Inside of the Foot Pass Performance Cue Checklists

Directions: Place a checkmark on the line of each of the performance cues that were demonstrated by your partner.

Date: _____ Evaluator's Name: _____

Preparation

_____ face target
_____ place non-kicking foot beside ball
_____ bend support foot slightly
_____ swing kicking leg back
_____ turn kicking foot outward
_____ arms out to side for balance
_____ focus on ball

Execution

_____ body over the ball
_____ swing kicking leg forward
_____ keep kicking ankle firm
_____ contact the center of the ball with inside surface of foot

Follow-through

_____ transfer weight forward
_____ swing through the ball
_____ smooth follow-through

Learning Activity #7: Passing to a Moving Partner Self Assessment

(7-10 Awesome, 5-6 Good, 0-4 Needs more practice)

1. I was able to pass the ball slightly ahead of my partner who was moving, so that he/she was able to move to the ball and easily gain control of it _____ times out of 10.

2. I was able to move to a pass from my partner and gain control of it _____ times out of 10.

(continued)

Figure 9.10   *(continued)*

Self Assessment #8: Passing to a Moving Partner From a Dribble

(7-10 Awesome, 5-6 Good, 0-4 Needs more practice)

1. I was able to make _____ out of 10 passes from a dribble to my partner who was also moving.

2. While moving, I was able to receive _____ out of 10 passes from my partner, and keep control of the ball until I passed again.

Self Assessment #9: Two-on-One Passing in a Small Area to a Partner Against an Opponent

Directions: After playing 2 vs. 1 "keep away" for a couple of minutes, with your group of three discuss and answer the following questions about strategies for passing and defending.

1. When you had possession of the ball, what did your teammate do to help you make a successful pass to him/her without getting intercepted?

2. When another player had possession of the ball and you were on defense, what did you do that helped you be successful at intercepting a pass and gaining possession of the ball?'

Peer Assessment #10: Two-on-Two Keep Away—Assessing Your Passing and Intercepting Efficiency

Name: _____ Evaluator's Name: _____ Date: _____

Try to use the passing and defending strategies that seemed to work well for you and those identified by other students in your discussions after your 2 vs. 1 games.

Directions: For this activity you will work in groups of 8 students. Four students will play for two minutes, while the other four will keep track of the successful passes and pass interceptions that are made by the players. Each student will record one students game statistics. Please give your form to the student who will be recording your performance.

Directions: When your player is on offense: place a slash mark through the number of the pass if it was not intercepted or was successfully received by the passer's partner. When your player is on defense: mark a line each time he/she intercepts a pass or takes the ball away from the player who has the ball.

Passes

1 2 3 4 5 6 7 8 9 10 11 12 13 14 15 16 17 18 19 20 21 22 23 24 25 26 27 28

29 30 31 32 33 34 35 36 37 38 39 40 41 42 43 44 45 46 47 48 49 50 51 52 53

- Total number of passes attempted: _____
- Total number of successful passes: _____
- Passing percentage: _____
- To calculate passing percentage: divide the number of successful passes by the total number of passes attempted. (20/10 = 50%)

Intercepted Passes

Total number of intercepted passes: _____

Successful Tackles

Total number of tackles: _____

Self Assessment #11: Shooting the Ball at a Goal Without a Defender

Directions: Using two cones set 8 feet apart as your target, place a hot spot 15 ft. from the goal, attept five shots at the goal from a dribble. Move the hot spot back to 20 ft, take five shots at the goal from a dribble. Repeat from 25 ft. Record your performance results below. Use both the kick with the inside of the foot and the kick with the instep while you practice.

(continued)

Figure 9.10   *(continued)*

Kick With the Inside of the Foot

I made _____ goals out of five from 15 ft.

I made _____ goals out of five from 20 ft.

I made _____ goals out of five from 25 ft.

Kick With the Instep

I made _____ goals out of five from 15 ft.

I made _____ goals out of five from 20 ft.

I made _____ goals out of five from 25 ft.

My shot percentage is _____. (divide the number of goals by the total number of shots)

I was more accurate when I shot at the goal from _____ distance.

I was more successful when I _____

Self Assessment #12: Shooting for a Goal From a Pass/Making an Assist

Directions: With a partner, dribble toward the goal, lead your partner with a pass so that he or she can take a quick shot at the goal from about 10 to 15 ft away from a side angle. Do this 10 times then switch.

1. I was made _____ goals from my teammate's pass. My shooting percentage was _____.

2. My partner made _____ goals from my passes. I made _____ assists. My assist percentage is _____.

Self Assessment #13: With a Partner, Shooting for Goals Against One Defender

Directions: Same as above but you and your partner must shoot with a goalie guarding the goal. Keep track of the number of times that each of you passes and shoots.

1. I kicked _____ goals from passes from my partner. My shooting percentage is _____.

2. My partner scored _____ goals. My assist percentage is _____.

2. I used the following strategies did you use to score a goal: _____

_____

Assessment Form #14: Three-on-Three Modified Soccer Game

Directions: After playing this modified game for three minutes, meet with the members of your team, discuss the offensive and defensive strategies with your team that worked well. What did you have difficulty with and what different strategy might you use. Remember when on offensive the goal is to maintain possession of the ball and to score goals. When on defense your goal is to gain possession of the ball and to prevent the other team from scoring. Your strategies should help you accomplish these goals.

1. What offensive strategies did your team use successfully to keep the ball away from your opponents and to move the ball toward the goal? _____

It may be helpful to also draw a picture with X's for your team and O's for your opponent's and to use arrows to show how the members of your team moved to demonstrate your strategies. Also draw the lines of your playing field. Do that in the space below.

(continued)

Figure 9.10 *(continued)*

2. What defensive strategies did your team use to successfully get the ball away from your opponents and to prevent them from scoring? Describe what you did that worked well. What did you do that did not work. What can you do differently that might work. _____

Use the space below to show what you did with drawings. Use X's and O's as you did for offensive strategies.

Plan a Team Practice Session

Based on your teams performance and your discussion of offensive and defensive strategies, plan a 20-minute practice session for your team. You will want to concentrate your work on those skills/strategies that did not work very well or ones that you need to develop. Use the space below to write out your practice plan. You may use activities/drills that we have already used in class or you may create your own.

Assessment Form #15: How Does Soccer Contribute to the Improvement of My Physical Fitness?

What fitness components can I improve through playing soccer? _____

_____

How can I tell if playing soccer improves my cardiorespiratory endurance? While playing a 3 vs. 3 game of soccer in class, the teacher will ask you to stop and take your pulse rate to see if you are in your target heart rate zone.

- My pulse rate was: _____ (count pulse for 10 seconds)
- My heart rate per minute was: _____ (multiply pulse rate $\times$ 6)
- My maximum heart rate: _____ (220 – your age)
- My target heart rate zone is: _____ (multiply your maximum hr $\times$ .60 = lower limit/multiply maximum hr $\times$ .85 = upper limit)
- Was my hr within my target heart rate zone? _____
- What does this mean? _____
- In order to improve my cardiorespiratory endurance by playing soccer, I must: _____
_____

Assessment Form #16: Four-on-Four Modified Soccer Tournament

For the next five days, all teams will participate in a round robin tournament. You will complete a number of learning activities that center around the tournament. Every student will sign-up for a tournament committee. There will be no more than five students on a committee. Each committee will have a specific assignment to prepare for the tournament. The committees and the assignments are explained below.

Assessment Form #16 a: Conducting a Tournament

Tournament committee:

In a round robin tournament, every team plays every other team the same number of times. Won-loss records are kept and the teams with the best records play for the championship at the end. If there are seven teams in our class tournament, how would you set up the tournament? You may need to collaborate with your teammates, go to the library to find a book on how to conduct tournaments, or search the internet for information. Most tournament directors develop entry forms for teams to fill out to enter a tournament. You may want to do that. Please use the space on this and the next page to complete the task. You may also want to make a tournament poster with the schedule, and a won-loss and team standing chart, so all the teams can keep track.

(continued)

Figure 9.10 *(continued)*

Members of the committee

1. _____
2. _____
3. _____
4. _____
5. _____

Rules committee:

The rules committee establishes or selects the version of rules that will be used in the tournament. Since we are playing a modified game, the rules committee must make up the rules that will be followed in the tournament games. When you develop the rules think about rules that will make the game fair, fun and safe for everyone. Some other questions for the committee to ask:

1. What area will the game be played on? What are the boundaries? How big are the goals?
2. What do players do when the ball goes over the sideline? the end line?
3. How will the game begin?
4. What are the fouls? Or illegal plays? What is the consequence?
5. What privileges will the goalie have?
6. How will a team score? How many points will be awarded for a score? Is there more than one way to score?
7. How long will a game last?

Use these questions to help the committee establish the rules. Please write the rules below. Once the rules are established then the committee must have a rules meeting for the coaches and teams.

1. _____
2. _____
3. _____
4. _____
5. _____

Awards/souvenirs committee:

This committee decides what each participant will receive as a souvenir for participating in the tournament and then they must make them. The committee must also make awards for the champion and runner-up teams. At the end of the tournament, the committee will be responsible for the awards ceremony and presenting the awards. You may also decide to give individual awards such as: outstanding boy player, outstanding girl player, most improved boy and girl, best sportspersonship award etc. Please write a report below in which you indicate what you will do. Then gather materials and make the awards.

Members of the committee

1. _____
2. _____
3. _____
4. _____
5. _____

(continued)

Figure 9.10 *(continued)*

Media/news/sports information committee

This committee is responsible for reporting the news and tournament results through the various news media forms: newspapers, radio, tv. The assignments on this committee are listed below:

1. Sports reporter for the River Ridge Gazette (a lap top computer will be provided).
2. Sports photographer for the river ridge gazette (a camera will be provided).
3. Sports announcer for WRRM 14.20 fm who will broadcast the selected games of the day on tape delay (tape recorder).
4. Xyz television crew: camera person (video camera).
5. TV play-by-play announcer.
6. River Ridge Sports information director—provides information about teams and players to the news media, prepares a media guide/program.

Each news media person must gather necessary equipment and supplies and make sure they are set up and ready to go for game time. You will provide a product that will be shared with the class. Below explain what your job will be and what yoou will do to prepare for your job. Describe the product that you produced for this project.

Members of the committee

1. _____
2. _____
3. _____
4. _____
5. _____

Score keeper/statistician committee

The scorekeeper/statisticians will work a game and keep game statistics for each player and a score sheet for each game. Part of the committee's responsibilities is to develop a statistics form that can be easily used to collect game statistics for each team and player and a score sheet. Then to use the sheets to record game stats and to tally the results after the game for the teams. Please use the space below to develop the layout of your forms. You may want to include such things as assists, scores, accurate passes, turnovers, steals, tackles, minutes played, etc. Once you develop your form layout, then you will type it on the computer.

Members of the committee

1. _____
2. _____
3. _____
4. _____
5. _____

Assessment Form #16 b: My Tournament Participation Evaluation

My team name: _____ Members of my team: _____

My team record: Wins: _____ Losses: _____ Place: _____

Individual Awards Received: _____

• My tournament stats:
• # of goals: _____ goal percentage: _____ goal average per game: _____
• # of assists: _____ assist percentage: _____ assists average per game: _____

(continued)

Figure 9.10   *(continued)*

- My tournament stats:
- No. of goals: _____ goal percentage: _____ goal average per game: _____
- No. of assists: _____ assist percentage: _____ assists average per game: _____
- No. of turnovers: _____ turnover percentage: _____ turnover average per game: _____
- No. of steals: _____ steal percentage: _____ steal average per game: _____
- No. of saves: _____ saves percentage: _____ saves average per game: _____
- The best part of the class soccer tournament was: _____
- What I liked the least about participating in the tournament: _____
- The special contributions of each of my team members were: _____
- I would like to participate in another class tournament. Why? Why not?

Assessment Form #17: Group Soccer Skills Teaching Project

Group members:

1. Your group of three will decide on a soccer skill that you would like to teach to the third grade physical education class at your elementary school.

   The soccer skill that you group chose:

2. Someone in your group will demonstrate the the skill to the third grade students. Your group will identify no more than five performance learning cues, that you will give the students to help them remember how to perform the skill correctly, when they practice. Your group will also complete a poster on which you will write each cue. You will also include either a drawing or pictures of someone performing each learning cue, on the poster. Make it large enough so that the third graders will be able to look at it while they practice if they need to be reminded of the cues. Turn your poster in with this assessment form. Be sure that you write your names on the bottom left corner of the poster.

   Write your learning cues below:

3. Write down and explain three practice activities (from easy to harder) that a third grade student who is just learning your skill should participate to improve his or her skill performance.

Assessment Form #18: Soccer: A Choice to Be Physically Active

1. Soccer is my choice of a physical activity that I would like to pursue as a lifetime physical activity. Why? Why not?

   _____

2. In my community, what resources are available to me so that I can continue to practice and play soccer, both as a youth and as an adult? I have completed some research to answer this question. _____

   _____

Assessment Form #19: My Final Evaluation of My Soccer Performance and Progress

1. My strong areas are (the skills/strategies that I perform well): _____

   _____

2. The skills/strategies that I need to continue to practice are: _____

   _____

3. New soccer skills and strategies that I would like to learn are: _____

   _____

Figure 9.10   *(continued)*

CHAPTER TEN

Effective Grading in Physical Education

For most teachers, the giving of a single grade is always a hard and sometimes ugly compromise—all the more so as classes become more heterogeneous through mainstreaming and detracking. Without agreed-upon program goals, assessment procedures, and performance standards, there is little the individual teacher can do beyond muddling through, even though it means continued unfairness and well-meaning dishonesty in reports. (Wiggins 1998, 287-288).

Calculating grades for a report card has caused many physical education teachers many headaches. Should you grade strictly on achievement, or should other factors such as attitude, behavior, and effort enter into the calculations? If you grade on achievement, what components of achievement are used? Should students be graded on fitness, game play ability, motor skill competence, or a combination of these? What about the skilled mover who has

exerted little effort but still performs at levels higher than other students in the class? All these factors are issues in calculating grades, and they are all addressed in this chapter.

According to Guskey (1996a), grades should indicate the proportion of targets students have mastered. Based on achievement of program objectives, grades are designed to report student accomplishments to others—parents, administrators, potential employers, college officials, and so on. Grade reports, if done correctly, represent a summary of students' major strengths and weaknesses. They report them with rich detail while at the same time are user-friendly so that others understand what the grade means.

With standards-based curriculums, not only are different types of assessment used, but the grading format changes as well. Instead of merely summing all assessments that contributed to a grade during a marking period, teachers formulate a grading plan before beginning instruction. Teachers design assessments that indicate the level of mastery for the content covered. Other assessments may also be given to provide feedback on performance but may not necessarily contribute to a student's final grade.

Each assessment should be part of the total assessment picture, similar to pieces of a puzzle. When all the pieces are in place and fit together, you have a picture of student achievement and mastery of content, which accurately tells the story of student learning. To assemble a complete picture, assessments must be planned before starting a marking period to ensure that they align with the teacher's vision of student achievement. Some teachers fail to do this, and it results in a "shotgun" approach to grading. Just as you would not begin painting a wall by flicking a brush loaded with paint at a wall, you should not do student assessment in a similar, haphazard manner, hoping that everything will eventually be covered. "Building assessment to improve performance . . . requires that grades and reports reflect our values and provide apt feedback" (Wiggins 1998a, 288).

Problems With Traditional Grading Practices

When teachers try to factor in effort, achievement, progress, class participation, quality of work, homework assignments, and a host of other variables, the meaning of the grade becomes distorted and confusing (Wiggins 1998). Because a grade should represent achievement, we feel that grades should not be calculated on these other areas (see figure 10.1). In this next section, we provide a rationale for our position.

Attendance and "dressing out"

Effort

Attitude and behavior

Improvement

Grading on a curve

Figure 10.1   Grades should reflect the degree to which a student has achieved learning objectives. These grading practices are not based on achievement.

Attendance and "Dressing Out"

Some physical education teachers use attendance and student participation habits to calculate grades. In these classes, students who attend, dress for class ("dressing out"), participate on a regular basis, and don't cause discipline problems end up with high grades. Attendance and dressing out are often used to calculate grades because numbers are easy to count and teachers have measurable factors and tangible items to use for determining grades. Students readily understand what they must do to get a certain grade. Unfortunately, teachers who grade on managerial concerns must realize that this method of decreasing subjectivity serves to decrease the validity of the grade as well.

A grade in physical education should represent the degree to which a student has achieved course objectives. It should not represent whether a student has dressed for activity and has been on time and acted in an appropriate manner. These items are managerial concerns; they should be addressed through class rules, school policies, and they should be handled administratively. Unfortunately, the practice of grading on managerial concerns has become a traditional way of calculating physical education grades. The tradition is passed from one generation of teachers to the next because teachers grade their students as they themselves were graded or because veteran teachers socialize student and beginning teachers pulling them into the "system." In some physical education programs, teachers are forced to follow departmental grading policies that reflect managerial concerns.

Teachers who use managerial concerns rationalize that students have to be present to learn and that dressing out is necessary for health and safety reasons. However, when teachers hold students accountable only for showing up on time and in proper uniform, the importance of physical education is significantly diminished. Grading on achievement involves defining what achievement means. This definition can be determined in a fair and objective manner when teachers carefully consider course objectives.

Teachers can reward students who have regular attendance by giving activity quizzes that cannot be made up if a student is absent or not dressed for activity. (Note: These were included in the original grading plan.) Missing one or two activity quizzes in a unit would not jeopardize a grade; however, over the course of a unit, several misses would adversely affect a grade. An activity quiz might require students to perform a folk dance learned the previous day or do some type of skill assessment or challenge for points. Students could play small-sided games and receive points. The assessment rewards students who are there, while at the same time providing the teacher with information about student progress toward learning objectives.

Effort

Coaches and physical education teachers often tell their students to give 100% effort (figure 10.2). The implication is that students should work as hard as possible and give their all. Teachers expect students to work hard and stay on task. While 100% effort is a noble goal, to define this level of participation is a difficult task. If one were to ask 10 physical education teachers to define effort, each would probably give a different response.

Problems arise when students perceive that they are giving 100% effort, but teachers perceive that they are not. Students who carry extra weight are often victims of this problem (i.e., low-fit individuals). Given the extra weight they carry, they may be working as hard or harder than their lean counterparts in terms of cardiovascular rate, but in terms of observable work, they appear to be slacking off. Unless teachers use heart rate monitors and systematically track this factor, measuring effort is

Figure 10.2   Effort is very difficult to judge or measure.

just not possible. Also, consider the skilled athletes whose movements are so efficient that they could be performing well above others in the class but exert little effort to do so. In fact, skilled performance is often demonstrated in seemingly effortless performance.

The best approach for evaluating effort is to set goals that *require* effort on the part of the students to achieve. Students who complete the assessment booklet or packet (as shown in chapter 9 for soccer) are demonstrating effort. The degree of quality indicates the effort they put into doing the assessment. Teachers might also use a "sponge," or instant activity, available to students as they enter class. These activities require little or no teacher explanation and can be started by the students whenever they enter class. Results can be recorded on a chart. A teacher could individualize these instant activities, making different levels of difficulty for low, medium, or highly skilled students. Teachers can also allow students to select their personal level of challenge for the activity. When this method is used, students are challenged to work at an appropriate level of difficulty while simultaneously developing and improving skill. Eventually, students are able to perform various activities at an enjoyable level of participation. Some students with lower initial skill probably require longer periods of time to reach these goals, hence they put forth greater effort. These students may not appear to be giving 100% effort as they simply are not working at the intensity of other more skilled or more fit students; however, because they must work longer to demonstrate comparable levels of achievement, the total exerted effort is equal.

Aggressive students as well may be perceived as putting forth greater effort. For example, while watching some volleyball games, you may observe aggressive players trying to play the ball every time the ball comes on their side of the court. Some aggressive players actually lack the desired psychomotor skills and may attempt to camouflage this lack of skill through aggressive play. Additionally, although they play aggressively, they are probably not meeting the teacher's goals with regard to game play and cooperation. Nonaggressive students are not necessarily trying less hard; they just might not have an opportunity to play the ball because of aggressive classmates. Because of the problems surrounding effort, a teacher should avoid using it as a grading category and instead let it manifest itself in other forms of student achievement or performance.

Attitude and Behavior

Some teachers grade on attitude as a way to control student behavior. Students who behave badly in class usually cannot get a good grade (Guskey 1996a). Although poor attitude and behavior are frustrating, they should not be used to calculate grades unless they affect student performance and directly cause a student not to meet instructional goals.

Teachers who use attitude as a factor in grading may do so in an attempt to get even with a student for causing problems for the teacher. When goals and expectations are lowered in return for student compliance, teachers trade off good behavior for good grades. Thus, the content of the class is greatly diminished in exchange for student compliance. You see this exemplified when watching teachers who roll out the ball and allow students to play day after day without requiring them to learn new skills or information.

It's better to deal with attitudes by talking directly with a student to explain teacher expectations regarding behavior, making phone calls home, or having a separate attitude evaluation (either through a narrative or descriptive rubric), than trying to factor attitude into a grade. O'Sullivan and Henninger (2000) created a "Physical Education Behavior Profile" for grading student behavior. In a ninth-grade sport education class, they assessed attitudes and observed behavior by including the following categories: displays teamwork at all times, respects the rights of others, shows prompt attention to teacher instruction, demonstrates a positive attitude and dresses for active participation.

When attitude is factored into a grade, teacher bias may determine the final outcome. When a student makes a poor impression early in the grading period, the teacher's opinion toward him or her probably doesn't change despite anything the student does. This judgment clearly is not fair to a student, so the grade in this case would be impossible to justify. When grades are based on clear goals and expectations, the student can't cop out on a low grade by saying, "The teacher just doesn't like me." We recommend that teachers keep grading separate from punishment and not use poor attitude as a factor for grading.

Reviewing the fifth, sixth, and seventh content standards (NASPE 1995) provides some useful ideas for assessing the affective domain. Students should do the following:

▶ Demonstrate responsibility to the teacher and other classmates whether working individually or in groups.

▶ Be sensitive to the needs of others, and respect the entire scope of differences in others, such as skill and ability level, gender differences, fitness level, and so on.

▶ Willingly accept the challenges and learning opportunities presented whether participating voluntarily in familiar activities or learning new ones.

Holding students accountable for good behavior is acceptable as long as the objective is written in clear, measurable, defensible terms so that students understand what they must do to reach these criteria. Defining appropriate student behavior and fair play toward others can be a difficult task. However, if these are part of the program's goals, teachers should include these items in class objectives, designate appropriate behaviors for them, and hold students accountable for meeting them. Goals such as "Students will respect the effort of others," "Students will accept calls made by officials," or "All team members will collect or distribute their own equipment" would address appropriate student behavior.

Improvement

In an effort to motivate lower-skilled and lower-fit individuals, some teachers attempt to grade on improvement. Grading on improvement poses a host of problems. When a teacher genuinely grades on improvement, at least two assessments are indicated: one before beginning a unit of study and one at the conclusion. If the skill were truly novel for students, an attempt to assess it before instruction is an inefficient use of instructional time.

When students have prior experience in an activity, a second problem emerges. When

learning a new skill, the novice experiences the greatest learning gains or improvement. When a teacher grades on improvement, it means that students who improve the most have the greatest gains and therefore receive the highest grades. Thus, a student might be higher skilled, but they may make less improvement and have a lower grade than a lesser-skilled classmate who showed greater improvement.

This problem leads to a third consideration—undependable gain scores commonly known as *sandbagging*. In other words, students perform poorly during initial testing and then make "miraculous" gains as the unit concludes. The sandbagger receives a high grade because so much improvement is documented.

The fourth problem associated with the practice of grading on improvement is that students might improve and still not achieve the unit objectives for reasonable skill achievement. The teacher's goals of making students skillful participants remains unfulfilled.

When the teacher is truly committed to achieving student competence, the practice of grading on improvement is not used. With standards or criteria for performance firmly in place, the moving target caused by grading on improvement becomes stabilized. When students are informed on the first day of instruction about unit goals and the appropriate instruction follows, they should have an adequate chance to reach these goals. Some units might require nine weeks of instruction and practice to allow for change and improvement. Both of us have taught these extended units and found that students enjoy attaining the higher levels of skill that these longer units make possible. When students are successful in developing competence, their enjoyment surrounding participation in the activity increases.

Grading on a Curve

When teachers grade on a curve, a certain percentage of students are assigned each grade, A through F (e.g., 10% As, 25% Bs, etc.). When grades are based on rank order rather than achievement, the students know how they finished when compared with others, but they know nothing about the quality of the performance. Basing grades on rank order of students can camouflage student results and feedback. It is much more informative to tell runners that they ran 100 meters in 11.6 seconds than it is to say that they placed third in the race. Future improvement is far easier when current performance is known. When grades represent specific achievement, those with a substandard performance know exactly what they must do to improve. Effective grading practices should point out to students strengths and areas needing improvement.

Grade Formats in Physical Education

Although narratives and checklists are sometimes used at the elementary level, letter grades are the most commonly used form of grading at the secondary level (Hensley et al. 1987). Narratives are written descriptions of student achievement. Teachers can cover a variety of topics in the narrative, including achievement, behavior, effort, improvement, and so on. Although they provide a lot of information, parents don't always know the implications of the narrative. Also, being creative while writing narratives for an entire class is difficult. After the first five or six, many of the comments made about different students are alike. Narratives are also the most time-consuming of any reporting form to complete (Guskey 1996a). Considering the number of students a secondary physical education instructor teaches, creating narratives for all these students would be a near impossible task. Computer programs have been developed that generate comments. Teachers can select the appropriate comments and the computer combines them into a narrative. These computer-generated narratives lose impact if students compare their narratives with those of others and discover the similarities between them.

Checklists contain a list of topics or skills that are considered the content of the class. Teachers can indicate with a scoring system whether a student has obtained proficiency for the characteristic. They are useful for diagnosis and prescription because of the detail they contain. Unfortunately, parents don't understand checklists. Although they report student progress, they rarely report the appropriateness of student progress. Parents read a narrative or checklist and then ask the question, "So what?" Parents want to know student achievement, how their child compares with others in the class, and what the child should be doing. In other words, they want to know, "Is my child above or below grade level expectations or on target?"

Although letter grades really don't address problems previously identified with other grading formats, people are more accustomed to them and therefore are less critical of their shortcomings. Parents have prior experience on interpreting student achievement through a grade. Grading with a letter grade, symbol, or meaningful word (e.g., *outstanding, satisfactory, pass, fail*) is the process of abstracting a great deal of information into a single sign, character, or word for communication. Of all the grading forms used, letter grades are probably the most easily misinterpreted (Guskey 1996a). The problem with letter grades is not the symbol, rather the lack of stable and clear points of reference while using these symbols (Wiggins 1998a). Although the move to changing the grading system from one based on participation and dressing for class to one based on measurable student achievement is positive, parents need to be educated about what the grade really represents. When teachers give parents and students rubrics and explain where students are in reference to them, some of the mystery surrounding a grade fades away.

Grades in physical education typically fall into the A or B range, more often due to low expectations than superior student achievement. Standards-based grades in physical education can represent qualities other than those to which parents are accustomed. Parents may question a student's physical education grade with comments like "Isn't he dressing for class?" or "Is she causing problems in class?" Too often their physical education classes in the past were graded only on these areas.

A grade should reflect student achievement for the grading period; however, capturing the work of six or nine weeks in a single letter or category is difficult. The main purpose of a grade is to communicate to others (parents, administrators, employers, college officials) each student's level of mastery for programmatic goals. Because teachers should inform students of their goals for the class as well as keep students informed of their progress on a regular basis, it is important for a program to have well-articulated goals so that others know what the grade actually means. Students are more likely to be motivated when they understand what they must do to be successful. These goals can be sent home at the beginning of a semester and again with a report card so that parents know what students have achieved and what the grade represents.

Effectively Grading Physical Education

When physical education was in its infancy, the emphasis was on improving health by making people physically fit. As various sports grew in popularity, other aspects of physical activity became more important. In 1910, Clark Hetherington, one of the early leaders in physical education, proposed that physical education should address four different concerns: organic, psychomotor, intellectual, and character (Siedentop 2001) (see figure 10.3). Today these four areas continue to be the basis of most physical education program objectives. When you read *Moving Into the Future* (NASPE 1995) and examine NASPE's content standards, all four areas are visible and carry a prominent role throughout the document. Hetherington used the term *psychomotor* to denote achievement with regard to motor skills, while *intellectual* referred to the knowledge components important to physical education. Hetherington's *organic* dealt with fitness components,

Figure 10.3   Hetherington's four areas of physical education.

and *character* referred to those aspects of learning associated with the affective domain such as leadership, positive sports behavior toward others, teamwork, respect, and caring for others.

In an attempt to dispel some of the mystery of turning student achievement into a single symbol, the Cincinnati Academy of Physical Education (CAPE) provided results of evaluations for several different areas on its report card. Students were evaluated on each of three areas: cognitive understanding, affective sensations, and motor performance. Under "cognitive understanding," students were given a score and rated either superior, good, average, fair, or poor in each of the follow subcategories: rules, strategies, written assignments, knowledge test, and oral test. Although "affective sensations" did not receive a score, the subcategories were also rated superior, good, average, fair, or poor. The subcategories under affective sensations included attitude, group play/interaction, safety, and confidence. Motor performance had no subcategories, but it did provide space for instructors to list various skills for the units taught. These skills were given a score then rated as superior, good, average, fair, or poor. Because these components were broken down into subcategories, students and parents had a much clearer understanding about student performance versus all of this information being combined into a single letter grade.

We admire Hetherington's insight and vision to have defined physical education in a manner that would still be used almost 100 years later.

Although all four areas are still considered important in physical education, some of these areas are emphasized to different extents in various programs. Some physical education curriculums are moving toward the development of fitness with little concern about the development of sport skills. Other programs have shifted to a sport education emphasis, assuming that fitness just "happens" when students develop competence in a sport area and participate in that activity on a regular basis. Adventure education programs promote development of Hetherington's components by giving special attention to the affective domain and selecting activities to promote growth of character. Some programs combine activities from several curricular models, seeking to provide students with achievement in all four of Hetherington's components.

The purpose of this book is not to argue in favor of any one curriculum but rather to show how performance assessments can evaluate student performance in physical education. The items and areas used to calculate grades in physical education are dependent upon the goals or objectives for the program. If teachers are promoting a fitness curriculum, then this component should receive the greatest emphasis in the grading scheme. If increasing student ability to play various sports or perform a range of physical activities (e.g., dance, swimming, gymnastics) is the main programmatic goal, then the psychomotor area should have greatest emphasis. Regardless of the curriculum selected, standards-based grades should be based on preset standards of achievement rather than a class rank or standard set on normative scores. When reading the rubrics in chapter 3, please note that all of them are based on a description of student skill, rather than comparing student performances to that of others.

To illustrate a way to determine student grades, let's assume that the physical education program philosophy is to develop skillful movers and that 50% of the student grade comes from demonstrating competence in this area. Because there is a cognitive component connected to this scheme, 25% of the grade is based upon competence relative to the knowledge component. The grading plan used in the example also values achievement in the affective domain, so 10% of the grade is based upon affective components and 15% is based upon fitness activities. (Note: Most physical education professionals do not feel that grading on fitness levels and achievement is appropriate; however, process measures of fitness are appropriate to use for grading.) After deciding where to place emphasis for creating the grade, teachers next must select units of study or a curriculum that achieves these programmatic goals.

In this example, the teacher decides that volleyball and weight training/conditioning will be taught during this nine-week grading period because these two units complement each other and will allow students to attain program objectives. Next, the teacher writes unit goals and develops assessments that determine whether students have achieved the stated goals. When this process is completed, the teacher then goes back to the original percentages determined for programmatic goals ensuring that unit percentages equal those set for the program. Teachers can leave the numbers as percentages or, if they find it easier, convert the percentages to points, which the example illustrates (see figure 10.4). Some computer grading programs are designed to calculate grades from percentages without converting individual test scores to points.

The teacher decides to appropriate 150 points to weight training/conditioning and 250 points to volleyball because volleyball covers 30 days of the 45-day grading period. Because students are more likely to achieve fitness components in a strength and conditioning unit, the 60 points allocated to fitness come from assessment in that unit. Both units involve skills, but since the volleyball is taught for a longer period of time, the majority of the 200 points allotted to psychomotor domain comes from volleyball. Figure 10.5 shows the game play analysis that is used for the unit—in this case, volleyball. Similar decisions about distribution of points are made about the other areas as the teacher designates assessments areas. The important thing to remember here is that the teacher must continually go back to program goals when deciding how to weight the assessments.

With performance-based assessments, the grade is determined by the rubric. When point systems are used, the points for the various

Unit Goals		Points
50%	Psychomotor skill	200 points
25%	Knowledge	100 points
10%	Affective	40 points
15%	Fitness	60 points
100%	Total	400 points

Volleyball = 250 points

Weight training = 150 points

Psychomotor

Volleyball
60 points	Game play assessments (4 @ 15 points each)
60 points	Volleyball practice log
10 points	Serving test
10 points	Wall volley test
10 points	Continuous rally test

Weight training
20 points	Lifting technique assessment (2 @ 10 points each – teacher checklist)
30 points	Lifting log

Knowledge

Volleyball
15 points	Game play officiating (3 @ 5 points each)
20 points	Game play assessment (2 @ 10 points each)
25 points	Student project choice (write article for newspaper, create a game broadcast, analysis of a video tape of game play)

Weight training
40 points	Weight training brochure

Affective

Volleyball
20 points	Journal
10 points	Peer assessment (2 @ 5 points each)
10 points	Teacher assessment (2 @ 5 points each)

Fitness

Weight training
45 points	Strength goals (9 stations @ 5 points each)
15 points	FITNESSGRAM Pacer assessments (3 @ 5 points each)

Grading Scale

A	360-400 points
B	320-359 points
C	280-319 points
D	240-279 points
F	239 and below

Figure 10.4   This figure illustrates a plan for grading student achievement.

The student	Never	Sometimes	Often	Always
	1	2	3	4
1. Uses correct form to make solid contact when serving the ball.	1	2	3	4
2. Places ball to open areas when serving.	1	2	3	4
3. Performs the set using correct form.	1	2	3	4
4. Performs the forearm pass using correct form.	1	2	3	4
5. Uses body parts sequentially to build force for the spike.	1	2	3	4
6. Maintains good body control during net play.	1	2	3	4
7. Shifts defensively in response to ball movement.	1	2	3	4
8. Demonstrates and uses offensive strategy and movement.	1	2	3	4
9. Knows the rules and applies them correctly during game play.	1	2	3	4
10. Moves to support teammates on the court.	1	2	3	4
11. Communicates with teammates both on and off the court.	1	2	3	4
12. Plays own position on court ("stays home").	1	2	3	4
13. Congratulates teammates and others for good play.	1	2	3	4
14. Accepts ruling by officials and makes fair calls during self-officiated games.	1	2	3	4
15. Uses emergency techniques sparingly.	1	2	3	4

Figure 10.5   This volleyball game play assessment was used with the grading plan in figure 10.4.

assessment pieces are designated on the scoring guide. Analytic rubrics pose a problem: The teacher must devise a system for converting the various components contained on an analytic rubric into grades. By converting an analytic rubric to a holistic one for final grading purposes, a paragraph describing the level of performance for each grade level can be written (see figure 3.6, the holistic rubric in chapter 3, for an example). The teacher simply matches student performance with the paragraph that best describes it. If certain qualities must be present for an A-performance, these must be indicated in the rubric. Some components, although important, might not be considered essential for performance. If the less important components are at a lower level than indicated on the holistic rubric, but the key elements are present at the upper level, students would receive the higher grade. Using this method, student performance is evaluated from a more holistic and big-picture perspective, which is often more accurate than when many individual elements are assessed separately then added together to determine the final grade.

It is very important to decide the total points or percentages at the beginning of the marking period and determine which assessments are administered. Once this has been done, teachers should not add additional assessments as the unit proceeds because these can negate the impact of major assessments (see figure 10.6). The following is an example of what not to do. In this scenario, the teacher required students to choreograph a dance and to videotape the performance. The assessment was assigned 100 points and required a major portion of the time spent in physical education for the grading period. After those points were assigned, the teacher began to give several quizzes and homework assignments to keep students on task and motivated as the unit progressed. These quizzes and homework assignments required minimal effort, perhaps an hour of total student time. By the end of the grading period, 100 points worth of homework and quizzes were included in the grade, which was equal to the project requiring four to five weeks to complete. Thus, insignificant student work had as much impact on the grade as did the major choreography assignment.

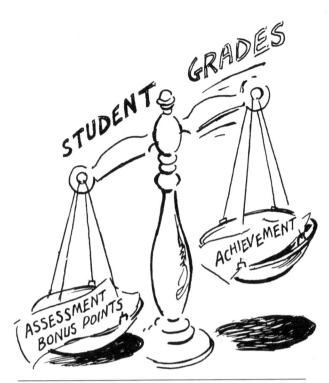

Figure 10.6   Bonus points can disrupt the balance of a sound grading system based on student achievement.

When teachers decide in advance what factors to use to calculate student grades and when they resist the temptation to pad the grade with additional points, the grading system remains true to the unit and program objectives.

Challenges in Effective Grading Practices

With regard to grading, physical educators face many problems. When these factors are known in advance, they can be avoided or circumvented, thus resulting in a fair and equitable system for grading. When teachers address issues related to validity, reliability, and select assessments that evaluate students themselves without regard to the skill of a partner or team and when they adjust a curriculum to accommodate a wide range of skills, grades are fair and can be defended. The following section gives suggestions for facing common problems associated with grading students.

Validity and Reliability

Grades must represent the degree to which a student meets the program's goals. When grades are based on measures other than achievement, the grade is not valid. Teachers must articulate to students, parents, and administrators the method used to determine the grade. Additionally, if the grade is determined from invalid assessments, the grade becomes invalid as well. Teachers must identify what they accept as evidence that a student has met instructional goals. Grades become accurate representations of student achievement when teachers use valid, reliable assessments and when they base the grade on the degree to which the student truly met the instructional goals.

Dependence on Other Students

When designing assessments, teachers must make sure that skills of other students don't influence another student's grade. For instance, during a volleyball game, a student has to receive a pass in order to demonstrate a spike. If the setup is poorly executed, students then have no opportunity to demonstrate their spiking ability. When an assessment requires a prior response (e.g., a tennis rally, game play, double dutch routine), the teacher needs to make sure that students providing the setup (i.e., the support for a skill) have enough ability to do so correctly. To provide consistency in this situation, a teacher might consider providing the prior response themselves, using a student aide who has good skills, or organizing game play with several different partners on several different days (multiple evaluation opportunities) so that teachers can accurately evaluate and determine student competence and achievement.

Student Skill Levels and Prior Experience

Setting the criteria for an activity or unit in which you have very high-skilled and very low-skilled students is difficult. Students with prior experience should score higher on assessments. When the standards are too high, low-skilled students may feel as though this level of achievement is unobtainable. When standards are too low, high-skilled students remain unchallenged, as they actually may be able to achieve the required level of achievement before the onset of instruction.

One solution to this problem might be to not teach familiar units or activities in which some students may already have competence. Since many students are required to enroll in a limited number of physical education classes, teaching unfamiliar activities seems educationally prudent as most teachers want students to gain competence in several sport areas. However, trying to select activities in which *no* student has previous experience is also difficult. If the department has more than one physical education instructor, teachers could elect to offer different activities, and require students to sign up for an activity in which they had not had previous experience.

When you are teaching a class with a wide range of skill and ability, skilled players might be assessed on a basic skill level that contributes to their grade. Upon passing this evaluation, the students can be given additional activities and drills that provide psychomotor challenges. Station work can also allow every student to improve skill, regardless of ability, when several levels of challenges are given and students are allowed to self-select the level on which they wish to participate. These extra levels may not be related to a grade, but they do provide ways for students to improve their skills while at the same time providing challenge for students. Sport education curriculums offer yet another solution to this dilemma. Because students have the opportunity to play a variety of sport roles during an activity, higher-skilled students might assume some other aspect of the game that they had not previously experienced. Students who have had a lot of playing experience could benefit from being a coach or referee, thus experiencing the game through another lens. Dancers could choreograph or direct production of dance pieces. Gymnasts could spot classmates or choreograph routines for others.

Another way to address the problem of wide ranges in skill and ability level is to select a variety of units within a grading period. Dance might be coupled with a volleyball unit or an individual sport with a team sport. When an activity requires strength and power to be successful, teachers can pair it with another activity that requires other equally valued traits such as balance or rhythmic activity. When this practice is utilized, students have a balanced curriculum, and a grade is not determined by any one motor skill characteristic.

When addressing the issue of a wide variation of skill levels within a class, a return to unit objectives should reveal goals in areas

away from the psychomotor domain. Because psychomotor skill is only one of the areas on which a grade is usually determined, lower-skilled students can emphasize other areas such as knowledge, homework, teamwork, and affective attitudes that are important factors when calculating the final grade. When considering the total grade, all students undoubtedly have at least one area in which they can succeed, even though the bar on psychomotor skill is still high. Since the final grade reflects the total picture of how well students have met program goals, each student can excel at some area.

Hints and Suggestions for More Effective Grading Practices

While working in secondary schools, we changed our grading policies every year in search for the "best" system. We're not sure that we have arrived at utopia yet, but we are much closer than when we began teaching. We have developed several ideas over the years that we feel enhance grading practices (see table 10.1).

• **Establish High Standards for Achievement** Some teachers try to motivate students by giving high grades in physical education for minimal effort. Actually, this is counterproductive to having students enjoy and respect physical education. When only minimal effort is required, students, parents, administrators, and others tend to lose respect for the subject. Meaningful learning is intrinsically motivating (Herman, Aschbacher, and Winters 1992). When people have to work hard to be successful in an endeavor, they appreciate the achievement more. They must, however, know what they are required to do for this learning. The key is to define success in terms that students clearly understand, so they know what is expected to reach the desired outcomes. Then, teachers simply need to provide the vehicle for reaching these targets and outcomes. Assessments shouldn't be watered down so that students putting forth minimal levels of achievement receive high grades.

• **Set "the Bar" at an Appropriate Level of Achievement** Students usually meet teacher expectations but don't often exceed them unless motivated by something other than a

Table 10.1 Hints and Suggestions for Highly Effective Grading Practices

Achievement

Establish high standards for achievement.

Set the bar at an appropriate level of achievement.

Look at achievement through a variety of lenses.

Fairness

Show the assessment plan early in the instructional unit.

Keep the grading system balanced.

Use formative assessments for determining grades.

Conduct grading practices with less-skilled students.

Minimize subjectivity on assessments leading to a grade.

Don't give low grades to motivate students to try harder.

Avoid averaging scores to arrive at a student grade.

Teaching

Use assessment for multiple purposes, rather than just to give grades.

Give extra credit for extra learning, not just doing extra work.

These suggestions are the result of several years of trial and error and are offered to help you develop highly effective grading practices.

grade. You want to set your standards high, but not *too* high. Setting the criteria the first time an assessment is used is difficult.

Goals and objectives determine where the bar of achievement is to be placed. If the teacher's objective is for students to have adequate skill to engage in game play at a recreational level, the bar on achievement should be set at that level. The teacher must determine which skills are involved and the level of expertise necessary for each of these skills when setting the bar. Assessments are then created that evaluate these skills.

Criteria on assessments can be based on the skills of those who have the level of expertise that the teacher wants the class to reach. By observing recreational play and noting what those players are capable of doing, a teacher can develop a sense of where to place expectations for assessments. Another way might be to see what athletes (junior varsity or varsity) are capable of doing on certain assessments and make appropriate adjustments. If the teacher has a reasonable amount of skill in the sport or activity, a third way to set the bar might be to do a self-administered assessment.

When the teacher merely sets the bar at the point that students currently are performing

(which, in essence, are norm-referenced criteria), students never become motivated to surpass this level (Wiggins 1998a). Setting goals at a level that ensures student success during game play (or during an appropriate culminating activity for the unit) requires most students to stretch their current limits to gain more skills or higher levels of existing skill.

• **Look at Achievement Through a Variety of Lenses** When grades are based on a variety of different goals, they provide several lenses with which to evaluate students. This technique is similar to using triangulation, a practice used by qualitative researchers that involves evaluation of several types of data about the same topic or subjects in an attempt to gain a clearer picture of what they are studying. This method is also somewhat analogous to a detective trying to solve a case—the more clues that point to the same conclusion, the stronger the argument. When several indicators lead to the same conclusion with student grades, the teacher becomes more certain that the degree of student learning and achievement has been correctly identified. Physical education is based on an array of skills, knowledge, and attitudinal dispositions, all of which contribute to a physically educated person. This scope should be considered when determining student grades. We recommend that no one area be used to decide or determine a grade. When a teacher bases grades on several types of assessments (psychomotor, cognitive, affective domain, and fitness), then students who are low-skilled or low-fit should have a legitimate chance for an acceptable grade.

• **Show the Assessment Plan Early in the Instructional Unit**   Some students have difficulty achieving psychomotor goals. By showing the assessments early in the unit, clearly stating the criteria for each, and giving students opportunities to master this material, students should have ample opportunity to achieve these goals. Those preparations should give students reasonable and realistic opportunities to master the material. When students know how they are evaluated (i.e., they know the criteria and assessment that are used), they can self-assess or peer-assess during the instructional process. They know what they must do to reach the goals and whether more practice is necessary.

• **Keep the Grading System Balanced**   Figure 10.7 shows a sample grading plan that is not unlike many of those typically used in a high school physical education program. On first glance, it looks as though students are graded on four different areas. Students must achieve a certain level of skill on the psychomotor domain as well as on written tests, and they must show positive direction and leadership. Actually, dressing for class overrides each of these areas, thus destroying the balance of the grading scheme. Regardless of performance on areas one, two, and three, students fail when they don't dress for class.

When looking at the F grade, only dress cuts and absences are listed. Despite exceptional performance in the other areas, dress cuts and excessive absences determine the grade. Thus, even though skill, knowledge, and leadership seem to be grading considerations, they are not because failure to dress for class overrides all other achievement. Additionally, three of the four categories listed for evaluation (cooperation and attitude, skill improvement, and learning achievement) are not clearly explained on the grade explanation sheet.

The stated grading plan should be the one actually used. One category, such as dressing

for class or attendance, should *not* override the other areas. Poor attendance undoubtedly decreases levels of performance and achievement on psychomotor, cognitive, and fitness areas, but it should not be used as a sole determinant of a grade. Note the lack of specificity between this grading plan and the one presented in figure 10.4. Teachers should clearly state what areas they grade on and not allow one area to disrupt the balance in a grading format.

Teachers should focus on poor achievement and learning rather than simply counting the number of dress cuts. Teachers use grades to hold students accountable for dressing for activity. However, if dressing for class determines the student grade and if the grade represents the degree to which a student has met class objectives, then the objectives of this class must be to have students dress for class. We suspect this is not the message most physical education teachers want to convey about their programs.

• **Use Formative Assessments for Determining Grades**   Grades should be indicators of the degree to which a student achieved the teacher's objectives for the course. Although it is difficult (if not impossible) to collapse student work into a single letter grade, current grading policies often require teachers to do just that. To further complicate the process, some teachers use assessment results from a single day to influence a student's grade. Imagine a student who has worked hard during a six-week volleyball unit then "bombs" the one-shot assessment on the day it was administered, resulting in scores that are not really indicative of the degree of achievement relative to the course or unit objectives.

Because assessments have a dual purpose of providing feedback while assessing performance, doing multiple administrations of assessments makes sense from a pedagogical point of view, as well as an evaluative one. Using formative assessments eliminates the problem of a student doing well for most of a unit and then having an off day when grading was done. If teachers allow multiple attempts to demonstrate mastery, grades are then more representative of actual student achievement.

• **Allow Extra Practice Time for Lesser-Skilled Students**   When lesser-skilled students don't have enough time in class, extra practice time outside of the regular class is necessary. Before the formal start of a day's

The four areas of evaluation:

1. Attendance and participation
2. Cooperation and attitude
3. Skill improvement
4. Learning achievement

A grade

- 90% to 100% on written tests
- 90% to 100% on skill tests
- Demonstrated leadership and positive direction
- Dressed and participated all but two days of a grading period

B grade

- 80% to 89% on written tests
- 80% to 89% on skill tests
- Demonstrated leadership and positive direction
- Dressed and participated all but four days of a grading period

C grade

- 70% to 79% on written tests
- 70% to 79% on skill tests
- Demonstrated leadership and positive direction
- Dressed and participated all but seven days of a grading period

D grade

- 60% to 69% on written tests
- 60% to 69% on skill tests
- Demonstrated leadership and positive direction
- Dressed and participated all but 10 days of a grading period

F grade

- Five or more dress cuts equals an F
- Eleven days absent equals an F
- Five unexcused nonparticipation days
- Combination of any of the above

    An accumulation of five dress cuts in one nine-week period constitutes failure for that nine-week period!

    Excused absence days may be made up within five school days following the absence for class credit. Unexcused absences, expulsions, suspensions, truancy, or dress cuts cannot be made up.

    Despite receiving passing grades for the first, second, and third items, you can still fail for the nine weeks because of excessive absenteeism, nonparticipation, or dress cuts.

Figure 10.7   Although this sample grading system appears to assess cognitive, affective, and psychomotor learning, dress and participation actually override student achievement.

class, the teacher may allow for additional skill practice while others are still dressing for class. A class routine could be established whereby students enter the gym and begin working on an activity predetermined by the teacher. This instant activity could be a carryover from the previous day's instruction or a novel task posted on a bulletin board as students enter the gym. Adequate practice time for lower-skilled student *must* be built into the program.

Students could also practice drills or assessments as homework. Teachers could allow students to check out a piece of equipment for practice outside of the school day. Another option for encouraging success for lower-skilled students is to provide multiple opportunities for taking an assessment, making it a formative assessment. When students achieve the goal on the assessment, the grade is recorded. With the use of formative assessments, lower-skilled students have more chances to achieve success. In addition, they learn an important life lesson—hard work pays off. Teachers should not hesitate to use achievement to determine student grades. Establishing clear and specific targets takes the mystery out of the grading process.

• **Use Assessments for Multiple Purposes, Rather Than Just to Give Grades**   The primary purpose of assessment should be to give feedback to teachers and students; therefore, determining grades should be a *secondary* reason for doing assessment. Remember: Not all assessments need to contribute to a grade. A student teacher once told one of us that she was not allowed to administer skill tests in her classes because the district in which she was student teaching did not allow physical education teachers to give grades based on psychomotor skills. It did not occur to the student teacher that skill tests could be used for student learning or feedback, even if they did not contribute to the grade.

Additionally, students should not be graded while they are trying to learn something. It is better to use assessment for feedback while a student is learning than to attempt to use it as part of the grade. Only after students have gained mastery should a teacher consider recording grades. Intermediate and formative assessments provide teachers and students feedback, but these don't have to contribute to the student's final, report card grade.

• **Avoid Averaging Scores to Arrive at a Student Grade**   With performance-based assessment, new grades and scores should not be averaged with prior ones. A student with minimal experience in an activity could perform so poorly in the initial part of a unit that even if mastery were achieved by the time the unit concluded, the low initial grades would drag the final grade down. Because a grade represents the degree to which the student achieved mastery of the teacher's goals, an averaged grade does not accurately reflect the extent of achievement. When formative assessments are given, the new grade should be used, rather than an average of the new and old scores.

When a teacher wants to show the scores on assessment that didn't contribute to a grade, grading programs are available that can show a student profile of scores on various assignments and assessments. Even though assessments don't contribute to a grade, they can be useful for demonstrating improvement and progress.

Parents enjoy getting grade reports from teachers because they can see what their child is doing in class in relation to the type of instructional activities occurring in class. On the example shown in figure 10.8, student skill assessments are shown, as are quiz scores and homework. Although not all assignments contribute to a grade, they are all displayed for the parent and student to view. Many types of grading programs exist. Often teachers can customize the printout to fit their particular class needs. Some programs also print behavior reports for parents along with reports of student achievement.

• **Don't Give Lower Grades to Motivate Students to Try Harder**   During the early part of a grading unit or semester, a teacher may give borderline students a lower grade in hopes of encouraging students to try a little harder. Highly skilled athletes are sometimes victimized in this way as well, in an attempt to motivate them to work harder. This practice may cause a student to become discouraged and therefore put forth even less effort than previously expended. When grades are based on clearly stated goals and standards, teachers should reward students with precisely what they have earned. A grade is a representation of the degree to which a student has mastered the teacher's goals. It should not be manipulated in this manner in an attempt to increase student motivation. Borderline students should be given additional evaluations to determine the extent to which they mastered the content (see the previous hint about looking at achievement through a variety of lenses). Formative assessments are also useful with borderline students, as they can help pinpoint student achievement accurately and let them know what they must do to move to the next level.

Riverside High School   Tuesday, September 29
Progress Report for Jackson, Susan L.
ID: 12047
Ms. King   Physical Education 101
Room #: Gymnasium   Section #: 01
Final average: 96.8
Final grade: A

Name	Score	Max	Grade
SKL #1	6	10	None
SKL #2	7	10	None
SKL #3	8	10	B
Quiz #1	9	10	A
SKL #4	10	10	A
SKL #5	14	15	A
SKL #6	13	15	None
SKL #7	18	20	A
HW #1	17	18	A
Fit #1	14	15	A

Figure 10.8   Computer grading programs can help streamline record keeping and inform both students and parents about achievement during a grading period.

• **Minimize Subjectivity on Assessments Leading to a Grade** Students must know grading criteria, understanding in advance teacher expectations and how they will be graded. The less mystery surrounding teacher goals and the grading system, the more likely students are able to hit achievement targets. When targets are clear, students can peer-assess and self-evaluate. This moves the sole responsibility for achievement away from the teacher, making the student responsible for learning as well. Additional detail should be included with grade reports when necessary. With this additional information, teachers can indicate which assessments were used for calculating a grade.

Teachers could report student work habits in this additional information without incorporating them into the final grade. A grade report, explanation of program goals, and a rubric or scoring guide all would provide additional explanation of how the grade was determined, clarifying for parents what the grade represents and eliminating some of the confusion that can occur when a letter grade represents several weeks of achievement. When any grading practices or policies lead to miscommunication with parents or students, teachers should make adjustments that clarify the process.

• **Give Extra Credit for Extra Learning, Not Just Doing Extra Work** The final grade a teacher gives a student should be a reflection of the degree to which a student achieved the teacher's goals. When a teacher gives extra credit, it should be for additional learning, not just more work on the same topic or area. When extra credit is given for additional work (rather than learning), it distorts the weighting of course percentages discussed earlier in this chapter. Sometimes at the end of a grading period, when students discover that their grades are less than what they wanted, teachers allow students to do extra credit assignments. These usually are meaningless in terms of student knowledge or course content. Remembering that a grade should reflect the degree of student achievement of teacher goals, the practice of letting a student boost a grade at the end of a grading period goes contrary to that philosophy and therefore should not be used. Students should not be allowed to gain extra credit points unless they are a reward for tackling a task more difficult than expected of others in the class that leads to learning and achievement beyond the scope of the normal class.

Conclusion

Guskey (1996a) reports that when parents design report cards, they look very different than when teachers design them. A survey might be conducted allowing parents and students to indicate the information they consider important concerning student achievement. Because they are the primary consumers of student grades, their needs must be considered when planning the reporting system.

Grades should not be used as weapons (Cotten and Cotten, 1985). Teachers have far more success when they think of a grade as a reward for student achievement that must be earned. Basing grades on specific, clear, and defensible targets gives students the greatest opportunity for success.

Incorporating effort, improvement, attitude, and aptitude into a grade greatly increases the subjectivity surrounding the grading system, as well as the mystery of what is necessary for success. Confusion and miscommunication decrease when the grading system is kept focused on student achievement and when the teacher lets the grade truly represent the degree to which a student achieved the goals for the class. Explicitly defining achievement in understandable terms enhances program credibility while at the same time letting parents know how they can help their child achieve higher levels of learning.

When calculating student grades, we have found the best policy is to revisit the objectives, weight them accordingly, and then decide which assessments best indicate student achievement. When this method is determined before the instructional unit begins, both teachers and students know the guidelines, and there are no surprises when instruction concludes.

CHAPTER ELEVEN

Acquiring Assessment Savvy

The task of the excellent teacher is to stimulate "apparently ordinary" people to unusual effort. The tough problem is not identifying winners: it is in making winners out of ordinary people. (K. Patricia Cross)

When you switch to a performance-based assessment format, you should start with a few new assessments, then make additional changes over time. To begin the process of climbing the planning staircase, teachers should step back and decide what they are really trying to teach. When teachers look at the final outcomes first, they can determine the path they wish their programs to take. Some curricular goals are left to the discretion of the teacher, while other times these final outcomes are determined by state or district educational goals. Regardless of the source, teachers usually have some input with the direction they take to get students to meet class objectives. Teachers can determine what they want graduates of their programs to know and be able to do by using personal judgment, by taking goals from external sources into account, and by blending these with personal convictions about how effective physical education programs should be run.

Review of the Five-Step, Standards-Based Planning Process

The first question teachers must address is, "What are the most important concepts and skills relative to activity or to physical education?" The second question to ask is, "How are these concepts and skills used in the real world?" If the concepts are used in the real world and are important for students to know and be able to use or do as adults, then they are worthwhile and should be included in your physical education curriculum.

After the major goals and unit focus have been written, teachers continue to climb the planning staircase outlined in chapter 8 by developing a culminating performance to determine whether students have met the goals as intended by the teachers. If teachers are not going to measure something that requires the use of higher-level skills and thinking, then they should forget the idea of using performance-based assessments. If teachers want students to analyze, evaluate, or synthesize information to demonstrate knowledge acquired, then performance-based assessments are ideal.

After teachers have determined the culminating performance that allows students to demonstrate unit goals, the next step is to identify actions or behaviors that they will accept as evidence that students have accomplished programmatic goals. The question asked here is, "What should my students be able to do as a result of participation in this physical education program?" Since most teachers want students to be competent movers, the answer to this question sometimes depends on the amount of time available and where the teacher is teaching. Will teachers have students develop competence in a team or individual sport, an activity such as dance or gymnastics, or in a leisure activity such as orienteering or in-line skating? Some of these decisions are undoubtedly based on the time table used and the geographical area in which the teachers are located. Students also should possess relevant cognitive knowledge about sport performance. Knowledge about fitness and wellness also falls into this area. Although there are several concepts that generalize across activities, the specifics of this content knowledge vary slightly. Student behavior and disposition toward activity should also be addressed when teachers consider indicators of successful completion of a physical education program. Cognitive and affective indicators are a little more difficult to identify because they represent things that are less overt or visible. Nonetheless, these latter two areas should also be addressed and included.

After the assessments are developed, teachers write criteria to evaluate student performance. As stated in chapter 3, one of the hardest steps of the assessment process is to write the rubrics. Unfortunately, it is also the one most frequently omitted by teachers. Teachers should realize that the criteria for assessments must be determined sooner or later, and it is most advantageous to determine them before students begin to work on the assessment. The rubric is usually not perfect the first time the assessment is used. It is, however, important to have something written that informs students about how the assessment will be evaluated.

Step four of building a standards-based unit of instruction involves the development of a series of performance-based assessments that move students from initial stages of learning to the competence necessary for success on the culminating performance. These assessments provide students and teachers with feedback on student progress so that lessons are developed that maximize a teacher's effectiveness.

The final step in the curricular planning process is to arrange the resources necessary for student success. The best assessments and unit plans cannot overcome poor planning of resources. Teachers need to think ahead so that resources linked to outside agencies or people can be arranged or scheduled. When teachers develop a time line, it helps them ensure that resources, facilities, and support are ready when *they* are ready to begin instruction. Schedules can be adjusted if the teacher knows in advance that some key element will not be available on a given day. Preplanning resources might not seem to be an important component of the planning process, but it can save a lot of stress and prevent instructional disasters!

Lund and Kirk's 35 Tips for Acquiring Assessment Savvy

The prospect of switching to a performance-based assessment format can be a little scary, but when one considers the benefits, these thoughts soon disappear. After teachers make the decision to use performance-based assessments, the question many ask is, "Where do I begin?" We have been through the process of creating assessments many times. The purpose of this last chapter is to give some final suggestions—the dos and don'ts, so to speak—for beginning the transition to performance-based assessment in physical education. This final chapter offers suggestions and words of wisdom to teachers as they begin the road toward the creation of an effective assessment plan for their physical education programs. We have identified 35 ways to help make the assessment process in physical education more efficient and meaningful for teachers, students, parents, and administrators (see figure 11.1).

So here you have it. We'd like to introduce now Lund and Kirk's 35 Tips for Acquiring Assessment Savvy.

1. Think Big, Start Small

When teachers switch to performance-based assessments, they should not throw out all their old assessments immediately. By looking at the various assessments used, teachers can determine which ones are keepers, which ones will be changed eventually, and what needs to be tossed immediately. If teachers incorporate performance-based assessments a little at a time, the task then becomes doable, rather than formidable (figure 11.2). In some instances, performance-based assessments are not even the best alternative. With factual information, for example, traditional testing formats are the most efficient way to measure learning. When teachers, however, are trying to get students to apply their learning, performance-based assessments are better alternatives. Teachers must look at what information they are trying to measure when they determine whether to keep or toss an assessment. If the current assessment does not really measure the desired student outcome, changes should be made. The key to this suggestion is to have a plan and implement it in stages. Purposeful change done gradually makes the switch to performance-based assessments easier.

2. Teach for Depth, Not Breadth

With performance-based assessment, teachers must offer units of sufficient length to allow students to develop skill. In the first place, there is no point in doing assessments when learning is not occurring. Units that last one to two weeks do not allow sufficient time for students to develop the skills necessary for a meaningful experience. Any skill and ability measured during short units were probably developed in other places at other times, rather than as a result of instruction in this class. Second, because performance-based assessments usually require several days to complete, short units don't provide the time necessary for students to get "into" the assessment. We both have found that students enjoy longer units. Students have the necessary time to develop enough skill to participate in the activity at a recreational or meaningful level. When students are successful at an activity, they don't get bored, provided that instruction continues to occur throughout the unit. We also feel it is not acceptable for a teacher to present five days of lessons then allow students to play games for the next five weeks. Lessons taught during in-depth units must be educational and they must challenge. When students sense that their skills are improving as they experience success during the learning process, they do not become bored. Assessments help show students just how much they have learned by providing feedback about this progress. Assessments are motivational for students because they provide concrete goals that students can strive to achieve. Performance-based assessments require students to thoroughly understand the activity and unit in which they are engaged. This understanding is only possible through in-depth coverage of the activity or unit.

3. Become a Facilitator of Learning

One of the features of performance-based assessment is that teachers serve as facilitators of learning rather than the sole source of information. When students take ownership for their learning, they tend to become more engaged and interested. This is not to say that teaching should cease with performance-based assessment. On the contrary, students

Lund and Kirk's 35 Tips for Acquiring Assessment Savvy

1. Think Big, Start Small
2. Teach for Depth, Not Breadth
3. Become a Facilitator of Learning
4. Write Down Instructional Goals So That You Clearly State What You Want
5. Make Learning and Assessment As Authentic As Possible
6. Remember That Learning and Assessment Should Be Inseparable
7. Align Instruction With Assessment
8. Design Assessments So That Novice Levels of Learning Can Be Detected
9. Measure Affective Domain Dispositions if You Want Students to Acquire Them
10. Differentiate the Performance Task to Meet the Needs of Diverse Students
11. Use a Variety of Assessments to Measure All Aspects of Student Learning
12. Give Students Choices About Assessment
13. Keep Optional Assignments Equivalent
14. Write the Prompt So That Students Have Enough Information to Succeed
15. Write Rubrics Carefully
16. Specify Levels of Achievement
17. Present Assessments Early in the Unit
18. Use Assessment Continuously
19. Use Assessments for Multiple Purposes
20. Establish Checkpoints for Assessments
21. Develop Your Assessment Strategies
22. Keep Assessment From Being a Burden
23. Be Prepared to Revise Assessments
24. Use Assessments to Showcase Student Learning and Promote the Physical Education Program
25. Help Your Students Be Assessable
26. Allow Adequate Time for Students to Complete Performance Assessments
27. Weight More Difficult Assessments to Give Proper Credit for Extra Effort
28. Give Students the Opportunity to Improve or Correct Performance
29. Have Students take Assessments Seriously
30. Engage the Student, Not the Parents
31. Avoid Activities That Are Culturally Biased
32. Don't Trust Your Memory When Grading Students
33. Make Sure the Pieces Fit
34. Share Your Ideas With Other Colleagues
35. Be Part of the Solution, Not Part of the Problem

Figure 11.1   By addressing these elements, you can begin your journey to improve student assessment practices.

Figure 11.2   Think big, start small. When moving toward a performance-based assessment system, first consider which of your current assessment practices can still be used and then change others a few at a time.

can learn from sources other than the teacher, which is something teachers can actually facilitate with their assessments. With performance-based assessments, teachers are encouraged to step out of the front of the room and see what is happening from the back. When teachers learn to become facilitators and when they encourage genuine learning, an exciting phenomenon happens in the gymnasium: Other forms of learning begin to occur. Results are impressive when teachers coach students to learn and help them reach the outcomes or goals of the physical education program.

4. Write Down Instructional Goals So That You Clearly State What You Want   Teachers should begin to plan for assessment by asking themselves, "What should my students be able to do as the result of instruction?" This question helps focus the unit and should point teachers to the knowledge they assess and the type of assessments they use to determine student learning. Unfortunately, some teachers know what they want to teach, but they never put it in writing. By writing the intended goals instead of "knowing" them in their heads, teachers will have a much clearer idea about what they want students to learn. Too often teachers have a general idea about what they

want students to accomplish, but until they actually write the goals down, they really haven't clearly articulated the content or goals for the unit. After committing the goals to paper, teachers should create a list of the key understandings students should have at the completion of learning, and they should also develop a list of essential questions to address these. With formal written plans, instruction becomes much more deliberate, and assessments target the desired learning.

5. Make Learning and Assessment As Authentic As Possible   Some students question the relevance of an assignment or assessment. Teachers must ask, "Is this important?" before they decide what to assess. If teachers add a degree of authenticity to the assessment, students can then readily see the purpose of what teachers have them do and the value of doing it. When creating performance-based assessments, teachers should look for ways to make them as realistic as possible. Newspapers can provide ideas and so can television and other forms of media. Teachers should look to those people associated with sport to determine what they do and the knowledge base they must have to do their jobs well. When this knowledge base is compatible with what a teacher is covering in physical education and when it can be used to measure learning, a new assessment may have just been born. Performance-based assessments are great ways for teachers to let students know that this information is important beyond class and in the real world. Knowing that something is important can be an excellent motivator for students, of all skill levels, beginner to advanced. As the meaning of the task increases, so too does motivation, interest, and the amount of time students, are willing to spend completing it. When assessments engage students, as opposed to being a chore, they'll be easier for students to complete and easier for teachers to administer.

6. Remember That Learning and Assessment Should Be Inseparable   Effective, formative performance-based assessments provide feedback to students about their performance, making them fantastic teaching and learning tools. Assessments that fail to provide feedback for students do not do everything for a teacher's program that they can do, and they should be adjusted to do so. The ultimate goal of assessment should be to intertwine assessment and learning so that it is seamless and impossible to separate one from the other.

Assessment does not have to be an enemy of instruction; rather, it should be seen as an integral part of the learning process. It points out strengths and weaknesses, and it provides feedback for both teachers and students. When teachers design assessments, they should ask themselves, "How can I create assessments that make students perform better than they think they can, or better than even I think they can?" An assessment can provide challenges to learning and move students beyond their own personal expectations. When teachers design assessments with that in mind, students have greater opportunities to learn.

7. Align Instruction With Assessment Assess what you teach; teach what you assess. This sounds rather simple; however, too many times it just doesn't happen. Remember the class where the teacher lectured about all kinds of topics and the test covered the book that the instructor never mentioned? An assessment should measure the degree to which students learned the designated material. When the wrong evaluation tool is used, this won't happen. Teachers might hear about a new assessment at a conference or read about it in a journal and decide to use it. Unfortunately, the assessment chosen might not be the best way to access the desired student learning in their programs. Assessments must be selected carefully so that they evaluate what the teacher is teaching. Teachers must define what they want students to know and be able to do and then devise appropriate assessments to determine whether students have reached these goals. If the goal is for students to have adequate skill and information to play a game at a recreational level, then this is what should be assessed. If the goal is for students to play a game with a reasonable level of skill, a skill test measuring skill in a closed environment may be an intermediary step in the process, but it won't actually assess game play ability. Teachers can devise rubrics designed to evaluate student ability to play a game. Similarly, if a teacher wants students to perform or choreograph dances, then assessments must be designed to measure this ability and knowledge. Because physical education is

performance oriented, performance-based assessments are logical and very appropriate ways to measure learning. With a little planning, physical education teachers can have excellent instructional alignment and genuinely measure what they want students to achieve.

8. Design Assessments So That Novice Levels of Learning Can Be Detected Assessment should be about finding out what students can do, instead of what they cannot. As stated earlier, the purpose of assessment should be to provide feedback to students to improve performance. All students have *some* content knowledge, and they shouldn't be punished for what they don't have. This is analogous to the pull-up test—every child has some upper-body strength, but can't always demonstrate it on that test. Assessments should be sensitive enough to detect lower levels of achievement, as well as being able to discriminate upper levels of performance. Students of both lower ability and higher ability should be able to demonstrate achievement and learning on valid assessments. This task is challenging, but as teachers begin to understand the various components involved in the assessment process, it can be accomplished.

9. Measure Affective Domain Dispositions if You Want Students to Acquire Them Many performance-based assessments are designed to measure content knowledge and skill in the world of physical education and physical activity. Other affective domain attributes are important as well, and they can easily be incorporated into the assessment if the rubrics or scoring guides address them. Dispositions such as cooperation, fair play, caring, perseverance, resourcefulness, and responsibility are highly desirable traits for adults to possess. If these behaviors are taught to students and are addressed in assessments, then students are more likely to develop them. Since behaviors do not develop spontaneously, teachers need to assume the onus of teaching the desired ones to students. For example, highly able students haven't always learned the art of persistence because the tasks come so easy for them. Performance-based assessments can be structured so that highly skilled athletes must work to achieve the highest levels of performance and learn valuable work habits. Game play rubrics should address cooperation and fair play issues. These types of qualities are essential ingredients for success in life. Because they fit so well into physical education programs, failing to include them in the learning and assessment process represents an oversight on the part of the teacher or physical education program.

10. Differentiate the Performance Task to Meet the Needs of Diverse Students Students come to physical education with diverse talents, skills, and a variety of learning profiles, yet many teachers require them to all do the same assessments. When students are given choices with assessments, they can personalize both learning and performance. Instruction is most successful when teachers teach one step above current levels of performance. Every student *has* a current level of performance—low, medium, or high. When teachers use assessment to inform instruction, they can provide just the right amount of stimulation to students. The work should not be so easy that students are bored or so challenging that students give up. Either state causes the brain to shut down, and students therefore fail to learn (Callahan 1997). Performance tasks should be challenging to each student, with every student capable of some degree of success.

11. Use a Variety of Assessments to Measure All Aspects of Student Learning Teachers should add variety to their assessment vocabularies. Some students do poorly on one type of assessment despite good content knowledge. With a variety of assessments, students have an opportunity to use an assessment format that addresses their strengths while still measuring their achievement. Some states use specific testing formats (e.g., open-response questions, on-demand tasks) to assess student learning. In these states, teachers must give students opportunities to practice that testing format prior to completing statewide assessment formats. When students are unfamiliar with a testing format, they may have the desired content knowledge but may be unable to demonstrate it. However, the testing formats used by the state should not become the only assessment format used in a physical education program. Role plays, fictitious interviews with famous people, and play-by-play commentary are just a few of the performance-based assessments that give students the opportunity to demonstrate their many talents that might otherwise go unnoticed. Also remember that assessments shouldn't be chosen because they are cute or fun but because they allow students to demonstrate their competence in a given area. Variety in assessment practices is a positive way for teachers to ensure that students are assessed on their content knowledge and that test format does not interfere with students demonstrating what they know.

12. Give Students Choices About Assessment Adults can usually choose what they want to learn; students rarely have that luxury. Students are required to do exactly what the teacher decides they should do. Giving students choices about the type of assessment to complete allows them to take ownership in the assessment process, thus providing additional motivation to achieve. Brain research tells us that student choice enhances motivation (Harrison, Blakemore, and Buck 2001). Giving students choices about the type of assessment to complete allows them to take ownership in the assessment process and provides an incentive to do better. Students won't have to question, "Why are we doing this?" because they are the ones who have selected the task and assessment. Too often the answer to "Why am I doing this?" is "For the grade," or "Because the teacher wants to do it," which, to some, is not very motivating. Giving students assessment options that measure a given body of knowledge in different ways is a positive assessment strategy. Too often in traditional assessment formats, students learn something only for the test—and then it's over. Learning becomes more meaningful and longer lasting when teachers let students use information and take some ownership in the learning process.

13. Keep Optional Assignments Equivalent When allowing differentiation or choice in assessments, teachers must make sure that the various options are equivalent. The options must require equal time and effort to complete. Also, they must measure the same content knowledge. When differentiated assignments are done correctly, each one should have some students who choose to complete it. If every student chooses the same option, then teachers should reexamine the assignment because one option may require less work than others. Teachers should look at the learning goals set

I recently required students to submit artifacts for a portfolio on sport. Because I was rushed, I did not include a rubric. Although I was very specific about what should be included when I explained the list of required components, my students turned in work that was minimal and disappointing to me. For the next portfolio assignment, I included a rubric that specified levels of acceptable and unacceptable performance. The results were vastly different from the products turned in for the first assessment. When I clearly specified my expectations through a rubric, the students' work improved dramatically.

for the unit and make sure that all assessments measure the degree to which students achieve them. Sometimes differentiated assignments are fun to complete, but really they have little to do with assessing instructional goals.

14. Write the Prompt So That Students Have Enough Information to Succeed Teachers should be explicit with the directions given to students so that they know exactly what they are expected to accomplish and do. Tasks should be clearly written with adequate detail so that teachers get the desired results and behaviors that they wish to assess. The rubric is often a critical addition because it helps to define desired performance, and it signals students about what teachers will look for in the final product or performance. Students can be more successful when they understand what the assessment entails before they begin to work.

15. Write Rubrics Carefully Rubrics should be written in a positive light in terms of what students can do, rather than what they cannot (e.g., student does not show balance as opposed to student performs the move but is shaky or wobbles when trying to hold the pose). Too many times rubrics indicate deficiencies rather than recognize what students can do. A student might not be capable of performing at an expert level, but some level of competence should be present, which should be reflected in the rubric. If a student is judged as totally inept, then little learning has occurred and the teacher should question why an assessment is being administered at all. It also is more motivating for students when rubrics are written in a positive framework because even the least-skilled students can identify some things they are capable of doing. Teachers must also remember to choose

criteria carefully. Criteria should be the key elements that differentiate the lowest levels of performance from the highest levels of performance. Descriptive criteria help distinguish levels of performance and indicate things that an expert does to make the performance exceptional. By selecting criteria that differentiate achievement teachers can see what students have learned.

16. Specify Levels of Achievement When teachers create performance-based assessments, they must establish the *requirements* for performance. It is not enough to require students to submit a portfolio without giving any parameters or guidelines for what should be included. Teachers must envision what they expect students to include in the portfolio to satisfy their expectations for learning.

If teachers fail to set an acceptable level of achievement for student work when it is possible to do so, then the assessment decreases in value: The assignment merely becomes a matter of completion, rather than trying to demonstrate excellence. When levels of quality are formally stated, students know teacher expectations and can strive to do their best. By determining levels of quality, teachers can differentiate the efforts of students and justifiably reward those who submit higher-quality work. Teachers find that when criteria for excellence are clearly articulated, either through verbal descriptions or exemplars, overall student performance improves.

17. Present Assessments Early in the Unit When students know how they are assessed, they can practice during downtime (e.g., before class when others are dressing, during game play when their team is not playing). This is true whether teachers use traditional or performance-based assessments. Because students know how they are assessed, the assessment can have an impact *throughout* the unit, rather than just on "assessment day," as students know what they are expected to do. Also, when students are familiar with the assessment protocol, the assessment can be administered much more quickly, decreasing the time needed for an explanation. Giving students a chance to prepare for assessment is worthwhile from both an instructional standpoint, as well as an assessment one.

18. Use Assessment Continuously Too many teachers do assessments only when they must determine student grades. The main purpose of assessment should be to provide feedback to students. If students are going to improve, they need continuous information regarding their performance throughout the unit. For this reason, assessment should be a continuous, ongoing process. Teachers must continually move students toward their culminating performance or accomplishment that demonstrates both learning and competence. Assessments provide feedback to students about how well they are doing and if they are on target to achieve final goals for instruction. Final or culminating assessments can and should be graded. However, given the paperwork connected with recording grades for the number of students secondary teachers have on their rosters, assessments that lead to this final assessment might not be incorporated into final student grades.

When some type of assessment is given every day, either alone or integrated with learning activities, students have continuous feedback on how their learning is progressing. Teachers can use this information to shape subsequent lessons. When students are unable to perform a given assessment, this signals the teacher that students are not ready to move on to the next skill. When assessment is done continuously, it can assume multiple roles, rather than just contribute to a grade.

19. Use Assessments for Multiple Purposes When appropriate rubrics are written, assessments can serve multiple purposes, thus making efficient use of class time while still providing the required information about student achievement. A jump rope routine can demonstrate psychomotor performance, cognitive understanding of choreography and jumping techniques, cooperation with others, and the ability to count rhythms, perform steps, and jump to the beat. The teacher can assess many programmatic goals using a single assessment.

20. Establish Checkpoints for Assessments Teachers usually use different drills on different days. If instead the teacher used the same or similar drill on successive days, then students could note improvement over time. These repetitive drills or checkpoints give feedback to students and teachers alike about improvement because they are done on multiple occasions. A teacher might ask students at the completion of a checkpoint drill whether their performance reached the criterion set by the teacher or ask whether their performance had improved from a previous day or practice attempt. When students are given three or four chances on these checkpoint activities and assessments each day, they should see improvement during a single class. Checkpoint drills could be incorporated into assessments later on in the unit, thus transforming instruction into assessment. Students are motivated when they know that they are improving. Repetitive drills or checkpoints can provide concrete ways for students to see their skills improve.

21. Develop Your Assessment Strategies With large numbers of students, one way to integrate assessment with learning and practice tasks is to utilize peer assessment and self-evaluation. Teachers might, for example, develop learning progressions that have concrete goals, as in the table tennis progression shown in figure 11.3. Students self-evaluate or peer-assess tasks throughout the progression but are not allowed to move to the next level of learning until performing the final task of a given level for the teacher. The final task of each level should represent an application of knowledge or require students to combine several skills previously mastered in the progression. On the example shown, the teacher is required to assess one skill or drill out of seven. Because students move through this progression at different rates, teacher evaluations are generally spread out and students are not required to wait for their turn to be assessed by the teacher.

Table Tennis Skill Assessment

Level I

1. Six returns of serve using a forehand push shot
   a. Must be consecutive
   b. Any placement on the table permitted
2. Six returns of serve using a backhand push shot
   a. Must be consecutive
   b. Any placement on the table permitted
3. Six **consecutive** returns of serve using a forehand pick shot
   a. Any placement on the table permitted
4. Six **consecutive** returns of serve using a backhand pick shot
   a. Any placement on the court is permitted
5. Six **consecutive** forehand serves using backspin
   a. Must start from the right-hand side of the table and be diagonal
6. Six **consecutive** forehand serves using topspin
   a. Must start from the right-hand side of the table and be diagonal
7. Ten-hit rally using any combination of shots
   a. May be started with a serve; this is not the **first** hit
   b. If started with a bounce, this is not the **first** hit

Level II

1. Ten-hit forehand-to-forehand rally using only the push shot
   a. May be started with a serve; this is not the **first** hit
   b. If started with a bounce, this is not the **first** hit
2. Ten-hit backhand-to-backhand rally using only the push shot
   a. May be started with a serve; this is not the **first** hit
   b. If started with a bounce, this is not the **first** hit
3. Ten-hit forehand-to-forehand rally using only the pick shot
   a. May be started with a serve; this is not the **first** hit
   b. If started with a bounce, this is not the **first** hit
4. Ten-hit backhand-to-backhand rally using only the pick shot
   a. May be started with a serve; this is not the **first** hit
   b. If started with a bounce, this is not the **first** hit
5. Six consecutive returns of a topspin serve using the forehand chop shot
   a. No placement required for the chop
   b. Serve diagonally from right service court
6. Six consecutive returns of a topspin serve using the backhand chop
   a. No placement required for the chop
   b. Serve diagonally from right service court

(continued)

Figure 11.3 Since the teacher assesses only the final task in each level while students self- or peer-assess the previous tasks, teachers are able to hold students accountable for skill development while monitoring student progress and learning.

Level II (continued)

7. Sixteen-hit rally using any combination of shots
   a. May be started with a serve; this is not the **first** hit
   b. If started with a bounce, this is not the **first** hit
8. Six consecutive backhand serves using backspin
   a. Must serve from right-hand court
   b. No placement required on receiver's side of the table
9. Six consecutive backhand serves using topspin
   a. Must serve from right-hand court
   b. No placement required on receiver's side of the table
10. Four out of six slams: partner tosses the ball with slight topspin to bounce 10 to 12 inches high from the table for the performer to slam; partner catches the ball

Level III

1. Ten-hit backhand-to-forehand rally using the push shot
   a. May also be forehand to backhand
   b. Has to be done twice so that each person has a chance to do both forehand and backhand hits
   c. May be started with a serve; this is not the **first** hit
   d. If started with a bounce, this is not the **first** hit
2. Twenty-hit rally using half of the table and only the push shot
3. Ten-hit backhand-to-forehand rally using the pick shot
   a. May also be forehand to backhand
   b. Has to be done twice so that each person has a chance to do both forehand and backhand hits
   c. May be started with a serve; this is not the **first** hit
   d. If started with a bounce, this is not the **first** hit
4. Ten-hit rally using half of the table and only the pick shot
5. Eight out of 10 forehand serves, alternating topspin and backspin, to a sheet of paper (8-1/2 by 11) placed on the receiver's court.
6. Eight out of 10 backhand serves, alternating topspin and backspin, to a sheet of paper (8-1/2 by 11) placed on the receiver's court.
   a. Serve must be diagonal
7. Eight-hit rally using only the chop shot
   a. May be started with a serve; this is not the **first** hit
   b. If started with a bounce, this is not the **first** hit
8. Five **consecutive** returns of slam shots with a push or chop shot for multiple slam shots
   a. Both partners must do this
   b. Any placement of slam shot is allowed

Figure 11.3 *(continued)*

Teachers can also assess students in large classes by systematically evaluating a different set of students each day. Students know that 6 to 10 students are targeted each day for evaluation on a "good behavior" evaluation form. They don't, however, know which 6 to 10 students are being assessed. Eventually every student in class is evaluated, but the teacher is not overwhelmed in the process. When students know that teachers have this type of built-in accountability, they are more likely to stay on task. The teacher has a clearly stated method to assess student effort during class, rather than an abstract entity with an unclear definition.

22.   Keep Assessment From Being a Burden Although performance-based assessments are wonderful additions to the learning process, they are time-consuming to create, administer, and evaluate. When teachers rely exclusively on performance-based assessments, they might grow to dread the whole assessment process. To keep assessment from becoming a burden, try a variety of approaches. First of all, major assessments that require a lot of time to grade can be spread out. Teachers should not simultaneously give all of their students an assessment that requires significant time to grade. If teachers determine that a performance-based assessment is an appropriate measure of learning, they might then require it of one or two classes, while at the same time, other classes might complete other forms of assessment. With a rotation of performance-based assessments through the various classes, every student would eventually have an opportunity to do the performance-based assessment, but not all at once. Chapter 6 provides information on how to use portfolios in physical education. If teachers taught three different sport or activity units during a semester, a class would be expected to do one portfolio during the semester while other forms of performance-based assessment were used in the other two units. This way a teacher would only grade portfolios from two classes at any one time, instead of one from each class. All students would assemble a portfolio during the semester, but this would not occur simultaneously for the teacher.

A second approach to avoid having performance-based assessments become burdens might be to grade parts of the assessment when possible instead of requiring the assessment at the end of a unit. Obviously, some assessments could not be broken apart, making this approach unusable. In reasonable pieces, grading the entire culminating assessment becomes less of a burden and much more manageable.

23.   Be Prepared to Revise Assessments Good teachers tinker with assessments. Most assessments, performance-based or traditional, can be improved or fine-tuned. Expecting to write the perfect assessment the first time is unrealistic. Teachers should continually be on the alert for new slants or perspectives that further improve the evaluation instrument. Because performance-based assessments are written with an open format, which allows students to personalize them while remaining within the parameters set by the teacher, sometimes the new ideas for altering assessments come from students themselves. When teachers keep themselves open to different ways of addressing the various assessments, new and better assessments emerge. Just as a stone polisher continues smoothing the rough edges, teachers need to continually revise and refine assessments. Refining assessments helps teachers increase their clarity and vision about the things they want students to know, understand, and be able to do. A teacher must truly understand the learning that is necessary and what is involved before the assessment reaches excellence. Each time an assessment is used, teachers should seek to improve and refine it.

24.   Use Assessments to Showcase Student Learning and Promote the Physical Education Program There are many performance-based assessments that can both showcase and assess student learning, while at the same time add authenticity to the assessment. Excellent ways to assess student learning and to let others know what is happening in physical education include assignments that have students write articles for school newspapers, create newsletters that go home to parents, or even write to the local newspaper. Students must demonstrate knowledge of games and activities to write about them. Teachers could require students to research information to supplement an article about what is happening in class. Physical education "Back to School" nights can be culminating performances for a variety of activities. Physical educators might sponsor a dance and invite parents to participate with their children using dances that students learned in physical education class. An instructional assessment component could be added that has students teach these dances to adults. Half time performances at local sporting events provide other opportunities to showcase physical education accomplishments. When students know that they will have a live audience, they work harder to perfect their skills. Last, students might create videos that could become home exercise tapes or aerobic workouts for their families. All of these ideas can be excellent performance-based assessments that promote the physical education program, while at the same time serve as assessments for students.

25. Help Your Students Be Assessable Students must understand the purpose of assessment to do their best. When they understand the goals of learning and what they must accomplish to meet these goals, performance improves. Peer evaluations and self-assessments should be part of the total assessment package for a physical education program. Too many teachers make the mistake of assuming that students can already do these, and they fail to teach students how they should be done. As a result, the assessments are less effective than they should be. Students who don't understand that the purpose of an assessment is to give feedback to improve performance may be tempted to give classmates high marks on skill analysis peer assessments, even when these high marks are not warranted. Teachers should also remember their early days of teaching when the art of skill analysis was not very easy. Teaching students what to look for when they perform a skill analysis assessment, as well as where prominent errors might occur, is essential. Students must also see the whole assessment process as one designed to make them better performers. Also, clarifying expectations decreases the ambiguity about assessment and helps decrease the stress associated with the evaluation process.

26. Allow Adequate Time for Students to Complete Performance Assessments Effective performance-based assessments, those that are worthwhile and worth doing, require time to complete. Teachers should allot adequate time so that students can do their best. It's better to have fewer assessments, on which students can do quality work, rather than several assessments that don't let students really become engaged in the learning process. Short units don't provide adequate time for students to do their best on assessments. Also, when assessments are given during the later stages of a unit, adequate time may not be available for students to use this feedback. Student performance potential is maximized when students are informed about assessments as early as possible and when adequate time is allocated to complete the requirements in an instructional unit.

27. Weight More Difficult Assessments to Give Proper Credit for Extra Effort When teachers give students choices about what they need to do, teachers must make sure the projects and products are equivalent in terms of requirements or time. If they are not equivalent, teachers can weight them, giving additional credit to those who take on harder tasks. Students who are capable of doing difficult work usually will not take on this challenge unless they are rewarded for their extra effort. By making the difficult assessments worth more, teachers encourage able students to take on challenging assessments, thus encouraging the students to work at a level of difficulty appropriate for their talent.

28. Give Students the Opportunity to Improve or Correct Performance Many performance-based assessments are formative and provide students with multiple chances for evaluation. Formative assessments have many benefits. When students know in advance what they will be assessed on, they can prepare for the evaluation. Alexander (1982) found that grading was an excellent way to increase student performance. In one instance, when students were graded on a putting task (golf), student performance trials increased exponentially. This accountability can work on multiple days when students are given the opportunity to practice for the assessment (Lund 1992).

Students can best improve performance if they have the opportunity to use specific feedback that they're given. Students should be given the opportunity to ask, "How could I get better at doing this?" or "What did I do well and what could be improved?" A formative approach to assessment gives students the opportunity to hone their skills and make significant improvement.

29. Have Students Take Assessments Seriously While giving students multiple chances to improve performance (i.e., formative assessment) has merit, students must also understand that a teacher has a limited amount of time available. It should not be expended evaluating subpar performances. If allowed, some students will take the approach that they have nothing to lose, so why not show the teacher their skill. When students are given rubrics by which to self-evaluate and peer-assess, they can help the teacher avoid the evaluation of inferior student work. Students must understand that they do not have unlimited time and attempts to present material for evaluation. Although they should have more than one opportunity to demonstrate their competence, they also must understand that when they give the teacher something to evaluate, it should, in the students' minds, meet the criteria specified for the assessment. If the teacher is actually assessing students for a grade, then student skill levels should be developed enough for students to pass the assessment. Students must take assessments seriously, rather than diminishing their importance because they know they will have other opportunities to demonstrate competence.

30. Engage the Student, Not the Parents With performance-based assessment, students often work outside of class. If the result is a product, parents might be over-involved in its completion. With good performance tasks, you should find ways to engage the learner so that it is the learner who is ultimately graded, not the parent. Safeguards must be built in to ensure that the student has done the assessment rather than an outsider. With the addition of an in-class assignment—such as explaining the process used to complete the assessment—teachers can help to provide some assurance that students completed the work independently. The in-class work could be designed so that the student could not complete it without having personally done the outside-of-class work as well. Another tactic might be to have parents complete a log that documents student work on the project.

31. Avoid Activities That Are Culturally Biased One of the strengths of performance-based assessment identified by early advocates was that they were thought to be free from bias. Evaluators now realize that bias can also creep into performance-based assessments as well. Teachers should avoid biases connected with gender, socioeconomic status, ethnicity, disabilities, and so on when they select topics for performance-based assess-

ment projects. Some physical education programs promote bias when only team sports are included, which favor students with superior strength or power. Research projects may favor those students with home computers and Internet access unless provisions are made to give all students access to this technology. Teachers may unintentionally favor a written performance-based assessment that is word-processed or utilizes colorful clip-art images. Rubrics for written work must address content, as well as writing form. Teachers must take care to avoid bias when they select assessments and write criteria for the accompanying rubrics.

32. Don't Trust Your Memory When Grading Students When teachers assess students, they should record it in some way. There are a variety of ways to do this, from high-tech, palm-held computers to low-tech clipboards. Checklists allow teachers to record data quickly and effectively. Analytic rubrics can be used to compare student results and progress. Most secondary teachers have several classes that all do similar activities and drills. To remember performances from every student is a difficult, if not an impossible, task (figure 11.4). With a systematic way to record student performance, teachers are more likely

Figure 11.4 Trying to remember performances from every student during a grading a period is a difficult, if not impossible, task.

to have an accurate picture of student achievement, as well as an equitable grading format.

33. Make Sure the Pieces Fit Assessments must fit together so that the entire body of student learning is measured. Assessments should not just address the psychomotor domain. Although that is physical education's primary contribution to a school curriculum, it is not the only contribution. In addition to psychomotor skills, physical education contributes cognitive knowledge and important affective domain learning, as well as fitness and wellness components. Assessments should address all areas of a physical education program without shortchanging some important areas. A written test that covers only a handout that teachers used to supplement class information is not the only cognitive learning that occurred during the unit. While this information is important, knowledge covered in class should also be assessed. Performance-based assessments give teachers an opportunity to assess all information covered in class (figure 11.5). However, they must

Figure 11.5 Assessments must fit together so that the entire picture of student learning is measured.

be designed to fit together without leaving gaps in the measurement process.

34. Share Your Ideas With Other Colleagues Creating assessments and their accompanying rubrics is a time-consuming process. However, if teachers share ideas with colleagues, the process can be much less intimidating. Within a learning community, teachers can share assessments, use others as a sounding board for new ideas, and work as a team to develop and refine new assessment ideas. Teachers can share assessment ideas through

- Web sites such as PE Central, PE Talk, and so on,
- state, regional, and national conferences,
- colleagues within your district,
- former classmates from college,
- student teachers,
- mentor teachers,
- students who are classmates in postbaccalaureate classes,
- college professors, and
- departmental colleagues.

Conferences offer additional ways to get and present new assessment ideas, through formal presentations and informal sessions that occur during breaks and meals. Many conferences encourage physical education teachers to present lessons showing others what has worked for them in their own gymnasiums. By talking about assessment with others, teachers see new ideas emerge. Working with others makes creating assessments a more enjoyable process.

35. Be Part of the Solution, Not Part of the Problem Physical education can make a valuable contribution to a school curriculum when it is properly taught and administered. Physical education programs must be strong if they are to continue being a part of school curriculums in the future. Recent attention has been given to obesity and lack of physical activity of youth in the United States (NASPE, 2001). Problems also occur in the school culture, as students fail to respect the rights of others and don't know how to interact with one another in a positive manner. Physical education can have a positive influence on many school problems; it can address concerns in ways that no other subject area can. Physical education programs must be deliberate in their teaching and must be accountable to the larger school program. To measure learning in physical education and to document what is accomplished can increase the status of physical education in a school. This is not to say that assessment is the golden key to elevate the importance of physical education in a school. Rather, without assessment and the appropriate data, teachers cannot document the results of their teaching.

Conclusion

Assessment can be a burden, or it can be an opportunity to help students learn. We have chosen the latter because we see a strong connection between assessment and learning. The performance-based assessments described in this book provide teachers with a fresh way to look at student achievement. So much of physical education is performance oriented that these new forms of assessment seem to be tailor-made for physical education.

In their visionary article, Hensley and coauthors (1987) state that "much of what was being delivered in our professional training is not being put to use and that hundreds of published tests lie dormant because they are inappropriate for the typical classroom setting" (61). We sincerely believe that the assessment practices we suggest address many of the concerns outlined in that article. Further, we strongly feel that the assessments described in this text are appropriate for use in gymnasium settings. Teachers are encouraged to utilize performance-based assessments to provide students feedback on learning and, when appropriate, to contribute to student grade reports. Through self-assessments, peer assess-

ments, and evaluations done by teachers, the instructional process can be greatly enhanced. Although Hensley et al. concluded that the proposed changes might sound, "too radical, too abstract, too optimistic, or simply out of this world" (62), we disagree. The climate for change in assessment practices is ripe, and there is no better time than now to accept the challenges and the opportunities that follow.

We strongly encourage the readers to try these ideas in their classes as a means to enhance instruction and student learning. The thought of implementing them may be a bit overwhelming, which is why we suggest developing an "assessment buddy" to start the process. The buddy might be a colleague within the teacher's physical education department, one from another school, a college friend, or someone you meet over the Internet. Once teachers begin to use performance-based assessments, we think they'll discover that the assessments are actually fun to use. Performance-based assessments also address some of the assessment problems that have plagued physical education for years. Through refinements and revisions, the assessments can develop into tasks that are meaningful to both students and teachers.

We recognize that implementing a new assessment agenda is not an easy process, but as with any journey, the first step is probably the hardest. Teachers should start by trying some of the ideas found in this book and then modify them to fit the needs of the program.

When teachers keep initial attempts at performance-based assessment simple, success is more likely to happen. The results can be positive and rewarding. It's time to take that first step and begin climbing the stairs to a new way to assess student learning and a new assessment agenda.

accumulative—An accumulative portfolio includes documents that represent student learning across multiple units.

adventure education event tasks—Event tasks are activities that can be completed within a single class period. Adventure education event tasks would typically involve some type of cooperative challenge that could be finished during a single instructional period.

affective dispositions—The behaviors associated with students' attitudes, values, or beliefs.

affective domain—Learning dispositions concerning how students act and feel. Areas associated with the affective domain could include self-concept, effort, respect for others, assisting classmates and teachers, and so on.

alternative assessment—A term used to describe a performance-based assessment.

analytic rubric—A means of scoring an assessment that lists the various points or dimensions and allows the scorer to determine a level or degree of quality for the item. There are two types of analytic rubrics: qualitative (numerical) and quantitative.

application tasks—Learning or assessment tasks in which the student is required to apply learned skills, strategies, or knowledge, often in authentic situations.

artifact—Refers to a document that demonstrates student learning of specific goal or standard in an evaluation portfolio.

authentic assessment—A term used to describe a performance-based assessment.

backward mapping—A method of planning where the teacher begins by identifying the final student goal that students are expected to achieve and then designing learning experiences that allow students to achieve that final goal.

Bloom's taxonomy—A system for classifying levels of learning from simple to complex.

central organizer—A statement that focuses the unit content on a specific theme, concept, problem, skill, issue, or content in the backward mapping planning process.

characteristic—A term used to indicate the elements contained in a rubric to define excellence.

checklist—A type of rubric that lists characteristics or behaviors regarding a performance. It is scored as being present or not, with no judgment of quality made.

checkpoints—Also referred to as progress checkpoints. Assessments that are done several times that allow students to track progress and learning on a skill or activity.

cognitive knowledge—Knowledge related to the application, comprehension, evaluation, or synthesis of information relative to a given subject area.

competent bystander—A student who has good behavior but actually avoids participating in class activities.

concurrent validity—Measures a small sample of items that represent the total content measured.

content standards—Standards that establish the content that should be learned in various subjects.

construct validity—A type of validity that determines if the teacher is actually measuring what is intended to be measured. This is of greatest concern when developing performance-based rubrics.

content validity—Indicates the degree that the test items represent the total content of that which is to be measured.

criteria—The elements contained in a rubric or scoring guide that identify factors necessary for evaluating performance.

criterion referenced—Student learning is based on a preset standard of acceptable performance, without reference to performance of other students.

culminating assessment—A final performance or product that students complete that should provide evidence that the students have achieved unit goals and standards.

culminating performance—The final demonstration of skill that students are expected to present that requires students to apply the learning that occurred during the unit of study.

curriculum backward planning map—Guideline for planning a unit of study that begins with the identification of broad goals and standards that students achieve.

descriptor—A term used to indicate the elements contained in a rubric to define excellence.

essays—A performance assessment technique that involves having the students create some type of written product, such as a brochure, speech, dialogue, or critique of performance (e.g., a dance review).

essential questions--- The third component of the major focus of the curriculum planning map. Questions that students should be able to answer throughout and at the end of a unit to achieve the unit goals.

evaluation portfolio—A portfolio submitted for evaluation that contains artifacts that demonstrate competency in a subject or area. A written narrative accompanies the evaluation portfolio explaining the significance of each item included.

event tasks—An assessment technique that can be completed within a single class period or less. It usually involves some type of physical activity such as game play, creating a game or routine, choreographing a dance, rope skipping, or performing a dance.

exemplar—An example of student work used to exemplify acceptable performance.

extension tasks—Progression of learning tasks in which the situation, the criteria, or the task itself is changed to make it more difficult or easier to facilitate the extension of learning.

five-step standards-based planning process—Planning guideline model that uses backward mapping planning strategies, overall broad goals, and standards which students should achieve are identified on the top step. The teacher then moves down the steps in planning to identify the culminating assessment, essential questions, essential knowledge, skills, strategies, and learning and assessment activities and critical resources that students must learn to arrive at the top of the staircase to achieve goals and standards.

formative assessment—An assessment done during the learning process. Students are given feedback about areas that need additional learning so that they have the opportunity to correct or improve the final product.

game play—When students engage in an application task related to a competitive activity. Game play could include both small-sided or regulation games.

game play rubric—The set of criteria that a teacher uses to evaluate student ability to participate in a game or game-like activity.

generalized rubrics—Universal rubrics to assess a variety of performances, such as game play for team sports, writing samples, and so on.

group portfolio—A portfolio developed by a group effort in which each member of a small group contributes artifacts. Students are evaluated on group cooperation

holistic rubric—A means of evaluating an assessment that uses paragraphs to describe levels of performance. Several characteristics or traits are included within the paragraph, making these more suitable for evaluating culminating events or summative performances.

instructional alignment—A curricular planning technique where teachers test what they teach. Goals for student learning, instruction, and assessments are all concerned with the same knowledge or learning.

integrated assessment tasks—Assessment tasks that are completed along with learning or practice activities to provide students and teachers feedback about learning and level of progress.

interviews—An assessment technique where students are questioned by teachers to determine the extent of student learning. This form of assessment is best used when evaluating a small group of students.

journals—An assessment technique that allows students to write and reflect on various topics. Students are either given a specific topic to reflect on, or they are allowed to write on a topic of personal interest. Journals are excellent ways for teachers to look at student learning for affective domain components.

levels—Refers to a level of performance associated with analytic or holistic rubrics. Levels indicate varying degrees of student mastery of the subject matter.

multiple independent component question—A type of open response question that asks several questions about the same prompt. It has at least two questions or parts, and each answer is independent of the other questions.

multidimensional assessment—A student portfolio in which the student documents the attainment of two or more goals or standards.

multiyear portfolio—A portfolio that is developed by students to demonstrate learning across many years, (i.e., middle grades: 6th, 7th, and 8th grade).

narrative—A type of parental report that contains a written description of a student's achievement in a subject area. They are more widely used at the elementary level than they are at the secondary level.

norm referenced—Student learning is compared to the achievement of others who are equivalent in age or other characteristics and were assessed under similar circumstances.

numerical analytic rubric—Another term used for *quantitative analytic rubric.*

open response questions—An assessment technique that allows students to use knowledge learned in class and apply it to solve a problem presented in a real-world scenario. Many solutions to the problem are possible, and students are required to use higher-order thinking skills to create a solution.

peer evaluations or assessments—An assessment strategy that uses students to evaluate the performance of others in the class. Students observe the performance of a classmate and then provide feedback (written or verbal) to the person doing the activity.

peer observations—A peer assessment technique that requires students to watch one another and analyze the performance of a classmate. The teacher typically provides some type of guidelines, criteria, or rubric, which the student uses to complete the observation.

performance-based assessments—Assessments that look at students actively engaged in doing a task that represents achievement of a learning goal or standard. The task frequently is a performance or a simulation of one that someone actually in the field might do. Assessment and instruction are usually intertwined, making it impossible to separate the two. Students are given the criteria along with the assessment.

performance standards—These standards specify a level of performance for student learning. They indicate the nature of the evidence that is accepted to satisfy the standard, as well as a level of quality for the performance.

point system rubric—A scoring guide that consists of a list of characteristics by which to judge a performance or product that are assigned points and can be totaled to arrive at a final or overall score. There is no judgment about the level of quality for the trait or characteristic; however, the person creating the rubric can indicate a degree of overall importance by weighting the items—that is, assigning more points to those considered more important.

portfolio—Collection of materials or artifacts that, when considered collectively, demonstrate student competence or mastery of some subject or topic.

predictive validity—When a test is used to indicate future performance based on the score received.

progress checkpoints, see checkpoints—Points within a unit, that are identified by the teacher at which student progress is checked through assessment data.

product criteria—Criteria that refer to what a student produces or does. For example, 10 serves in tennis, 5 free throws, or 3 forward rolls.

process criteria—Criteria that refer to how the performance or product is completed. In physical education, process criteria are used to represent the critical elements of a given skill

progress criteria—Criteria used to determine student achievement toward a goal or standard. These are used to measure student improvement.

progressive assessment—A process whereby student progress is assessed from the performance of simple to more complex skills (i.e., those with increasing complex situations or settings).

progressive learning activities—Learning activities that build on previous activities to extend the difficulty of the task by changing the way the task is performed, the situation in which it is performed, or the criteria of the performance.

prompt—A scenario presented with a performance-based assessment that provides a setting for responding to the question being asked (usually a real-world situation).

qualitative analytic rubric—A type of analytic rubric that requires the scorer to determine a level of quality for each trait assessed using a verbal description for that trait. Useful for doing formative assessment of student learning.

quantitative analytic rubric—A type of analytic rubric that requires the scorer to determine a level of quality for each trait assessed using a number, which is grounded with a word or phrase (e.g., *sometimes,*

often, usually, or *never*) to indicate the meaning for that number. These are useful for assessing game play ability.

refinement task—A learning task in which the teacher directs the student's focus of learning to a particular learning cue or critical element of a skill performance, the purpose of which is to refine the performance of that particular element of the skill.

reliability—A means to ensure that the assessment measures what it says it measures each time the assessment is completed.

representative—A representative portfolio includes artifacts that document student learning across one unit of instruction.

response-to-provided-information open response question—A type of open response question that provides students with information (e.g., data from a fitness test, an excerpt from a journal article, diagram of a game strategy) to which a student must respond.

role-plays—When students are given a part in a scenario developed by a teacher to illustrate a point or discuss a class event. Role-plays typically involve some type of affective domain activity.

role-play assessments—An assessment technique. The teacher develops a scenario to assess some components of learning or activity. Often used for assessing affective domain dispositions.

rubric—The guidelines by which a performance or product is judged.

scaffolded open response question—An open response question containing a sequence of tasks that become increasingly more difficult. Each successive question depends on the response generated in the previous question.

self-evaluation—An assessment technique where students evaluate their performance against a set of criteria given by the teacher or an expert source.

single-dimensional assessment—Refers to a student portfolio in which students document learning that represents the attainment of a single goal or standard.

single dimension open response question—An open response question that requires students to respond to a single idea or concept. It often requires students to draw a conclusion or take a position and then justify that position.

standards-based assessment—An assessment designed to demonstrate that a student has achieved a level of performance designated by a content or performance standard.

standards-based instruction—A curriculum designed to enable students to meet instructional standards. The teacher uses a backward mapping planning strategy that begins with looking at the final goal of instruction and then designs learning experiences that allow students to reach that goal.

standards-based instructional format—A curriculum that is developed to allow students to gain competence on published standards. These standards are typically criterion referenced.

student choice open response question—A type of open response question where students can select the question they wish to address. The questions are basically similar but may differ in activity or subject area that the student is to address.

student log—Students are required to track performance by recording the incident each time it occurs. When appropriate, the time spent doing the activity or behavior (duration) is also recorded.

student project—An assessment technique where students are required to create some type of concrete product to demonstrate their learning or achievement on a topic or subject (e.g., a video of a workout routine or a piece of equipment designed to exercise certain muscles).

student performance—A method of assessing student achievement that requires students to demonstrate competence by presenting a piece that typically requires several days or weeks to prepare.

subjectivity—The amount of judgment used in assigning a score to a students assessment performance.

summative assessment—The final assessment of student learning. Typically comes at the conclusion of a unit of study.

task-specific rubric—A rubric written specifically for an individual assessment task. Criteria included in the rubric are specific to that assessment.

teaching to the test—When teachers know the content of an upcoming test and prepare students to do well on it. Usually when this is done teachers prepare students for a test rather than cover content they will need in the adult world, therefore giving it a negative connotation.

thematic portfolio—An assessment portfolio that focuses on a specific theme. For instance: improvement of personal fitness, development of cooperation and teamwork, skills, and attitudes, self-expression through movement.

traditional assessments—A term used to refer to tests typically used for assessment, such as written tests (e.g., multiple choice, true-false, matching formats), skill tests (e.g., a serving test in tennis), or fitness tests (e.g., sit-and-reach, one-minute sit-up test).

trait—A term used to indicate the elements contained in a rubric to define excellence.

transparency—When an assessment provides so much information that the student merely needs to follow the procedure outlined to complete the assessment without having to actually go through the thinking or problem-solving processes the assessment is designed to measure.

validity—A measurement technique designed to ensure that an assessment is measuring the construct that it says it measures.

working portfolio—Places where students can gather diverse information that demonstrates mastery of learning objectives. Artifacts are placed here in preparation for selecting materials to be used for the evaluation portfolio.

BIBLIOGRAPHY

Alexander, K.R. 1982. Behavior analysis of tasks and accountability in physical education. Ph.D. diss., The Ohio State University.

Arter, J. 1996. Performance criteria: The heart of the matter. Ed. R. E. Blum and J. A. Arter. *A Handbook for Student Performance Assessment*. vi-2:1-8. Alexandria, VA: Association for Supervision and Curriculum Development.

Black, P., and D. Wiliam. 1998. Inside the black box: Raising standards through classroom assessment. *Phi Delta Kappan* 80 (2): 139-148.

Bloom, B., G. Madaus, and J.T. Hastings 1981. *Evaluation to improve learning.* New York: McGraw-Hill Book Company.

Brown, J. 1995. *Tennis: Steps to success.* Champaign, IL: Human Kinetics.

Burke, K., R. Fogarty, and S. Belgrad. 1994. *The mindful school: The portfolio connection.* Palatine, IL: IRI/Skylight.

Callahan, C. 1997. *Using performance tasks and rubrics to differentiate instruction.* Read by author. Cassette recording no. 297069. Alexandria, VA: Association for Supervision and Curriculum Development.

Cohen, S.A. 1987. Instructional alignment: Searching for a magic bullet. *Educational Researcher* 16 (8): 16-20.

Cooper Institute for Aerobics Research. 1999. *FITNESS-GRAM test administration manual.* Champaign, IL: Human Kinetics.

Cotten, D., and M. Cotten. 1985. Grading: The ultimate weapon? *Journal of Physical Education, Recreation and Dance,* 56(2), 52-53.

Cunningham, G. 1998. *Assessment in the classroom: Constructing and interpreting tests.* Washington, D.C.: The Falmer Press.

Dick, E., H. Buecker, and K. Wilson. 1999. *Designing standards-based units of study.* Training manual prepared for the Oldham County Summer Institute for Teachers, 14-17 June.

Fredrickson, J.R., and A. Collins. 1989. A systems approach to educational testing. *Educational Researcher* 18 (9): 27-32.

French, K., J. Rink, L. Rikard, A. Mays, S. Lynn, and P. Werner. 1991. The effects of practice progressions on learning two volleyball skills. *Journal of Teaching Physical Education* 10 (3): 261-274.

Graham, G., S. Holt-Hale, and M. Parker. 1998. *Children Moving: A Reflective Approach to Teaching Physical Education* (third Ed) Mountain View, CA: Mayfield.

Graham, G., S. Holt-Hale, and M. Parker. 2001. *A reflective approach to teaching physical education* (fifth Ed). Mountain View, CA: Mayfield.

Griffin, L., S. Mitchell, and J. Oslin. 1997. *Teaching sport concepts and skills: A tactical games approach.* Champaign, IL: Human Kinetics.

Guskey, T. 1996a. *Alternative ways to document and communicate student learning.* Read by author. Cassette recording no. 296211. Alexandria, VA: Association for Supervision and Curriculum Development.

———. 1996b. Three kinds of criteria, *Educational Update* 38 (6): 1, 4-7.

Harrison, J., C. Blakemore, and M. Buck. 2001. *Instructional Strategies for Secondary School Physical Education* (fifth Ed.). New York: McGraw-Hill.

Haywood, C., and C. Lewis. 1997. *Archery: Steps to success.* Champaign, IL: Human Kinetics.

Hensley, L., L. Lambert, T. Baumgartner, and J. Stillwell. 1987. Is evaluation worth the effort? *Journal of Physical Education, Recreation and Dance* 58 (6): 59-62.

Herman, J., P. Aschbacher, and L. Winters. 1992. *A practical guide to alternative assessment.* Alexandria, VA: Association for Supervision and Curriculum Development.

———. 1996. Setting criteria. Ed. R. E. Blum and J. A. Arter. *A Handbook for Student Performance Assessment.* vi-4:1-19. Alexandria, VA: Association for Supervision and Curriculum Development.

Hopple, C.J. 1995. *Teaching for outcomes in elementary physical education.* Champaign, IL: Human Kinetics.

Jennings, J. 1995. School reform based on what is taught and learned. *Phi Delta Kappan* 76 (10): 765-769.

Kentucky Department of Education. (1993). Transformations: Kentucky's Curriculum Framework, Volume II. Frankfurt, KY: Kentucky Department of Education.

Kimeldorf, M. 1994. *A teacher's guide to creating portfolios.* Minneapolis, MN: Free Spirit Publishing.

Kirk, M.F. 1997. Using portfolio to enhance student learning and assessment. *Journal of Physical Education, Recreation and Dance* 68 (7): 29-33.

Kulinna, P.H., W. Zhu, M. Behnke, R.O. Johnson, D. McMullen, M.E. Turner, and G. Wolff. 1999. Six steps in developing and using fitness portfolios. *Teaching Elementary Physical Education* 10 (5): 15-17, 28.

Lambert, L. 1999. *Standards-based assessment of student learning: A comprehensive approach.* Reston, VA: National Association for Sport and Physical Education, an association of the American Alliance for Health, Physical Education, Recreation and Dance.

Lazzaro, W. 1996. Empowering students with instructional rubrics. Ed. R. E. Blum and J. A. Arter. *A Handbook for Student Performance Assessment.* vi-3:1-9. Alexandria, VA: Association for Supervision and Curriculum Development.

Lewis, A. 1995. An overview of the standards movement. *Phi Delta Kappan* 76 (10): 744-750.

Lund, J. 1992. Assessment and accountability in secondary physical education. *Quest* 44: 352-360.

Lund, J. 1997. Authentic assessment: Its development and applications. *Journal for Physical Education, Recreation and Dance* 68 (7): 25-28, 40.

Luxbacher, J.A. 1996. *Soccer: Steps to success.* Champaign, IL: Human Kinetics.

Marmo, D. 1994. "'Sport' folios: On the road to outcomes-based education". Paper presented at the American Alliance for Health, Physical Education, Recreation and Dance National Convention, April, Denver, CO.

Marzano, R., D. Pickering, and J. McTighe. 1993. *Assessing student outcomes: Performance assessment using the dimensions of learning model.* Alexandria, VA: Association for Supervision and Curriculum Development.

Melograno, V.J. 1994. Portfolio assessment: Documenting authentic student learning. *Journal of Physical Education, Recreation and Dance* 65 (8): 50-55, 58-61.

———. 1998. *Professional and student portfolios for physical education.* Champaign, IL: Human Kinetics.

———. 1999. *Preservice professional portfolio system.* Reston, VA: National Association for Sport and Physical Education, an association of the American Alliance for Health, Physical Education, Recreation, and Dance.

———. 2000. *Portfolio Assessment for K-12 Physical Education.* Reston, VA: National Association for Sport and Physical Education.

Mitchell, R. 1992. *Testing for learning: How new approaches to evaluation can improve American school.* New York: The Free Press.

Mohnsen, B.J. 2000. *Using technology in physical education.* Champaign, IL: Human Kinetics.

National Association for Sport and Physical Education. 1995. *Moving into the future: National standards for physical education.* Reston, VA: National Association for Sport and Physical Education, an association of the American Alliance for Health, Physical Education, Recreation and Dance.

National Association for Sport and Physical Education. 2001. *Shape of the nation report.* Reston, VA: National Association for Sport and Physical Education, an association of the American Alliance for Health, Physical Education, Recreation and Dance.

National Commission on Excellence in Education. 1983. *A nation at risk: The imperative for educational reform. A report to the nation and the secretary of education.* Washington, DC: GPO.

O'Sullivan, M., and M. Henniger. 2000. *Assessing Student Responsibility and Teamwork.* Reston, VA: National Association for Sport and Physical Education.

Owens, D., and L. Bunker. 1995. *Golf: Steps to success.* Champaign, IL: Human Kinetics.

Pangrazi, R. 2001. *Dynamic Physical Education for Elementary School Children* (13th Ed.). Allyn and Bacon, Boston, MA.

Popham, J. 1997. What's wrong—and what's right—with rubrics. *Educational Leadership* 55 (2): 72-75.

Rink, J.E. 1998. *Teaching physical education for learning.* Boston: McGraw-Hill.

Siedentop, D. 2001. *Introduction to physical education, fitness, and sport.* 4th ed. Mountain View, CA: Mayfield.

Siedentop, D., and D. Tannehill. 2000. *Developing teaching skills in physical education.* Mountain View, CA: Mayfield.

Stiggins, R. 1997. *Student centered classroom assessment.* 2d ed. Upper Saddle River, NJ: Prentice Hall.

Tousignant, M. 1981. *A qualitative analysis of task structures in required physical education.* Unpublished doctoral dissertation, The Ohio State University.

U.S. Department of Health and Human Services. 1996. *Physical activity and health: A report of the surgeon general.* Atlanta: U.S. Department of Health and Human Services, Centers for Disease Control and Prevention. National Center for Chronic Disease Prevention and Health Promotion.

United States Gymnastics Federation. 1992. *I can do gymnastics: Essential skills for beginning gymnastics.* Indianapolis: Master Press.

Vickers, J. 1990. *Instructional design for teaching physical activities: A knowledge structures approach.* Champaign, IL: Human Kinetics.

Westfall. 1998. Setting your sights on assessment: Describing student performance in physical education. *Teaching Elementary Physical Education* 9(6), 5-9.

Wiggins, G. 1989a. A true test: Toward more authentic and equitable assessment. *Phi Delta Kappan* 69: 703-713.

———. 1989b. Teaching to the (authentic) test. *Educational Leadership* 46 (9): 41-47.

———. 1996. What is a rubric? A dialogue on design and use. Ed. R. E. Blum and J. A. Arter. *A Handbook for Student Performance Assessment.* vi-5: 1-13. Alexandria, VA: Association for Supervision and Curriculum Development.

———. 1998a. *Educative assessment: Designing assessments to inform and improve student performance.* San Francisco: Jossey-Bass.

———. 1998b. *Sophisticated and naïve vs. right and wrong: How to teach and assess for intellectual progress.* Read by author. Cassette recording no. 298303. Alexandria, VA: Association for Supervision and Curriculum Development.

Wiggins, G., and J. McTighe. 1998. *Understanding by design.* Alexandria, VA: Association for Supervision and Curriculum Development.

Wilson, S., and K. Roof. 1999. Establishing a portfolio process for K-8 learners. *Teaching Elementary Physical Education* 10 (5): 10-14.

Note: The italicized *t* or *f* following a page number denotes a table or figure. The italicized *ff* following a page number denotes multiple figures.

Jacalyn Lea Lund, PhD, is an associate professor of physical education at Ball State University. She also has 16 years of experience teaching in public secondary schools. Lund was on the National Association for Sport and Physical Education (NASPE) team that developed the national content standards for physical education. She also has served on the writing team for the Kentucky Department of Education to create assessments for new physical education teachers. She is working to develop middle school assessments for the Indiana Physical Education Content Standards.

Lund earned an MS in physical education from the University of Northern Colorado in 1974 and a PhD in physical education from Ohio State University in 1990. She is a lifetime member of the American Alliance for Health, Physical Education, Recreation and Dance (AAHPERD).

Mary Fortman Kirk, PhD, is a professor of physical education at Northern Kentucky University, where she coordinates health and physical education programs. She also taught physical education at the high school level for 10 years. Kirk has given many presentations on portfolios and alternative assessment at conferences including AAHPERD, NASPE, and the National Association for Physical Education in Higher Education. She was appointed by the Kentucky commissioner of education to serve on the state task force for the development of physical education assessment and new teacher performance assessments.

Kirk earned an MA in motor learning and physical education from Michigan State University in 1973 and a PhD in motor development and teacher preparation from Ohio State University in 1989. She is the author of two books on pre-sport development programs for the National Alliance of Youth Sport and the Girl Scouts of the USA.